A FAITH WORTH DEFENDING

A FAITH WORTH DEFENDING

The Synod of Dort's Enduring Heritage

Edited by
Jon D. Payne and Sebastian Heck

REFORMATION HERITAGE BOOKS
Grand Rapids, Michigan

Reformation Heritage Books
2965 Leonard St. NE
Grand Rapids, MI 49525
616-977-0889
orders@heritagebooks.org
www.heritagebooks.org

Printed in the United States of America
19 20 21 22 23 24/10 9 8 7 6 5 4 3 2 1

Library of Congress Cataloging-in-Publication Data

Names: Payne, Jon D., editor. | Heck, Sebastian, editor.
Title: A faith worth defending : the Synod of Dort's enduring heritage / edited by Jon D. Payne and Sebastian Heck.
Description: Grand Rapids, Michigan : Reformation Heritage Books, 2019. | Includes bibliographical references. | Summary: "Contains essays on the history and theology of the Canons of Dort"— Provided by publisher.
Identifiers: LCCN 2019028992 | ISBN 9781601787408 (hardback) | ISBN 9781601787415 (epub)
Subjects: LCSH: Synod of Dort (1618-1619 : Dordrecht, Netherlands)
Classification: LCC BX9478 .F35 2019 | DDC 238/.42—dc23
LC record available at https://lccn.loc.gov/2019028992

For additional Reformed literature, request a free book list from Reformation Heritage Books at the above regular or e-mail address.

CONTENTS

With loving appreciation for our two congregations:

Christ Church Presbyterian, Charleston, South Carolina,

and

Selbständige Evangelisch-Reformierte Kirche, Heidelberg, Germany.

Therefore, my brothers, whom I love and long for, my joy and crown, stand firm thus in the Lord, my beloved.
—PHILIPPIANS 4:1 ESV

PREFACE

In every age the Reformed church faces serious challenges to its faith and confession. We are experiencing them today. In the early decades of the seventeenth century, a significant challenge was sparked by the Dutch theologian Jacobus Arminius (1560–1609) and his devoted followers. Arminian doctrine was undermining the free gospel of grace and causing more than a little confusion in the churches and seminaries.

In response to this divisive threat and under the protection of the States-General of the United Republic of the Netherlands, the Dutch church called for a national synod. The purpose of the synod was to deliberate and determine whether or not Arminianism was a true interpretation of God's Word and a faithful expression of the Reformed faith, especially in relation to the doctrines of grace. Representative ministers from Dutch churches, as well as several respected international delegates, were invited to participate.

The synod met in Dordrecht, Netherlands, from November 1618 to May 1619, thus marking 2018-2019 as the 400th anniversary of the Synod of Dort. It is upon this special occasion, therefore, that we are pleased to produce *A Faith Worth Defending*, a commemorative volume of essays on the history, theology, and pastoral implications of the Synod of Dort.

As with *A Faith Worth Teaching,* our previous commemorative volume on the 450th anniversary of the Heidelberg Catechism (1563)*,* the contributors are pastors and scholars who hail from an array of Reformed traditions. With biblical clarity and heartfelt conviction, the writers demonstrate how Arminianism compromises a true understanding of the nature and effects of sin, the extent of the atonement, the scope of God's sovereignty (i.e., predestination), and the essence of assurance, among other things. They also set forth a positive and biblical view of these truths and highlight how one's belief regarding these key doctrines is critical to faith, piety, and practice. In these pages you will not find cold and supercilious theological discourse, but warm and edifying instruction on the five heads of doctrine in the Canons of Dort. In short, this book is a defense and declaration of the gospel. It will not only inform the mind, but feed the soul.

Arminianism continues to plague the broad evangelical church in our day, and its effects are ubiquitous. Therefore, it's important that Christians (Reformed and otherwise) understand what they believe and confess about God, sin, and salvation and why sound doctrine matters.

A book project like this does not come to fruition without the work of many hands. First of all, we want to express deep and profound gratitude to each author who contributed to this volume. We know you are busy. Thank you for your valuable contribution to this volume. Many thanks to our two churches—Christ Church Presbyterian (PCA) in Charleston, South Carolina, and Selbständige Evangelisch-Reformierte Kirche, Heidelberg, Germany—for encouraging us to take on projects like this that will benefit not only you but also the wider church. We also want to express deep gratitude to our families. Your unswerving support, steadfast love, and constant encouragement are unmatched, and this book would have never seen the light of day without it. We also want to thank Joel Beeke, Jay Collier, and the entire team at Reformation Heritage Books. As always, it is a joy and privilege to work with you. Thank you for your wisdom and direction on this project. We appreciate Dr. Beeke's and Ian Turner's editing of the manuscript.

Most of all, we give glory, thanksgiving, and praise to our blessed and sovereign triune God, who "hath been pleased in His infinite mercy to give His only begotten Son for our surety, who was made sin, and became a curse for us and in our stead, that He might make satisfaction to divine justice on our behalf."[1]

—Jon D. Payne
Sebastian Heck

---

1. Canons of Dort, II, 2.

CHAPTER 1

Preserving the Reformation: A Historical Portrait of the Synod of Dort

W. Robert Godfrey

In 2017 many churches, Christians, and historians marked the 500th anniversary of the first public act of reformation when Martin Luther nailed his Ninety-Five Theses to the church door of the castle church in Wittenberg. In 2018–2019 far fewer people will note the 400th anniversary of the meetings of the Synod of Dordrecht, a national synod of the Dutch Reformed church. Yet this synod was not only vitally important to the health and strength of the Dutch Reformed church for centuries to come but in a profound sense it restated and preserved the message of the Reformation in the face of the greatest Protestant threat to the gospel since the beginning of the Reformation.[1] The message of Dort remains vital and necessary for the church today.

This synod, usually called in English the Synod of Dort, was indeed a national synod with delegates from various local synods as well as a delegation of professors of theology from several Dutch universities. It was also, however, an international synod with delegates from Reformed churches throughout Europe, specifically from Great Britain, Switzerland, and various German states and cities. The French were also invited but were not permitted to attend by the French king. The international delegates were full members of the synod. This makes the Synod of Dort the only truly international ecclesiastical synod in the history of the Reformed churches—a synod

---

1. The following are some basic books on the Dutch Reformation, Arminius, and the Synod of Dort: *Handbook of Dutch Church History,* ed. Herman J. Selderhuis (Göettingen: Vandenhoeck & Ruprecht, 2014); Jonathan Israel, *The Dutch Republic, Its Rise, Greatness, and Fall 1477–1806* (Oxford: Clarendon Press, 1998); P. Y. DeJong, ed., *Crisis in the Reformed Churches* (Middleville, Mich.: Reformed Fellowship, 2008); Carl Bangs, *Arminius* (Nashville: Abingdon Press, 1971); Keith Stanglin and Thomas McCall, *Jacob Arminius* (Oxford: Oxford University Press, 2012); Aza Goudriaan and F. A. van Lieburg, eds., *Revisiting the Synod of Dordt* (Leiden: Brill, 2011); and W. Robert Godfrey, *Saving the Reformation: The Pastoral Theology of the Synod of Dort* (Orlando: Reformation Trust, 2019).

of about ninety delegates which met from November 13, 1618, to May 29, 1619. The calling of this synod was the culmination of nearly a century of great religious and political changes in the Netherlands. In a remarkable way the synod spoke for all the Reformed churches.

In the first part of the sixteenth century, the Netherlands, or Low Countries, were seventeen provinces, or small countries, each with its own history. Each of these provinces had passed into the hands of the Hapsburg dynasty, and they were ruled over by Charles V, who had heard Luther at the Diet of Worms in 1521. Charles, was the greatest of the Hapsburg rulers, possessing sovereignty over vast lands in Europe. He was the Holy Roman Emperor and king of Spain, as well as ruler of parts of Austria, Italy, France, and the Low Countries. After Charles abdicated, the Holy Roman Empire passed to his brother, while Spain and the Netherlands passed to his son Philip, who became Philip II of Spain.

In the days of Charles, the first Lutheran martyrs died in Brussels in 1522. Lutheranism did not become widely popular in the Netherlands; rather, Anabaptism became the first widespread variety of reform. Menno Simons came from Friesland in the north of the Low Countries. Calvinism did not begin to spread significantly in the Netherlands until the 1550s.

The early Reformed preachers in the Netherlands came from Geneva and from the French Reformed church. They brought not only the theological message of the Reformed but also the goal of establishing congregations, following Reformed convictions of polity, worship, and piety. Reformed polity called for the local congregations to be governed by a council of ministers, elders, and deacons elected by the congregation. This council had a great responsibility:

> By this means true relation is preserved; true doctrine is able to take its course; and evil men are corrected spiritually and held in check, so that also the poor and all the afflicted may be helped and comforted according to their need (Belgic Confession, art. 30).[2]

In time the congregations also began to create broader ecclesiastical structures and government in the form of local gatherings of congregations, called classes, as well as broader regional synods. The regional synods were provincial synods except in the case of the province of Holland which, because of its large population, had two particular synods. Following the example of

---

2. Citations from the Belgic Confession are taken from the translation in the *Trinity Psalter Hymnal* (Willow Grove, Pa.: Trinity Psalter Hymnal Joint Venture, 2018).

the French Reformed church, they also held national synods. These broader assemblies also adopted as the confessional standards of the Dutch Reformed churches both the Belgic Confession (1561) and the Heidelberg Catechism (1563). Ministers, elders, deacons, and professors were required to subscribe to these confessions and accept all their teachings.

The early Reformed churches in the Low Countries experienced severe persecution. The reality of that persecution is reflected in the Belgic Confession, written by the Reformed preacher Guido de Brès, who himself became a martyr in 1567. In article 28 on the duties of church members, the Confession states:

> And to preserve this unity more effectively, it is the duty of all believers, according to God's Word, to separate themselves from those who do not belong to the church, in order to join this assembly wherever God has established it, even if civil authorities and royal decrees forbid and death and physical punishment result.

Also in the last article of the Confession, article 37 on the last judgment, de Brès returned to thoughts of the persecution he had seen:

> Therefore, with good reason the thought of this judgment is horrible and dreadful to wicked and evil people. But it is very pleasant and a great comfort to the righteous and elect, since their total redemption will then be accomplished. They will then receive the fruits of their labor and of the trouble they have suffered; their innocence will be openly recognized by all; and they will see the terrible vengeance that God will bring on the evil one who tyrannized, oppressed, and tormented them in this world.

For decades the threat and reality of persecution was a way of life for many Reformed Christians in the Netherlands. Persecution made most of the Reformed strict, disciplined, and determined in their religious convictions.

Philip's vigorous persecution—along with various political and economic issues—sparked the beginning of a revolt in 1568, which would become a war that lasted formally for eighty years. By the 1580s the war had in effect split the Low Countries into two parts, which ultimately became the United Provinces, or the modern Netherlands, composed of seven provinces in the north, with modern Belgium composing most of the ten provinces in the south. In the United Provinces, important decisions about religion were left to each province with the understanding that a national synod could be called only by the unanimous decision of all seven provinces at the States General (a kind of parliament representing the provinces). The Reformation and the revolt in the Low Countries would lead to a new country as well as a new church in that region.

In the sixteenth century, most Roman Catholics and Protestants shared the conviction that social stability depended upon the cooperation of the civil government and the one true church. The civil government used the sword to enforce the true church, suppressing those groups that it regarded as heretical and dangerous to the public health. Where the state changed its allegiance on the true church, the church in various ways came to depend on the state. So it was for the Reformed in the United Provinces. The Reformed churches needed the permission of the civil government locally for certain acts of ecclesiastical discipline. They also needed the permission of the States General for the calling of a national synod. A few such synods had been held in the days of persecution and then after the establishment of the United Provinces. The last national synod before the Synod of Dort had been called in 1586.

The calling of a national synod in 1618, therefore, was a very remarkable event. The civil government had sought to limit the power, influence, and independence of the church by not allowing the meetings of national synods. The calling of the great synod of 1618–1619 did not actually change that government strategy. After the Synod of Dort, no national synod was held in the Netherlands until after the Napoleonic era in 1816. But the Dutch Reformed church was so well served by the Synod of Dort that it flourished in many ways for the next two centuries.

Why did the civil government approve the meeting of the national synod of Dort in 1618? The synod was called to deal with a great crisis in the life of the Dutch Reformed church so serious that the United Provinces had been brought to the verge of civil war (and this on the eve of renewed war with Spain) just before the synod was called. This crisis goes back to the life and influence of the Dutch Reformed minister and theologian Jacobus Arminius (1560–1609).

Arminius had been a bright student who received an orthodox Reformed education at Leiden, Geneva, and Basel. He returned to Amsterdam after his studies and was ordained to the ministry there in 1588. He served as a pastor in Amsterdam for fifteen years, and then from 1603 served as a professor of theology at Leiden until his death in 1609. In his years as a minister and professor he wrote a number of treatises (now collected in an English translation in three volumes), but did not publish any of them in his lifetime. Arminius's decision not to publish was unusual and shows that he was aware that his theological views would be very controversial. His writings show that he was furiously opposed to a Calvinist approach to predestination called supralapsarianism. But his rejection of supralapsarianism led him to abandon all Calvinist views of predestination. He seems to have adopted instead the teaching on predestination of the Spanish Jesuit Molina known as middle knowledge. He knew that the large majority of his Reformed ministerial colleagues would regard Molina's views as semi-Pelagian.

The influence of Arminius during his lifetime spread not through his writings but through his teaching and friendships. His teaching attracted a small but influential following of ministers. The year after the death of Arminius, some forty-two ministers who had been influenced by him realized that their position in the church was at risk as his views were becoming better known. So they prepared a petition to the civil government asking for protection. The petition—or "remonstrance," as it was then called—summarized the views that they wanted tolerated and protected in five points. This petition became known as the Remonstrance of 1610. Here are those critical five points from their remonstrance:[3]

> Article 1: God—by an eternal and unchangeable decree in Jesus Christ, His Son, before the foundation of the world—has determined, out of the fallen and sinful human race, to save in Christ, because of Christ, and through Christ those who, through the grace of the Holy Spirit, believe in His Son Jesus and persevere in this belief and obedience even to the end, through His grace. On the other hand, God has determined to leave the unconverted and unbelieving in their sin and under wrath and to condemn them as separate from Christ. This is the word of the holy gospel in John 3:36, "He who believes in the Son has eternal life, and he who is disobedient to the Son shall not see life, but the wrath of God remains on him." Other passages teach the same.

> Article 2: From this it follows that Jesus Christ, the Savior of the world, died for all men and for each man. He earned for them all, through the death of the cross, reconciliation and the forgiveness of sins. Still Christ died in such a way that no one actually shares in this forgiveness of sins except those who believe. This is the word of the gospel of John 3:16, "God so loved the world that he gave his only Son, so that whoever believes in him, should not perish but have eternal life." And in the First Letter of John 2:2, "He is the reconciliation of our sins, and not only ours, but the sins of the whole world."

> Article 3: Man does not have this saving faith from himself nor out of the power of his free will. Man in the state of apostasy and sin cannot,

---

3. This is my translation, which can be found in my book *Saving the Reformation*.

out of or from himself, think, will, or do any good that is truly good (as is particularly saving faith). But it is necessary that by God, in Christ, through His Holy Spirit, he be born again and renewed in understanding, affections, and will, and all powers so that he may rightly think, will, and do the truly good. This is the word of Christ, John 13:5, "Without me you can do nothing."

Article 4: This grace of God is the beginning, continuance, and completion of all good so much so that even the regenerate man can neither think, will, or do the good nor resist any temptation to evil without prevenient or assisting, awakening, following, and cooperating grace. So all the good deeds or works of which man can think must be ascribed to the grace of God in Christ. But as to the manner of the working of this grace, it is not irresistible. It is written of many that they have resisted the Holy Spirit, as in Acts 7 and many other places.

Article 5: Those who are united to Jesus Christ by a true faith and so come to share in His life-giving Spirit have abundant power to fight against Satan, sin, the world, and their own sin and to win the victory. But whether they of themselves through neglect can lose the beginning of their being in Christ, again take up with this present world, reject the Holy Spirit once given to them, lose their good conscience, and abandon grace, must first be sought out further from the Holy Scriptures before we can ourselves teach it with the full confidence of our minds.

These five articles became the center of all the ensuing controversy between the Calvinists and Arminians. It is vital to remember that this struggle started with the Arminians summarizing their theological views in five points. In a profound sense Calvinism does not have five points, but rather has five answers to the five errors of Arminianism. The Arminian position has often been expressed as conditional election, unlimited atonement, real depravity, resistible grace, and uncertainty on perseverance. By contrast the Calvinist answers were unconditional election, limited atonement, total depravity, irresistible grace, and the perseverance of the saints.

On receiving the Remonstrance of 1610, the leader of the civil government, Jan van Oldenbarnevelt, recognized the explosive character of this document and tried to keep it a secret. Of course it leaked out, and the Calvinists were furious. The classes and synods wanted to take disciplinary action, but the civil government blocked such moves. As the controversy grew, it affected both church and state. The large Calvinist majority in the church became more and more frustrated, and some even contemplated separating from the undisciplined church. The civil leader Oldenbarnevelt continued to protect the Arminians while the military leader Maurits, Prince of Orange, moved toward the Calvinist side. The polarization of Dutch society became so complete that the United Provinces moved toward the real possibility of civil war. Prince Maurits arrested Oldenbarnevelt in a coup d'etat in 1618, and the new government authorized the calling of a national synod.

Theologically, most of the attention on the Synod of Dort has gone to its decisions in response to the Arminian teaching, known as the Canons of Dort. Of great additional historical importance, however, were the decisions of the synod on various national church matters that needed to be addressed by a synod of the whole church. These decisions would ultimately come to be known as the Pro-Acta and the Post-Acta of the synod, as they were made before and after the work on the Canons.

In the Pro-Acta, the synod appointed a committee to prepare a new Dutch translation of the Bible, which would come to be known as the *Statenvertaling*, or the State translation. This version would come to have the same influence in the history of the Dutch churches that the King James Version has had in the English-speaking churches. The synod also encouraged the churches to instruct more carefully and fully the teaching of the Heidelberg Catechism to the young people. Finally, the synod discussed a question arising from Dutch trading contacts in the Far East. Should the children born to servants who were not Christians but were living in Christian households be baptized on the basis of the household baptisms recorded in the book of Acts? A minority of the synod, led by the British delegates, answered the question in the affirmative. The majority advised that the children should not be baptized until after they were catechized. This seems to have been the first time in European history that a missionary question was posed to a Protestant church assembly.

In the Post-Acta, undertaken after the international delegates were dismissed with thanks on May 6, 1619, the synod adopted an official text of the Belgic Confession to ensure that all the churches used the same text of the confession that had long guided them. The synod also adopted a form of subscription which clarified the binding character of all the teachings of the Confession and the Heidelberg Catechism, along with the Canons just adopted. It also adopted a church order that would direct the offices and the work of the churches for centuries. Further, it addressed a question on how the churches should understand and keep the Sabbath. The synod declared that it did not have time to deal definitely with that question, but did adopt six points on the Sabbath as a brief, provisional answer. The synod taught that Christians should keep Sunday as a perpetual, moral obligation to worship and rest from ordinary work, otherwise giving the rest of the day to renewing activities. Under the influence of the Bible, English Puritanism, and the decision of Dort, the Dutch Reformed churches and people would become strictly Sabbatarian.

When the representatives of the Arminians arrived at the synod, as they were required to do, they were asked to present their views orally and to answer the questions of the synod. After several weeks the president of the synod, Johannes Bogerman, lost his patience and dismissed the Arminians with sharp criticism. The Arminians were required to stay in Dordrecht to present their views in writing to the synod.

After the dismissal of the Arminians, the synod divided into its constituent delegations from the various Dutch synods and the various European states. These "colleges" each prepared suggested responses to the Arminian five points. Each of them responded to the third and fourth Arminian points together, as they must have been instructed to do. The third Arminian point on depravity sounded orthodox until viewed in light of their fourth point. The final version of the Canons adopted by the synod followed this same form, combining the two points into what came to be known as the third and fourth heads of doctrine.

Most of the colleges prepared their judgments in the technical theological language of the universities; that is to say, in scholastic language. This kind of technical language had developed among Protestant theologians, Lutheran as well as Reformed, in the late sixteenth and early seventeenth centuries. This approach was understandable and very efficient. But the drafting committee of the synod decided to write the Canons very differently. Several key decisions guided the form and character of the Canons.

First, and perhaps most importantly, the committee decided that the Canons should be written for the church and not for the universities. This decision meant that the language of the Canons would not be scholastic or technical, but "popular"—that is, for the people in the churches. The Canons were not written for theologians to answer the theology of the Arminians for them. The Canons rather were written to instruct, edify, and comfort the people of God in the truth and in holy living.

Second, the committee decided that each head of doctrine should be complete in itself. It did not want the reader of the fifth head of doctrine on the perseverance of the saints to have to remember all that had been said in the previous heads of doctrine, particularly on subjects such as human responsibility and the means of grace. As a result the reader will find a fair amount of repetition from one head of doctrine to another. Remembering this is of particular importance for the teacher who wants to teach straight through the Canons.

Third, the committee determined that the Canons in each head of doctrine should demonstrate the catholicity of Reformed theology. Each head of doctrine begins with at least one article that states a catholic doctrine—that is, a doctrine that in the early seventeenth century would have been accepted by Lutherans and Roman Catholics as well as the Reformed. From that catholic beginning, each head of doctrine develops the distinctively Reformed answer to the Arminians. The implicit point of this way of proceeding is to demonstrate that the Reformed theology is neither novel nor sectarian, but rather that the Arminian theology is both novel and sectarian.

Fourth, the Canons are written so that in each head of doctrine there are first positive articles expressing the Reformed position in straightforward terms without entering into explicit controversy. Then follows a section in which various errors are specifically rejected.

Fifth, the Canons as a whole and most of the articles seek to teach the truth theologically while at the same time showing the implications of that truth for Christian living and piety. We can see that, for example, in I, 9:

> This very election was made not on the basis of foreseen faith, or of the obedience of faith, or of holiness, or of any other good quality and disposition, as the prerequisite cause or condition for electing anyone. Rather, this election is to faith, to the obedience of faith, to holiness, etc. And so election is the fountain of all saving good. From election flow faith, holiness, and all other saving gifts, even eternal life itself, as fruit and effect. As the Apostle wrote: "He chose us in love [not because we were, but] so that we might be holy and blameless in His sight" (Eph. 1:4).

Here we see clearly stated the theological truth that election does not depend on any cause or condition in man, such as faith, obedience, or holiness. As said earlier in the Canons, election rests solely on the will and good pleasure of God. So election does not depend on faith and holiness, but faith and holiness depend on election. And here theology flows into piety. Election has effects in the lives of the elect.

This article makes clear that the elect will not remain unbelieving and utterly sinful, but will be brought to faith and a new life. Reformed theology is not indifferent to the importance of faith and holiness; the doctrine of election does not encourage any spiritual lethargy or moral indifference. Rather, election is the fountain of life and Christian living.

Sixth, the committee labored to write canons that would be acceptable to the all the members of the synod. That proved to be easy on most points. While both infralapsarians and supralapsarians were members of the synod, they were familiar with their differences and had learned how to live together. The Canons were written so that both the infralapsarians and supralapsarians would sign them. On one issue, however, the synod was surprised at the seriousness of the disagreements among the orthodox over whether to speak of the sufficiency as well as of the efficiency of the atonement. The second head of doctrine in the Canons is a very careful compromise that did unite the Synod. In the end every member of the synod voted to approve the Canons.

The Canons were prepared with a conclusion that has always been regarded as a part of the confessionally binding Canons. The conclusion summarizes some particularly outrageous accusations against the Reformed and rejects them utterly. It also calls on all Reformed theologians and preachers to be careful and edifying in speaking and writing about these subjects and closes with a prayer that Christians would be sanctified in the truth.

Some days after adopting the Canons, the synod adopted a preface to the Canons reviewing the history that led to the calling of the synod. That preface has never been regarded as part of the Canons and has seldom been printed with the Canons.

The following is a suggested outline of the Canons and their teaching:

I. First Head of Doctrine: God's Predestination—or Redemption Planned
   A. Common Christian Convictions, Articles 1–6
   B. Reformed Doctrine of Election Defined, Article 7
   C. Elaborations on the Doctrine of Election, Articles 8–11
   D. Answers to Alleged Problems Caused by Election, Articles 12–14
   E. Reformed Doctrine of Reprobation Defined, Article 15
   F. Answers to Alleged Problems Caused by Reprobation, Articles 16–17
   G. Election, Reprobation, and God-Centered Religion, Article 18
   H. Rejections of Errors

II. Second Head of Doctrine: The Death of Christ—or Redemption Accomplished
   A. Common Christian Convictions, Articles 1–7
   B. Reformed Doctrine of Limited Atonement Defined, Article 8

How then should we evaluate the importance and significance of the Canons for the church today? Are the Canons simply concerned with some rather minor matters of theology? Are they just icing on the Reformed cake? In fact, the Canons are a great treasure of the church and should be much better known, used, and appreciated than they have been. We can summarize that value in four points.

First, the Canons are true. Their aim is not to express or summarize all Reformed confessional commitments. For that we must turn to the Belgic Confession or the Westminster Confession of Faith. Nevertheless, the Canons define and clarify important elements of Reformed belief against the Arminian challenge. They do that by appealing to the Scriptures as their only ultimate authority.

In the positive articles, an explicit appeal to the Bible is only made occasionally, but in the rejections of errors biblical texts are often quoted, sometimes without comment. The authority and perspicuity of the Scriptures suffuse the Canons. Here is *sola Scriptura* at work.

Second, the teaching of the Canons is foundational. The clear teaching on election, total depravity, and irresistible grace is necessary to preserve and protect *sola gratia*. The teaching on the complete effectiveness of the saving death of Christ for the elect clarifies *solus Christus*. It elaborates on the statement of Belgic Confession, article 22: "Therefore, to say that Christ is not enough but that something else is needed as well is a most enormous blasphemy against God—for it then would follow that Jesus Christ is only half a Savior." While *sola fide* may not be so obvious in the Canons, faith is in fact referred to in more than half the articles. Faith receives the grace of God and is central to persevering in grace. While justification is not defined in the Canons—the definition in the Belgic Confession and in the Heidelberg Catechism is assumed—the Canons assert elements of theology necessary to protect and clarify the Reformation doctrine of justification.

In fact, the Canons promote God-centered and God-glorifying religion, living, and comfort. They teach that God is sovereign, that sin is deadly, that Jesus is the complete Savior, and that the Holy Spirit is successful. These teachings are foundational indeed.

Third, the Canons are comforting. The Canons speak repeatedly of the comfort worked in the hearts of God's people to know that their salvation is secure and certain in the hands of God. The Canons stress how important the ministry of the church and the means of grace are to work that comfort. The doctrine of election does not eliminate or undermine the necessity of the church and the Christian community. Rather, the comforting fruit of election is worked in and through the church.

The Canons stress the centrality of comfort by having a whole section on the assurance of salvation in the fifth head of doctrine, articles 9–13. This section is not strictly necessary as a response to the Arminian questions on perseverance. But it is a helpful and encouraging call to enjoy the certainty of salvation.

Fourth, the Canons are teachable. The Canons were designed not only to be understandable for the people of the church but also as a model for teaching the truths of Calvinism. Consider the way in which the first head of doctrine teaches the doctrine of election. In article 1, it wisely begins not in eternity with the decrees of God but in history with the human condition. For most people, it is much more comprehensible to begin with human deadness and helplessness and then to ask, Where must help come from for the helpless? It must come from God, according to His plan—a plan for His people.

The Canons are a great resource of the church that have been too little used. Most translations of the Canons have preserved the long sentences of the Latin original. Long sentences work in Latin but do not work well in English—especially in contemporary English.[4]

The writing of the Canons of Dort is not a minor moment in the history of church meetings. For the Reformed, the Canons saved the Reformation, undergirding and protecting its basic truths. Even more, the Canons are part of a significant pattern repeated throughout the history of the church—a pattern recognized and articulated in the New Testament by Jude in his general epistle. Jude not only described what was happening in his own day but presented a pattern that would be repeated over and over again in the life and history of the church. He wanted his focus to be on the "common salvation" that all Christians share and on "the faith" given by Jesus and the apostles to the people of God (v. 3). But he had to divert from what he wanted to do because he saw a great and pressing need that he had to address. "Sneaks" (v. 4) had come into the church, perverting the grace of God. They had to be refuted and warned of the judgment to come. And the effect of the perversion of the sneaks was division and separation (v. 19). The faith must be fought for and defended. Those who stand for the faith do not cause divisions, but those who attack the faith cause the divisions.

Here is the pattern: the faith, the fight, and the fracture. The Synod of Dort was one episode in the long struggle between God's wisdom and man's invention, between the truth and the lie, between grace and works, between faith in Christ and self-sufficiency. Its 400th anniversary is well worth celebrating. The church needs its teaching today as much as ever.

---

4. The new translation of the Canons in my book on the Synod of Dort will help students use the Canons more easily and help teachers teach them more effectively. Godfrey, *Saving the Reformation*.

CHAPTER 2

What's the Difference? A Historical and Theological Comparison of the Three Forms of Unity

Lyle D. Bierma

The title of this book, *A Faith Worth Defending*, has in view particularly the defense of the Christian faith in the 1619 Canons of Dort. The Canons of Dort (CD), however, have long been part of a triad of confessions known as the Three Forms of Unity, which include the 1561 Belgic Confession (BC) and the 1563 Heidelberg Catechism (HC). These confessional documents have together functioned as doctrinal standards for Reformed denominations with roots in the Netherlands ever since the Synod of Dort required all office-bearers in the Dutch Reformed Church to subscribe to them.[1] As an explanation or clarification of some of the teachings of the Belgic Confession and Heidelberg Catechism, the Canons of Dort stand in substantial doctrinal harmony with the other two forms of unity. At the same time, it should be recognized that "each of the confessions has its own peculiar function, since each was designed to meet specific needs of the church at a given time."[2] As part of this quadricentennial reflection on the Canons of Dort, therefore, this chapter will focus particularly on the distinguishing historical and theological characteristics of the Canons in comparison with the other two statements of faith. We will begin by comparing the Canons of Dort with the Belgic Confession, the document to which it had a closer historical,

---

1. Donald Sinnema, "The Origin of the Form of Subscription in the Dutch Reformed Tradition," *Calvin Theological Journal* 42 (November 2007): 256–82.

2. "Harmony of Heidelberg Catechism, Belgic Confession, and the Canons of Dort," in *Ecumenical Creeds and Reformed Confessions* (Grand Rapids: CRC Publications, 1988), 146. This harmony consists of a chart of comparative confessional references based on the order of the Heidelberg Catechism. The introduction to the harmony goes on to note that "a harmony of the confessions can be used with profit only when the independence and integrity of each confession is respected."

geographical, and theological affinity, and then turn to a comparison with the Heidelberg Catechism.

The Canons of Dort and the Belgic Confession

Historical Comparison

Geographically and historically, the Canons of Dort had something in common with the Belgic Confession because both had their origins in the region of Europe known as the Lowlands (today comprising the Netherlands, Belgium, Luxembourg, and parts of northern France), and both were written during the Lowlanders' long struggle for freedom from Spanish Catholic control. But that is where the similarity ends.

The Belgic Confession was composed in 1561 in French by Guido de Brès (1522–1567), a Reformed pastor in Tournai (Doornik) in what is today southern Belgium.[3] He had been born, raised, and drawn to Protestantism in the nearby city of Mons (Bergen), which had come under Reformed influence from French Calvinists escaping persecution in France. In 1548 he fled to London, England, where he joined a Reformed refugee congregation and experienced firsthand the Protestant reforms introduced into the Church of England during the reign of Edward VI. Returning to the Continent in 1552, de Brès served several congregations in the Lowlands and northern France and published his first major theological work, an anti-Catholic treatise entitled *Le Baston de la Foy Chrestienne* [*The Staff of the Christian Faith*] (1555). That same year he fled persecution again, this time to Frankfurt, and then moved on to Lausanne and Geneva for several years of theological study with Theodore Beza and John Calvin. In 1559 he took up residence in his birthplace of Tournai, where he drafted the Belgic Confession, until in late 1561 persecution forced him to escape again to France. Five years later he returned to the southern Lowlands city of Valenciennes, but in 1567, after several incidents of Protestant iconoclasm in the city, he was arrested by the Catholic authorities, imprisoned, tried, convicted, and finally hanged for his Protestant faith.

As we shall see in more detail later, de Brès had a twofold audience in mind when he wrote the Belgic Confession, both the persecutors and the persecuted. One of his purposes was to impress upon King Philip II in Spain and the king's proxies in the Lowlands that Reformed Protestants were not like the "Anabaptists, anarchists, [or] those who want to reject the authorities

---

3. For both an older and a more recent biography of de Brès, see Lambrecht A. van Langeraad, *Guido de Bray, zijn leven en werken: bijdrage tot de geschiedenis van het Zuid-Nederlandsche protestantisme* (Zierikzee: Ochtman & Zoon, 1884); and Émile Braekman and Erik de Boer, eds., *Guido de Brès: zijn leven, zijn belijden* (Utrecht: Kok, 2011).

and civil officers." On the contrary, they respected the fact that "God has ordained kings, princes, and civil officers" and that "everyone...must be subject to the government...and hold its representatives in honor and respect" (BC, art. 36).[4]

However, de Brès also intended that the Belgic Confession serve as a form of unity for persecuted believers in the underground Reformed congregations. The full title of the first edition indicates that the confession was made "by common consent" by adherents throughout the country, and as it gained more traction in the emerging churches in the northern Lowlands, ministers, elders, deacons, schoolteachers, and professors of theology were required to sign it as an expression of agreement with the Reformed faith. By the 1580s it was also functioning as a standard of doctrinal orthodoxy, and at the Synod of Dort it officially became one of the three confessions to which office-bearers were expected to subscribe.[5]

The roots of the Canons of Dort, composed fifty-eight years later, can be traced to the same area of Europe, but to the northern, Dutch-speaking part of the Lowlands, seven of whose provinces had declared their independence from Spain in 1581 and formed the Republic of the United Netherlands. Furthermore, whereas the Belgic Confession was composed during a time of intense persecution in the years before the outbreak of the Eighty Years War (1568–1648) between the Lowlands and Spain, the Synod of Dort was held during a twelve-year truce (1609–1621) in the middle of that war. Perhaps the biggest difference in the two contexts, however, was the improved status of the Reformed churches in the Lowlands at the time of the Synod of Dort. In 1561 Reformed Protestantism in the Lowlands consisted of a network of oppressed underground congregations located mostly in the southern provinces. By 1619 many of those believers had migrated to the independent provinces in the north, where they now enjoyed not only religious toleration but a favored status in the eyes of the Dutch government. They no longer had to defend themselves politically and theologically against an oppressive Spanish Catholic regime but now had the freedom to focus on disputes inside the family of Reformed churches—most notably the Arminian controversy—and to shape the religious landscape of the north.

Unlike the Belgic Confession, the Canons of Dort were composed not by an individual but by a national synod of the Reformed churches of the United

---

4. All quotations from the Belgic Confession are from "The Belgic Confession," in *Our Faith: Ecumenical Creeds, Reformed Confessions, and Other Resources* (Grand Rapids: Faith Alive Christian Resources, 2013), 25–68.

5. Sinnema, "Origin of the Form of Subscription," 257–77.

Netherlands convened by the Dutch government. The synod comprised fifty-eight ministers and elders from the various Dutch provinces, five professors of theology, and eighteen government delegates, the latter of whom monitored the plenary sessions, advised on matters of procedure, and certified the doctrinal decisions at the end. But the synod also had an international character: twenty-six Reformed theologians from eight foreign territories were invited and participated fully in the drafting, discussions, and voting related to the Canons of Dort. Thirteen Arminians were also in attendance to represent the doctrinal positions at the heart of the dispute, but after several weeks of theological and procedural bickering, the president of the synod expelled them from the gathering. Once they left, the synod went on to craft a rejection of the Arminian positions and an international Reformed alternative in "The Decision of the Synod of Dordt on the Five Main Points of Doctrine in Dispute in the Netherlands," more popularly known as the Canons of Dort.[6]

Complicating the doctrinal controversy was the fact that the Arminian stance was supported by certain political leaders who advocated peace with Spain, whereas the Calvinist party was backed by some who wished to continue the war. As Carl Bangs once described it,

> There would be a war party, militaristic, staunchly Calvinistic and anti-Catholic, predestinarian, centralist, politically even royalist, and ecclesiastically presbyterian. There would be a peace party, trademinded, theologically tolerant, republican, and Erastian. The first would support the war and fight Arminianism; the second would support a truce and fight Calvinism.[7]

This intertwining of political and theological sympathies led the Calvinist party to regard the Arminians not only as heretical but also politically subversive, the same epithets the Catholics had applied to de Brès and the Protestants in the south some sixty years earlier. Once the synod had adjourned, therefore, the government closed down the Arminian churches in the Dutch republic, and those Arminian ministers who refused to conform to the decisions of Dort were deposed from office. Some were even banished or fled the country until a measure of toleration was restored beginning in 1625. In addition, one of the most powerful political champions of the Arminian party, Johan van Oldenbarnevelt, was beheaded for treason on

---

6. Donald Sinnema, Christian Moser, and Herman Selderhuis, eds., *Acta et Documenta Synodi Nationalis Dordrechtanae (1618–1619)*, vol. 1 (Göttingen: Vandenhoeck & Ruprecht, 2015).
7. Carl Bangs, *Arminius: A Study in the Dutch Reformation* (Nashville: Abingdon, 1971), 275.

May 13, 1619—one more indication that in the nearly sixty years between the Belgic Confession and the Canons of Dort, the religious and political fortunes of the Reformed churches in the Lowlands had dramatically changed.[8]

Theological Comparison

Although there is definite overlap in the theology of the Canons of Dort and the Belgic Confession, the two documents differ in the scope, depth, and shape of their doctrinal material. First of all, the Belgic Confession covers all the major loci, or points of doctrine, of Christian theology, though not in great depth. Beginning with the doctrines of God and Scripture (arts. 1–11), it roughly follows the history of redemption by moving from the creation and fall of humanity (arts. 12–15) to the person and work of Christ (16–21), the ministry of the Holy Spirit in salvation (arts. 22–26), the church and the sacraments (arts. 27–36), and the last judgment (art. 37).

Second, as we have already noted, the theology of the Belgic Confession was molded in part by the two distinct audiences that de Brès had in mind, the persecutors and the persecuted. On the one hand, the Belgic Confession functioned as a kind of apology, or defense of the Reformed faith, to King Philip II of Spain, seeking to assure him that Protestant believers in the Low Countries not only respected civil government and its officers but also adhered to orthodox Christian doctrine. Almost the entire first half of the Belgic Confession contains "affirmations of the universal, apostolic Christian faith held in common with Roman Catholics": the being and attributes of God (art. 1), the inspiration of Scripture (art. 3), the Trinity (arts. 8–9), the deity of Christ (art. 10), the deity of the Holy Spirit (art. 11), creation (art. 12), providence (art. 13), original sin (art. 15), the incarnation and two natures of Christ (arts. 18–19), and the atonement (arts. 20–21).[9]

On the other hand, the Belgic Confession was also intended as an instruction manual in the basics of the Reformed faith for the underground congregations in the Lowlands. The second half of the confession, in particular, highlights some of the major differences between Protestant and Roman Catholic teaching. For example, Christ and His merits are all that are necessary for salvation (art. 22); we are justified through faith alone (art. 23); good works are the fruit, not the basis, of our salvation (art. 24); Christ alone, and not also the saints, intercedes for us before the Father

8. Philip Schaff, ed., *The Creeds of Christendom: With a History and Critical Notes*, 6th ed., vol. 1, *The History of Creeds* (1931; repr., Grand Rapids: Baker, 1990), 514–15.

9. John Bolt, "The Belgic Confession (1561): Testimony of an Oppressed Church," *Calvin Theological Seminary Forum* 20/1:7–8.

(art. 26); and the true church and false (i.e., Roman Catholic) church "are easy to recognize and thus to distinguish from each other" by their marks (art. 29). In applying the mark of "the pure administration of the sacraments," de Brès finds wanting both the Anabaptist and Catholic views on baptism (art. 34) as well as the Catholic doctrine of transubstantiation (art. 35).

Finally, de Brès intended the theology of the Belgic Confession to bring a word of comfort to his flock during a time of intense suffering. As he offers words of assurance to the persecuted, however, he still has the persecutors in his sights. "When the devils and the wicked act unjustly...this doctrine [of divine providence] gives us unspeakable comfort since it teaches that nothing can happen to us by chance but only by the arrangement of our gracious heavenly Father, who watches over us with fatherly care" (art. 13). The holy, catholic "church is preserved by God against the rage of the whole world, even though for a time it may appear very small to human eyes—as though it were snuffed out" (art. 27). And the final judgment will be a "very pleasant and a great comfort to the righteous and elect, since their total redemption will then be accomplished...and they will see the terrible vengeance that God will bring on the evil ones who tyrannized, oppressed, and tormented them in this world" (art. 37). Even these pastoral words of comfort are tinged with warnings to those instigating the persecution.

The theology of the Canons of Dort, by contrast, has a narrower scope, a greater depth, and a rather different shape from that of the Belgic Confession. Whereas the Belgic Confession is a systematic overview of all of Christian doctrine, summarizing the entire history of redemption from creation to consummation, the Canons of Dort focus on just the few points of doctrine that were in dispute during the Arminian controversy. But they explore these doctrines in much greater depth. In other words, the Belgic Confession has theological breadth but does not go very deep; the Canons of Dort have theological depth but do not go very wide.

The shape of the Canons of Dort was actually determined by an earlier Arminian document—namely, a 1610 Remonstrance (sharp protest) that laid out the Arminian position in five propositions:

1. God decreed to save those "who by the grace of the Holy Spirit shall believe" and "to leave the incorrigible and unbelieving in sin."

2. Christ died "for all men and for every man, so that He merited... forgiveness of sins for all...yet so that no one actually enjoys this forgiveness of sins except the believer."

3. "Man does not have saving faith of himself nor by the power of his own free will."

4. The grace of God must commence, progress, and complete any good in man "so that all good works…must be ascribed to the grace of God in Christ. But with respect to the mode of this grace, it is not irresistible, since it is written concerning many that they resisted the Holy Spirit."

5. Those who are "incorporated into Jesus Christ" are abundantly assisted in their struggle to persevere by the power of Christ and His Spirit, but "whether they can through negligence fall away…must first be more carefully determined from the Holy Scriptures."[10]

These five articles provided the structure for the later debates in the controversy and ultimately for the decisions of the Synod of Dort, which responded to the Remonstrance with a corresponding five heads of doctrine of its own in the Canons of Dort. These heads are often called "the five points of Calvinism," which is a misleading label because these points do not constitute the whole of Calvinist (Reformed) theology and do not in every respect represent the thinking of John Calvin. The five points are also often summarized using the acronym TULIP (Total depravity, Unconditional election, Limited atonement, Irresistible grace, Perseverance of the saints), a mnemonic device of relatively recent origin,[11] which has its own limitations. First, "tulip" is an English word and works as a memory aid only if one has a knowledge of the English language. Second, it does not accurately reflect the order of the five points of doctrine in the Canons of Dort, which are actually arranged as ULTIP rather than TULIP. Finally, the phrases suggested by each of the five "petals" of the TULIP oversimplify and sometimes even misrepresent the content of the doctrine to which they are attached. The term "total depravity," for example, could be misunderstood to mean that fallen humans are incapable of any moral good whatsoever, whereas the point of the Canons of Dort is that human depravity affects every part of a human being and renders us totally unable by ourselves to return to the favor of God. The head of doctrine on "unconditional election" is not just about election but about divine reprobation as well. The doctrine of "limited atonement" has to do not with shortcomings in the atonement but with the divine intention of the work of Christ and its

---

10. Jan N. Bakhuizen van den Brink, ed., *De Nederlandse Belijdenisgeschriften in Authentieke Teksten*, 2nd ed. (Amsterdam: Ton Bolland, 1976), 288–89. This abridgment of the five articles of the Remonstrance is found in Cornelius Plantinga Jr., *A Place to Stand: A Study of Ecumenical Creeds and Reformed Confessions* (Grand Rapids: Board of Publications of the Christian Reformed Church, 1979), 134.

11. Kenneth J. Stewart, "The Points of Calvinism: Retrospect and Prospect," *Scottish Bulletin of Evangelical Theology* 26.2 (2008): 187–203.

focus on the elect. The Canons of Dort also highlight in this point of doctrine the unlimited value and sufficiency of Christ's death and the proclamation of the gospel "without differentiation or discrimination to all nations and people" (II, art. 5).[12] "Irresistible grace" does not mean that God coerces people into relationship with Him against their will, but that His grace softens our resistance and "infuses new qualities into the will, making the dead will alive" (III/IV, art. 11). Finally, "perseverance of the saints" is possible, according to the Canons of Dort, only because of God's preservation of His elect.[13]

The Canons of Dort, therefore, serve as a kind of commentary, or long explanatory footnote, on certain teachings in the Belgic Confession and the Heidelberg Catechism that Arminius and his followers had called into question, particularly the doctrine of predestination (as in BC, art. 16). This role of the Canons of Dort as a fuller explanation of parts of the Belgic Confession is sometimes evident in the very wording of the two documents. Article 16 of the Belgic Confession, for example, builds its teaching on predestination around two of God's attributes, His mercy and His justice:

> We believe that—all Adam's descendants having thus fallen into perdition and ruin by the sin of Adam—God showed Himself to be as He is: *merciful* and *just*. God is *merciful* in withdrawing and saving from this perdition those who, in the eternal and unchangeable divine counsel, have been elected and chosen in Jesus Christ our Lord by His pure goodness, without any consideration of their works. God is *just* in leaving the others in their ruin and fall into which they plunged themselves (italics added).

The Canons of Dort's "commentary" on this article picks up the language of justice and mercy in its own more detailed description of predestination in the first main point of doctrine: the divine decree of election and reprobation is "God's act—unfathomable, and as *merciful* as it is *just*—of distinguishing between people equally lost" (art. 6, italics added). In election "God chose in Christ to salvation a definite number of particular people out of the entire human race...in order to demonstrate his *mercy*" (art. 7, italics added), and in reprobation "some have not been chosen or have been passed by in God's

---

12. All quotations from the Canons of Dort are from "The Canons of Dort," in *Our Faith: Ecumenical Creeds, Reformed Confessions, and Other Resources* (Grand Rapids: Faith Alive Christian Resources, 2013), 118–44.

13. For these reasons, those in the English-speaking world might find the FAITH acronym (Fallen humanity, Adopted by God, Intentional atonement, Transformed by the Holy Spirit, Held by God) more suitable for remembering the main points of the Canons of Dort. See Jim Osterhouse, *F.a.i.t.h. Unfolded: A Fresh Look at the Reformed Faith* (Grand Rapids: Faith Alive, 2011).

eternal election…in order to display his *justice*" (art. 15, italics added). Similarly, the Canons of Dort's Third Main Point of Doctrine (human corruption),
appears to elaborate on the statement in the Belgic Confession, article 14, that
fallen humanity "lost all their excellent gifts which they had received from
God, and retained none of them except for small traces which are enough to
make them inexcusable." The Canons of Dort echo and elaborate on some of
that language in its own assertion in article 4 that "a certain light of nature
remaining in all people after the fall" is inadequate to save them but enough
to "render themselves without excuse before God."

What we have here, therefore, is a second-generation Reformed confession
(CD) engaged in a deeper theological reflection on parts of a first-generation
confession (BC) that had come under attack in the intervening years. As the
formula of subscription adopted at the Synod of Dort described it, the Canons
of Dort were really an "explanation of some points of the aforesaid doctrine
[in the BC and HC] made by the National Synod of Dordrecht, 1619."[14]

The Canons of Dort and the Heidelberg Catechism
Historical Comparison
Historically and geographically, the Canons of Dort had less in common
with the Heidelberg Catechism than with the Belgic Confession. To be sure,
both the Canons of Dort and the Heidelberg Catechism came into existence
at the behest of rulers concerned about doctrinal disputes in their realms, but
the Heidelberg Catechism was composed two generations before the Canons
of Dort in a different part of Europe and on a much smaller stage. The Heidelberg Catechism was a territorial confession in a relatively small state in
the west-central region of the Holy Roman Empire (Germany); the Canons
of Dort were an international confession, drafted and adopted at a national
synod in the United Netherlands, which was still officially a part of the Holy
Roman Empire but had declared its independence in 1581.

Something of the history and purpose of the Heidelberg Catechism is
reflected in its full title: Catechism or Christian Instruction As This Is Conducted in Churches and Schools of the Electoral Palatinate.[15] First, although
the catechism was written, ratified, and published in the city of Heidelberg, it
was intended for use in the Electoral Palatinate, one of some three hundred

---

14. The full text of the formula in both English and the original Dutch can be found in
Sinnema, "Origin of the Form of Subscription," 273–74.

15. Parts of the following historical and theological summary are taken or adapted from
Lyle D. Bierma, "The Heidelberg Catechism," *Tabletalk* 32 (April 2008): 14–17, and are used
by permission of the publisher.

small states that made up the Holy Roman Empire in the sixteenth century. Second, the catechism was to provide "Instruction As This Is Conducted in Churches and Schools" of the territory. The Palatinate had become officially Protestant (Lutheran) in 1546, relatively late when one recalls that Luther had triggered the Reformation in another part of Germany almost thirty years earlier. When the political leader of the Palatinate, Elector Frederick III, came to power in 1559, he conducted a visitation of the churches in his realm to assess their spiritual progress. What he found was disheartening, especially the dearth of piety and knowledge of the Christian faith on the part of the young people. Where doctrinal instruction was being offered, teachers and preachers were using a variety of catechisms, and some instructors were confusing their students with irrelevant questions and unsound teachings. If we are really to bring about a reformation in our territory, Frederick III concluded, the place to begin is with the training of our children—youth ministry! And for that we need a single, clear guide to biblical truth and instructors who teach and live by that guide.[16]

Finally, the full title of the catechism refers to "Christian" instruction in the churches and schools. This may indicate a deliberate attempt on Frederick's part to avoid such labels as "Lutheran," "Calvinist," or "Zwinglian." The only legal form of Protestantism in the German Empire at that time was Lutheranism, as defined by the Augsburg Confession (1530). Frederick's predecessor, however, had opened the Palatinate to followers not only of Luther but also of Melanchthon, Bullinger, and Calvin, and Frederick III continued this policy as he became increasingly attracted to certain Reformed ideas. To help achieve religious and political stability in his realm, therefore, Frederick commissioned a catechism that would offer instruction in the fundamentals of the "Christian" faith, a summary of biblical doctrine that minimized differences and emphasized consensus among the Protestant factions in the territory.[17]

The production of such a catechism was assigned in 1562 to a team of Heidelberg ministers and university theologians under the watchful eye of Frederick himself. Two young members of the team, Zacharias Ursinus (1534–1583) and Caspar Olevianus (1536–1587), are often identified as the co-authors of the Heidelberg Catechism, but the consensus among scholars today

---

16. Lyle D. Bierma, "The Purpose and Authorship of the Heidelberg Catechism," in Lyle D. Bierma et al., *An Introduction to the Heidelberg Catechism: Sources, History, and Theology* (Grand Rapids: Baker Academic, 2005), 50–52.

17. Charles D. Gunnoe Jr., "The Reformation of the Palatinate and the Origins of the Heidelberg Catechism, 1500–1562," in Lyle D. Bierma et al., *An Introduction to the Heidelberg Catechism: Sources, History, and Theology* (Grand Rapids: Baker Academic, 2005), 15–47.

is that Ursinus was the primary writer and Olevianus had a lesser role. Ursinus was particularly well suited to the task not only because of his moderate, irenic disposition but also because he had studied under leading theologians from the different Protestant traditions in Wittenberg, Zurich, and Geneva.[18] The team perused and even borrowed language from a number of earlier catechisms, both Lutheran and Reformed, and the final draft of their work was adopted by a Palatinate synod in Heidelberg on January 18, 1563.

One of the major differences between the Heidelberg Catechism and Canons of Dort, therefore, was in their approach to overcoming intra-Protestant doctrinal differences in their respective realms. In the Heidelberg Catechism Frederick III sought to bring the Protestant parties in the Palatinate together by focusing largely on broadly Christian themes, common theological ground, and positive statements of doctrine. However, in the Netherlands nearly sixty years later, the matters in dispute were considered so fundamental to the Christian gospel that nothing short of a clear delineation of Reformed orthodoxy and a sharp rejection of errors was required. Frederick III was seeking to complete the Reformation; the Synod of Dort was seeking to preserve and defend it. The elector was constructing theological bridges (HC); the Synod of Dort, theological fences (CD).

Theological Comparison
The theological differences between the Canons of Dort and Heidelberg Catechism are found, once again, not in divergent doctrinal positions but in the shape, scope, and depth of their doctrinal contents. The shape and scope of the Heidelberg Catechism was determined, first of all, by the simple fact that it was a catechism. Like most other catechisms before and after it, the Heidelberg Catechism provides an explanation of the basic elements of the Christian faith: the Apostles' Creed, the Ten Commandments, the Lord's Prayer, and the sacraments. What is distinctive about the Heidelberg Catechism, however, is that it connects these expositions to a single, overarching theme—Christian comfort—introduced in the famous first question and answer: "What is your only comfort in life and in death? That I am not my own, but belong—body and soul—to my faithful Savior, Jesus Christ."[19]

To live and die in the joy of such comfort, I must know three things: how great my sin and *misery* are, how I am *delivered* from such sin and misery,

---

18. Bierma, "Purpose and Authorship," 52–74.

19. All quotations from the Heidelberg Catechism are from "The Heidelberg Catechism," in *Our Faith: Ecumenical Creeds, Reformed Confessions, and Other Resources* (Grand Rapids: Faith Alive Christian Resources, 2013), 69–117.

and how I can live in *gratitude* to God for such deliverance (HC 2). These subthemes of misery, deliverance, and gratitude form the three major divisions of the Heidelberg Catechism, and the expositions of the basic elements of Christianity are woven through them. We come to know our misery through a summary of the Ten Commandments (HC 3–5). We come to know our deliverance through the gospel as summarized in the Apostles' Creed (HC 19–58), which is signified and sealed through the sacraments (HC 65–85). Finally, it is through each of the Ten Commandments (HC 92–115) and the Lord's Prayer (HC 116–129) that we come to know ways of expressing our gratitude for this deliverance. In short, the Heidelberg Catechism directs all the fundamentals of the Christian faith toward the comfort of the believer.

In choosing comfort as the central motif of the Heidelberg Catechism, the authors were addressing the spiritual anxieties of the day. Against the background of a Catholic sacramental system that required acts of penance to help pay for one's sins, the Heidelberg Catechism proclaims the comfort of belonging to a Christ "who has *fully* paid for *all* my sins" (HC 1). In contrast to a late medieval piety that encouraged people to do their best and then hope for the best, the Heidelberg Catechism proclaims the comfort of belonging to a Christ who "by his Holy Spirit *assures* me of eternal life" (HC 1). Good works are not a means by which we must earn our righteousness before God (HC 62), but the "fruit of gratitude" (HC 64), rooted in the renewing work of the Holy Spirit (HC 86). Here, as in many other places, the Heidelberg Catechism shows itself as both a pastoral and a polemical document, sensitive to the spiritual *dis*comfort of an audience raised in the Roman Catholic tradition and responding with comforting truths from the gospel. Surprisingly, the Heidelberg Catechism is silent or at least muted on certain teachings that are usually associated with the Reformed theological tradition: election, reprobation, covenant, particular atonement, and perseverance of the saints. But this can probably be explained by the intent of the authors to instruct young people and uneducated adults in only the basics of the Christian faith, not some of its more complex doctrines, and to emphasize points of convergence, not divergence or dispute, among the various Protestant parties in the state.

The Canons of Dort, by contrast, represent an international but exclusively Reformed response to theological issues raised within the Reformed family of churches in the Netherlands. It also covers a much narrower range of doctrine, as we have seen, and, unlike the Heidelberg Catechism, amplifies rather than mutes such doctrines as predestination, particular atonement, and perseverance. As with respect to the Belgic Confession, the Canons of Dort serve as a kind of "commentary" on parts of the Heidelberg Catechism—

reiterating, defending, or further explicating certain teachings in the Heidelberg Catechism as it addresses the challenges of the Remonstrants. For example, in laying a foundation for the doctrine of limited atonement in the Second Main Point, the Canons of Dort employ some of the actual phrasing of the Heidelberg Catechism, again revolving around the justice and mercy of God:

Canons of Dort	**Heidelberg Catechism**
God is not only supremely merciful, but also supremely just (II, 1).	God is certainly merciful, but also just (11)
This justice requires…that the sins we have committed against His infinite majesty be punished with both temporal and eternal punishments, of soul as well as body (II, 1).	As a just judge, God will punish [our sins] both now and in eternity…. God's justice demands that sin, committed against His supreme majesty, be punished with the supreme penalty—eternal punishment of body and soul (10–11).
We cannot escape these punishments unless satisfaction is given to God's justice (II, 1).	How then can we escape this punishment and return to God's favor? God requires that His justice be satisfied (12).

Another example can be found in the third main point of doctrine ("total depravity"), where the Canons of Dort clarify the phrase "unable to do any good" in Heidelberg Catechism 8 ("But are we so corrupt that we are totally unable to do any good…? Yes, unless we are born again by the Spirit of God.") by interpreting it as our being "unfit for any *saving* good" (III/IV, 3, italics added).

Despite these differences in theological scope and depth, the Canons of Dort exhibit some surprising similarities with the Heidelberg Catechism as well. First, in a number of places the Canons of Dort manifest the same kind of pastoral and practical tone that we find throughout the catechism. When we reach article 12 of the first main point of doctrine on election and reprobation, for example, "suddenly the air warms and the atmosphere brightens. We pass from somewhat chilly and technical material into some articles of genuine pastoral concern."[20] Article 12 recognizes that in real life, assurance of election does not happen all at once but "in due time…by various stages and in differing measures." Article 16 assures believers worried about being

---

20. Plantinga, *A Place to Stand*, 140.

reprobate that it is not they but "those who have forgotten God and their Savior Jesus Christ and have abandoned themselves wholly to the cares of this world and the pleasures of the flesh [who] have every reason to stand in fear of this teaching." And article 14 cautions the church to teach election "with a spirit of discretion, in a godly and holy manner, at the appropriate time and place...for the glory of God's most holy name, and for the lively *comfort* of God's people" (italics added).

The Canons of Dort also share with the Heidelberg Catechism some awareness, unusual for the age, of the missional responsibility of the church. Heidelberg Catechism 86 concludes its answer to the question of why we should do good works with an explicit reference to evangelism by deed or example: "so that our neighbors may be won over to Christ." The Canons of Dort expand this view of the church's mission by underscoring the Word ministry of the church, even quoting in the first main point, article 3, Paul's famous "missionary" text in Romans 10:

> In order that people may be brought to faith, God mercifully sends messengers of this very joyful message to the people and at the time He wills. By this ministry people are called to repentance and faith in Christ crucified. For "how shall they believe in him of whom they have not heard? And how shall they hear without someone preaching? And how shall they preach unless they have been sent?" (vv. 14–15).

At a time when Protestant attention was still focused largely on the continent of Europe, the Canons of Dort calls these "messengers of this very joyful message" to engage in this ministry on a global scale: "Moreover, it is the promise of the gospel that whoever believes in Christ crucified shall not perish but have eternal life. This promise, together with the command to repent and believe, ought to be announced and declared without differentiation or discrimination to all nations and people, to whom God in His good pleasure sends the gospel" (II, 5). This universal "ministry of the gospel" is the means by which God brings His chosen ones to salvation (III/IV, 10).

As different, therefore, as the Belgic Confession, Heidelberg Catechism, and Canons of Dort are—historically, geographically, and theologically—they are still remarkably similar in their theological orientation, pastoral tone, and practical approach to doctrine. They also share a set of common purposes: to unify, educate, and comfort early modern communities of Reformed believers and to establish boundaries of orthodoxy in their particular contexts. The term "Three Forms of Unity," therefore, reflects not only the goal of these confessions but the very nature of the documents themselves.

CHAPTER 3

The English Delegation to the Synod of Dort

Kevin J. Bidwell

King James I of England, who was also King James VI of Scotland (1567–1625), was the central figure behind the selection of the English delegation to the Synod of Dort. This monarch was the first to rule the two kingdoms of England and Scotland with a freshly united crown, a situation which would inevitably lead England into unchartered challenges. What a momentous opportunity lay upon this king's shoulders to make a success of the newly constituted monarchy. It would be a far from easy task for the Stuart king to navigate his way through this stormy political season on the Continent in order to support the Dutch Calvinists. His leadership prowess had already been demonstrated though his prime legacy, that of the completion of the Authorized Bible translation (first published in 1611) and one that bears his name to this day, affectionately called the King James Bible.

Something lesser known, possibly because it has been airbrushed out of British Christian history, was that King James had a decisive hand in the Synod of Dort in the Low Countries (1618–1619). This synod's task was to clarify the definition of salvation according to a Calvinistic worldview in response to Arminian points that had been controversially proposed. The king's involvement through sending a delegation of ministers laboring in England to attend the Synod was most likely a move of royal pragmatism to uphold regional stability that was theologically driven and politically motivated.

The unfolding of events leading up to this international synod, which drafted articles to shape the church's understanding of the gospel until that point in the church's history, had an impact upon the English church in its own day. The king's decision to be involved and to send a delegation may have sent shock waves among some of the bishops in the Church of England at that time. The Stuart King James I (r. 1603–1625) had succeeded the Tudor Queen Elizabeth I (r. 1558–1603), whom some argue had produced only a "half-baked" English settlement of reform. Therefore, there may have been some trepidation among the clergy that James's Dutch Calvinistic support would then lead to an Arminian purge back in England. It did not.

Remnants of thought as espoused by Jacobus Arminius (1560–1609) would have found favor in many British circles in comparison to John Calvin's (1509–1564) perceived hardline presbyterian position, in which a presbyterian church model would have had little sympathy from many bishops. James undoubtedly would have been cognizant of the Dutch presbyterian leanings, and as one who asserted "no bishops, no King," his involvement would inevitably supply problems down the line for him and the Church of England. Elizabeth had supported the Dutch against the Spanish, and now James's support would have been a logical extension of that policy to endear favor with the United Provinces in the Low Countries against the Spanish.

While the background to the political and theological climate in the Low Countries was highly polarized, the same cannot be said of England. The backcloth out of which the English delegates were sent was a nuanced variation of views. The historical canvas of theological perspectives in England from 1600 to 1640 was far from simple. Anthony Milton writes that "there was a broad spectrum of views" between 1600 and 1640 "running from crypto-popish 'Arminian' zealots on the one hand, through to die-hard Puritan nonconformists on the other."[1] This diversity is confirmed by Chad Van Dixhoorn's understanding of the purpose of the Westminster Assembly. He believes the assembly's concern was mainly for religious unity so that England and Scotland could be Reformed in "doctrine, worship, discipline and government."[2] Therefore, historical theology should treat the first half of the seventeenth century in England with great care, because it appears that a rainbow of theology and ecclesiology existed among the Puritan and Calvinistic preachers.

Arguably, the Canons of Dort became later subsumed into the statements made by the Westminster Assembly (1643–1653)[3] and its catechisms, but few British churchmen are as familiar today with its ecclesial forerunner, the Synod of Dort, as with the Westminster Assembly in London. While many

---

1. Anthony Milton, *Catholic and Reformed: The Roman and Protestant Churches in English Protestant Thought, 1600–1640* (Cambridge: Cambridge University Press, 1995), 5.
2. Chad Van Dixhoorn, "The Making of the Westminster Larger Catechism" in http://www.the-highway.com/larger-catechism_Dixhoorn.html, 2.
3. "Of Christ the Mediator, Chapter 8 of The Westminster Confession of Faith," in Kevin J. Bidwell, *The Westminster Standards for Today: Recovering the Church and Worship for Everyday Christian Living* (Welwyn Garden City, U.K.: Evangelical Press, 2017), 185–88.

in the English-speaking world are familiar with the five points of Calvinism, summarized with the acronym TULIP, many would surely benefit from understanding more about the groundbreaking church synod in the Low Countries from 1618 to 1619. This essay forms part of a collection of essays that commemorates the 400th anniversary of the impact of the Synod and particularly examines the English delegation to it. In considering this delegation, it is insightful to learn about each of the delegates particularly, along with their collective influence at the Synod.

The Westminster Assembly sat in the years between 1643 and 1653 with most of its business being concluded prior to 1649. The period then between these two great assemblies in Dort and London was only twenty-five years. The Canons of Dort undoubtedly bore influence upon the deliberations in the Westminster Assembly. Therefore, the better we comprehend the English influence upon the Dort theological discussions, the better we can understand the English church in its run-up to the Westminster Assembly. Currently, the Synod of Dort is insufficiently discussed by many English-speaking Christians. It would serve the church in the English-speaking world well to revisit this synod and to learn from the Dordrecht divines.

The Background to the Synod of Dordrecht from an English Perspective

The town of Dordrecht in one of the United (Dutch) Provinces of the Low Countries provided the landmark stage for an assembling of Protestant divines. It commenced on November 13, 1618, and continued until May 9, 1619. Having completed their work, the English delegation left the assembly before the end in 1619 to return to England and report back about the proceedings.

It was only in 1648 that Dutch liberation was finally won after the bitter Eighty Years War. This war was waged against Roman Catholic hostility and persecution from King Philip of Spain. The liberation of the Dutch Protestant people was followed by theological controversy, and it led to the commencement of the Synod of Dort only eight years later. This "crucible of conflict" is the backcloth to this theological settlement, but all along, local Dutch delegates would have borne a fresh memory of this conflict. Memories of Protestant patriots during the time of Spanish persecution would have been burned into their consciences. The crux issue which fueled the death of thousands of Protestant Christians was that they simply refused to bow the knee at the Roman altar of *transubstantiation*. Therefore, a Protestant stand against compromise concerning salvation was not a simple matter. The English delegates would not have had to bear the consequences directly if the

Synod got it wrong. Therefore, we should always bear in mind that one's context impacts one's motivation and outlook. The Dutch national identity was at stake. It was being newly forged, and religion would be an integral component in the forming of that Calvinistic identity.

In the hand of the Lord's infallible providence, the Low Countries became an amphitheater of theological conflict. While the Reformed faith flowed from Geneva in many directions, the thought of Calvin and the Genevan church blueprint was the last theological stream to enter that part of the European world. Roman Catholic dogma, Anabaptist ideas, and Lutheranism were already present. Calvinism, as it is now known, was becoming firmly rooted in Dutch soil, but there was not yet a unified position. One of those positions, Arminianism, was becoming as popular as it was pernicious.

Jacobus Arminius is no stranger to contemporary evangelical religion. He is the founder of the doctrinal system for salvation called Arminianism. This Arminian theological system opposes Calvinism by proposing a weakened view of sin and election with the possibility of man's free choice to attain salvation. A supposed salvation freely available for all, without the caveat of God's gracious election, concludes that the individual alone makes the final decision for salvation. This, of course, diminishes the glory of God in salvation. This raises an important question: Who has the final casting vote in election and salvation, is it God or man? The followers of Arminius presented and signed a Remonstrance (1610) against the Calvinist orthodoxy of the University of Leiden theologian Franciscus Gomarus (1563–1641), who was the figurehead for the Counter-Remonstrants. This Remonstrance, probably unknowingly at the time, became the catalyst for a storm of ideological and religious thought. The battle lines were drawn, but the battle rages to the present day, despite the synod's conclusions.

As in most regions of Europe where loyalty to Rome divided parties, the newfound United Provinces was no exception. This theological storm was equivalent to a constitutional crisis, and there had to be a resolution. The Remonstrants, according to Milton, had support from the "famous international jurist Hugo Grotius and the distinguished statesman Johan van Oldenbarnevelt."[4] As the political struggle ensued, the greatest Counter-Remonstrant supporter was Count Maurice of Nassau (prince of Orange after 1617). K. H. D. Haley writes memorably that Count Maurice said: "He did not know whether predestination was blue or green, but even if

---

4. Anthony Milton, *The British Delegation and the Synod of Dort (1618–19)* (Woodbridge, Suffolk: Boydell Press, 2005), xvii.

he did know its colour, he decided by his support to make it orange."[5] The Orangist party affirmed Calvinistic predestinarian doctrine while the Contra-Remonstrants were at the same time busy imprisoning Grotius. The net result was the sense that the Arminian Remonstrants who first appeared at the Synod in December were effectually the accused and condemned, even before the hearings were given.

Had this synod been restricted to the regional parties of the Low Countries, it would never have gained such influence and recognition; it was its international character which precipitated its influence to the present day. There were delegates from the Palatinate, Switzerland, Geneva, Emden, Hesse, Bremen, Nassau/Wetteravia, as well as delegations from the Church of England (there were invitations sent to France and Brandenburg, but they did not attend).

The presence of delegates from the Church of England raised valid questions as to their Calvinist and Reformed identity or otherwise, both then and now. In researching this chapter, I visited a substantial Church of England library in Sheffield, England, only to find that they did not stock a single book on the Synod of Dort. The presence of English delegates sent by King James appears to have been erased from their history books and the Dort doctrinal formulations forgotten and buried. But why? Hopefully, this chapter will help to set the record of history straight and help us to consider recovering lost doctrines for the church in England and those of all English-speaking evangelical persuasions.

King James and His Choice of Delegates to the Synod

King James played his hand to support the Calvinistic party in the Dutch Republic. His team would have been carefully chosen, if not handpicked. Milton states that "James chose the delegates because he knew that they would not favour the Remonstrants. Indeed given the urgent need for a unified political settlement, it would have made little sense not to do so."[6] Milton astutely examines the representativeness of the delegates, and he rightly raises the question of episcopacy with the sending of Bishop Carleton of Llandaff.[7]

Our next section will highlight each of the king's delegates at the Synod. Apart from the choice of a single Scottish man Balcanquhall and his ministerial life in England, this was an English delegation. Despite the assertion

---

5. K. H. D. Haley, *Dutch in the Seventeenth Century* (New York: Thames and Hudson, 1972), 105.

6. Milton, *The British Delegation and the Synod of Dort (1618–19)*, xxviii.

7. Milton, *The British Delegation and the Synod of Dort (1618–19)*, xxviii–xxxvi.

by the distinguished historian and expert on this subject Anthony Milton, who prefers the notion of the "British Delegation," it was an English-oriented delegation, and King James gave little space for the Scots or the presence of manifest presbyterian sympathies among his chosen representatives. So was it representative of the British church? The answer is no, and thus the issue is how was the delegation representative of the Church of England?

The episcopal structures for the Church of England were never in serious threat until the years leading up to the Westminster Assembly, probably after the death of King James. It was not until the 1630s, after the death of King James, that future Westminster divines, such as Stanley Gower, began to offer a voice of dissent concerning this pattern of church government. He considered the church bishops to be "Babel's bricklayers," and he advised that "episcopacy should be abolished altogether or reduced to its 'first order'." Instead, he believed that "ultimate authority should be shared with the presbyters."[8]

It should not surprise us that a bishop is included in the king's lineup; indeed, we may wonder why more bishops were not included. It was undoubtedly an episcopal-leaning delegation, but to what degree did that shape their soteriology and Calvinistic theology? The general theological landscape was varied with Puritan ideals, bubbling separatist opinions, and calls for various amounts of reform in the Church of England.[9] Scotland had other issues to contend with, but the overall presbyterian trajectory was somewhat settled, though perhaps soteriology would have been less established. It is controversy that often forges the truth for the church upon the anvil of doctrinal dispute. The doctrine of salvation from a Calvinistic mind-set needed clarification for posterity's sake.

This royal delegation of five men was given a royal mandate at Newmarket, Suffolk, in October 1619. Michael Dewar mentions that they were to

8. Jacqueline Eales, *Puritans and Roundheads: The Harleys of Brampton Bryan and the Outbreak of the English Civil War* (Glasgow: Hardinge Simpole Publishing, 2002), 107, 111.

9. The historical context of English church reform during the late sixteenth and early seventeenth centuries is a much-discussed topic. Here are some references that are helpful to give some preliminary insights: Meic Pearse, *The Great Restoration* (Carlisle: Paternoster, 1998); Nick Lunn, "Laurence Chaderton—Puritan, Scholar, and Bible Translator," *Banner of Truth* 537 (June 2008): 1–7; J. I. Packer, *Among God's Giants* (1991; repr., Eastbourne: Kingsway, 2000); Basil Hall, "Puritanism: The Problem of Definition," in *Studies in Church History*, vol. 2, ed. G. J. Cunning (Nashville: Nelson, 1965); Francis J. Bremer, *The Puritan Experiment: New England Society from Bradford to Edwards* (Basingstoke: Palgrave Macmillan, 1976); and Patrick Collinson, *The Elizabethan Puritan Movement* (1967; repr., Wotton-Under-Edge: Clarendon Press, 1990), 86.

"inure themselves fully into the Latin tongue, to show unity among themselves, to keep to Scripture" and the Church of England doctrine.[10]

The English-Speaking Delegates at the Synod

The names of the delegates would have been illustrious, a well-chosen list—at least in the eyes of the king. However, according to Joel R. Beeke and Randall J. Pederson, history remembers some of the delegates as Puritans. The so-called Puritan movement, broadly spanning from 1560 to 1660, marks out such ministers who were known for pursuing a purity of doctrine, worship, and church government.

The historian Michael Dewar introduces ambiguity on our subject. On the one hand, he believes that King James's delegates "were Calvinists to a man." But on the other hand, he asserts that "they were 'Protestants,' not 'Puritans,' not cavilling at ceremonies or 'scrupling' at surplices."[11] But these assertions beg a question: What defines a Calvinist? It is well documented that the delegates were not necessarily entirely sympathetic to all the details of the Canons of Dort, which formulated a Calvinistic soteriology. Some delegates held to hypothetical universalism, a doctrine that doubts the doctrine of particular redemption espoused by the Dort divines. Therefore, we must ask serious questions, such as How can someone be identified as a Calvinist? What defines a Calvinist? Is it only soteriology that makes one a Calvinist, despite their ecclesiology? In the light of the Canons of Dort, it is suspect in my opinion to be called a Calvinist while expressing doubt on tenets of the faith such as particular redemption.

We know that the theological views of this delegation were far from homogeneous among each other and with respect to the views on the finalized Dort doctrinal formulations. With respect to the atonement discussion, it is known that the English "delegates expressed the existence of different opinions among the Episcopate."[12] Therefore, in defending their position of hypothetical universalism, they asserted that other learned English divines held the same position.[13] The English delegation was at variance with the Synod's fifth article on perseverance in urging that true believers and the regenerate could fall from the faith of justification and that people holding

---

10. Michael Dewar, "The British Delegation at the Synod of Dort: Assembling and Assembled; Returning and Returned," *Churchman* 106/2 (1992): 130–46.

11. Dewar, "The British Delegation at the Synod of Dort," 133.

12. Milton, *The British Delegation and the Synod of Dort (1618–19)*, xxxi.

13. Milton, *The British Delegation and the Synod of Dort (1618–19)*, xxxi.

such views should not be condemned.[14] These views are anomalous with a historic understanding of Reformed doctrine and seem to be a diluted form of Calvinism, a modified Calvinism, or some would contend if measured against the Canons of Dort, no Calvinism at all.

So, what did the Thirty-Nine Articles of the Church of England espouse on matters to which Dort deliberated? We must be reminded that the Church of England agreed upon their historic articles in 1562, and there is parity on salvation with other Reformed confessions. The Belgic Confession held by Dutch Calvinists was authored primarily by the Dutch Reformed minister Guido de Brès, and it was finished in 1561. A copy was sent to the king of Spain the following year, and it was adopted at the Synod of Dort. The Belgic Confession is Reformed and presbyterial in terms of its doctrine for church government, worship, and doctrine. The Thirty-Nine Articles of the Church of England are Calvinistic in part, though certainly Protestant in supporting doctrines such as predestination and election.[15] Therefore, had the English delegation been confessionally faithful to their own articles, there should have been greater English congruence with the Dutch on soteriology than there was. There are theological gaps in those 39 Articles that should be mentioned, such as little coverage being given to the doctrine of the perseverance of the saints. It was for this precise reason that in the 1640's the Westminster Assembly sought to produce a more robust Reformed statement of faith, to supersede the 39 Articles for the Church, which in fairness was a very early document of the Reformation.

This brief comment enables us to understand that there were differences in the theology of ministers in the Low Countries versus the 39 Article men from England; the 39 Articles were insufficiently robust to contend against the newly formed Arminian doctrines.

---

14. Milton, *The British Delegation and the Synod of Dort (1618–19)*, xxxi–xxxii.

15. In the Thirty-Nine Articles of Religion of the Church of England, article XVII is "Predestination and Election," and the first paragraph reads: "Predestination to Life is the everlasting purpose of God, whereby (before the foundations of the world were laid) he hath constantly decreed by His counsel secret to us, to deliver from curse and damnation those *whom he hath chosen in Christ out of mankind*, and to bring them by Christ to everlasting salvation, as vessels made to honour. Wherefore, they which be endued with so excellent a benefit of God be called according to God's purpose by His Spirit working in due season: they through Grace obey the calling: they be justified freely: they be made sons of God by adoption: they be made like the image of His only-begotten Son Jesus Christ: they walk religiously in good works, and at length, by God's mercy, they attain to everlasting felicity" (italics mine).

Let us now examine the persons and theology of each of King James's men sent to Dordrecht. The royal expectation laid upon them was their support of the Counter-Remonstrants, while still professing the views of the Church of England.

George Carleton (Bishop of Llandaff)

George Carleton (1557/8–1628) was born in Norham, Northumberland, and was serving as the bishop of Llandaff (South Wales) when he was sent to the Synod of Dort. Carleton was consecrated to his first bishopric in Llandaff on July 12, 1618, and it was just months afterward that he was required to attend the Synod. Nicholas W. S. Cranfield notes that he was "invited only as an observer at the synod" where he "spoke out against adopting article 31 of the Belgic Confession."[16] This article concerns church government, and Carleton was convinced of bishops and episcopacy rather than presbyterian elders.

At the time of the Synod, this bishop believed in episcopacy in terms of church government while supporting Calvinistic doctrine. Cranfield notes that when the articles of the Synod of Dort appeared in English in 1623 that "Carleton urged Archbishop Abbot to have a convocation to adopt them, in order to uphold Calvinist theology of grace as the official doctrine of the Church of England."[17] At the Synod itself, "Carleton knew that some bishops espoused a 'general redemption' instead of a particular one, even though it was not the official position of the Church of England."[18] He was politically astute, but he appears to have held the line on Dort's key points.

Carleton was no doubt lacking experience as a bishop when he arrived at Dort, but he can be considered to have reasonably supported Calvinism in his representation. He continued this influence in the years following the convocation and several of his writings are worthy of note. In 1615 he wrote "Directions to Know the True Church" where he espoused that the Church of Rome had remained true in doctrine until the time of Luther. Cranfield comments that this position was seconded by James Ussher, the puritan John White and his contemporary at Dort, Joseph Hall. He wrote of the failed 1605 Gunpowder Plot, in which the Roman Catholics attempted a political blow to Protestant England. Most noteworthy was an anti-Arminian tract that he wrote at the onset of Charles I's reign. Later Charles I promoted him to the bishopric of Chichester.

---

16. Nicholas W. S. Cranfield, "George Carleton," in *Oxford Dictionary of National Biography (Online)* (Oxford: Oxford University Press, 2008), https://doi.org/10.1093/ref:odnb/4671.

17. Cranfield, "George Carleton."

18. Milton, *The British Delegation and the Synod of Dort (1618–19)*, xxxii, n60.

Joseph Hall (Dean of Worcester)

Joseph Hall (1574–1656) straddles a crucial time frame, one that includes both the doctrinal struggles of Dort and the Westminster Assembly. Joseph Hall, together with John Davenant and Samuel Ward, may be considered Puritan, at least in broad terms.[19] It is believed that while Hall studied at Emmanuel College, Cambridge, he "gained a life-long love for Puritan piety, though he supported Anglican rather than Presbyterian ecclesiology."[20]

At the Synod "he worked for an amicable confessional settlement between the Reformed and the Arminians, albeit from a distinctly Reformed perspective."[21] Realistically, whether such a settlement is possible is doubtful. This may have led to his breakdown in health and his subsequent departure from Dort's deliberations. Dewar is less favorable in his evaluation of him because Hall's sudden departure from the Synod and return to England "always had an air of mystery." He writes about one whom he deems to quite possibly have been the theologically "ablest" of the English delegates.[22] His limited involvement, however, makes this claim hard to determine. Many years later in 1627, subsequent to his involvement in Dort, he was elevated to bishop of Exeter. There he was renowned to be a bishop with Calvinistic leanings. However, he maintained a toleration of the Roman Church. This theological trajectory undermined his Protestant convictions. It is hard to see how true Calvinism can sit in such compromised thinking.

John Davenant (Master of Queens College, Cambridge)

John Davenant (1572–1641) leaves for us a twin legacy: his attendance at the Synod of Dort and the production of his magisterial *Exposition of Colossians* (1627).[23] But what was his contribution at the Synod? Vivienne Larminie outlines that in arguing for a moderate position at Dort's debates "after painstaking

---

19. Joel R. Beeke and Randall J. Pederson, *Meet the Puritans: With a Guide to Modern Reprints* (Grand Rapids: Reformation Heritage Books, 2006). Beeke and Pederson did not include Ward in their book because they included only Puritans who had books reprinted in the last fifty years.

20. Beeke and Pederson, *Meet the Puritans,* 309. A valuable historical point is that he did not sit in the Westminster Assembly.

21. Beeke and Pederson, *Meet the Puritans,* 310.

22. Dewar, "The British Delegation at the Synod of Dort."

23. John Davenant, *An Exposition of the Epistle of Saint Paul to the Colossians* (Edinburgh: Banner of Truth, 2005). C. H. Spurgeon "placed Davenant on Colossians in the first rank of commentaries on this Pauline epistle." Charles Bridges stated that "I know no exposition upon which a detached portion of Scripture (with the single exception of Owen on the Hebrews) that will compare with it in all parts…in depth, accuracy and discursiveness." The book first appeared in Latin (Cambridge, 1627).

analysis of the issues dividing conservatives from the Arminian Remonstrants," that Davenant and his English friend Samuel Ward joined with ministers from Bremen in arguing for "hypothetical universalism."[24] He was what is adversarially called today a "four point Calvinist." It is a weakening of the doctrine of salvation through asserting that Christ died for all men, not just for the elect. It is the adopting of an Arminian tenet into Calvinism. W. B. Patterson asserts that "the other British representatives were persuaded to accept this view, and maintained it in the conflicts which followed, 'decisively,'" thus "influencing the Synod's final decrees." Further he writes that "although the decrees which were read out at Dort on 6 May 1619 were not universally to British taste, on the whole they represented a judicious compromise such as generally reflected Davenant's, Ward's, and also James I's own attitudes."[25] This is a fascinating insight. If Patterson is correct, then the English delegates led a charge to "water down" the doctrine of particular redemption.

Beeke and Pedersen note that "regrettably, Davenant held to 'hypothetical universalism,' a mild form of universal redemption, attested not only to James Ussher and Richard Baxter, but also by Davenant's 'A Dissertation on the Death of Christ,' which he finished shortly after leaving Dordrecht."[26] They write that, moreover, "Davenant and the English delegates won Synod over to the view that the debate on redemption must be worked out in terms of both sufficiency and efficiency"; however, Davenant went further by holding that "the Father and the Son had a conditional intention to save all, though that condition was not absolutely efficacious."[27]

A developing picture is emerging as we read the sketches of the English delegates. Their being sent to Dort by King James I led, in some measure, to their subsequent promotion in the English church. For Davenant, it came in 1621, and his sphere of influence increased as he became the bishop of Salisbury. His name is still affectionately associated with that town to this day.

---

24. Vivienne Larminie, "John Davenant," in *Oxford Dictionary of National Biography (Online)* (Oxford: Oxford University Press, 2008), https://doi.org/10.1093/ref:odnb/7196.

25. W. B. Patterson, *King James VI and I and the Reunion of Christendom* (Cambridge: Cambridge University Press, 1997), 276.

26. Beeke and Pederson, *Meet the Puritans*, 170.

27. Beeke and Pederson, *Meet the Puritans*, 170–71. See also W. Robert Godfrey, "Tensions with International Calvinism: The Debate on the Atonement at the Synod of Dort" (PhD diss., Stanford University, 1974), 179–88.

Samuel Ward (Master of Sydney Sussex College, Cambridge)

Samuel Ward (1572–1643) is a prime example of the doctrinal complexities held by some men who in every generation hold theological inconsistencies while still supporting Calvinism and Reformed orthodoxy. This does not mean that we turn a blind eye to error, but it does challenge us to know exactly where to draw lines for church unity. So what was Ward's theological trajectory at the Synod?

Ward was born at Bishop Middleham in County Durham. He studied at Cambridge, where he was influenced by the Puritans William Perkins and Laurence Chaderton. In 1610, he was elected to the mastership of the "newest Puritan foundation, Sydney Sussex College where he remained until his death."[28] It appears that Ward was given a host of other titles in which he nominally filled the role, such as his appointment in 1615 as archdeacon of Taunton. Todd explains that "evidence of Ward's activities outside of Cambridge is sparse…[and] his principal commitment was always to his college, to biblical and theological scholarship, and especially to the maintenance of Calvinist orthodoxy."[29] Despite being an outspoken Calvinist, Ward was sent by King James to the Synod of Dort, where Episcopius (the chief spokesman of the Remonstrants) perceived him to be "the most learned member" of the five English delegates. There was probably a nuanced difference between Davenant and Ward on the matter of universalism. Ward argued that "Christ's death won only the possibility of salvation for all and remained merely potential for the reprobate, God having selected some and not others."[30] In my mind, the notion of God calling freely and efficaciously from the mass of the reprobate is a far more satisfying proposition than Davenant on this issue. Suffice it to say, we must recognize that Ward joined all the other delegates in full support of all five articles of the Synod against the Remonstrants.[31]

Ward was given the title of Lady Margaret Professor of Divinity in 1623, and he continued to refute Arminianism and stood specifically against the Arminian doctrine of resistible grace. This faithful theologian remained a lifelong proponent of predestinarianism. Under his guidance, Sydney Sussex College attracted Puritans such as Oliver Cromwell, Thomas Edwards,

---

28. Margo Todd, "Samuel Ward," in *Oxford Dictionary of National Biography (Online)* (Oxford: Oxford University Press, 2008), https://doi.org/10.1093/ref:odnb/28705.

29. Todd, "Samuel Ward."

30. Todd, "Samuel Ward."

31. Debora Shuger, ed., *Religion in Early Stuart England, 1603–1638: An Anthology of Primary Sources* (Baylor, Tex.: Baylor University Press, 2012).

and Thomas Gataker, as well as refugees from Heidelberg.[32] If any of these delegates should be remembered as a Puritan, it was Samuel Ward. Upon his return from Dort, Ward had a towering influence in the 1620s and 1630s, not least in his association with Cromwell. He became a man who worked for a theological and reforming influence in the church in England in the years prior to the Westminster Assembly.

With the rise of Charles I (r. 1625–1649), Ward would have found himself in a precarious and marginalized position, not least with the king's choice of Arminian Archbishop William Laud (1573–1645). During civil hostilities in March 1643, Ward was unable to give financial support from the college to the king or to the opposing parliament. Following a brief imprisonment due to his lack of support for the parliament forces, Ward died in the master's lodge at the college on September 7, 1643. He was expected to attend the Westminster Assembly as part of 120 clergymen, from its commencement in July 1643. Illness prevented his participation. The fact that parliament included him highlights the respect and esteem he enjoyed from his peers.

Walter Balcanquhall (Fellow of Pembroke Hall, Cambridge)
This sole Scottish figure (c. 1586–1645) among the king's delegates to Dort was born and educated in Edinburgh. According to John Coffey, Balcanquhall became a "convinced Episcopalian." He took his first ministerial post as a vicar of a local Church of England parish in Harston, Cambridgeshire, in 1615.[33] In 1610, he began studies at Pembroke College, Cambridge, where he became a fellow the following year. His appointment as chaplain to the king on December 16, 1617, placed him in a prime position "to represent the Church of Scotland at the synod," according to Coffey. This begs many questions. Though Scottish by birth, how could a Scottish-convinced episcopalian represent the presbyterian church of Scotland? The answer is simple: he was sent as a delegate by the king, not by the church. Balcanquhall appears to have made up the numbers in the delegation as a token Scottish representative. The company of delegates overall were clearly English minded, episcopalian in their affiliation to the Church of England, and yet in some measure Calvinistic.

Dewar echoes similar thoughts as he writes that Balcanquhall is "often thought to represent the Church of Scotland," yet "he was neither a member of it, nor a Presbyterian minister."[34] The best way to think of King James's

---

32. Shuger, *Religion in Early Stuart England.*
33. John Coffey, "Walter Balcanquhall," in *Oxford Dictionary of National Biography (Online)* (Oxford: Oxford University Press, 2008), https://doi.org/10.1093/ref:odnb/1151.
34. Dewar, "The British Delegation at the Synod of Dort."

Erastian college of delegates is that it was effectually representing the Church of England and King James.[35]

Balcanquhall arrived late, just before Christmas of 1618. Coffey concludes that he "endorsed the Synod's condemnation of the Remonstrants, but distanced himself from militant Counter-Remonstrants like Gomarus and their doctrines of supralapsarianism and limited atonement."[36]

In 1625, he became dean of Rochester. Sadly, however, he later denounced Puritans before King Charles I, supported the Laudian agenda, and gathered intelligence against his fellow Scottish people, notably against the Covenanters in 1638. In 1641, the Scottish parliament condemned him as an incendiary. The Covenanters also denounced him, and Robert Baillie's letters reveal that "many Englishmen thought him a 'vile man.'"[37] Following his seeking refuge in Oxford, the headquarters of Charles I in the English Civil War, Balcanquhall died in Chirk Castle Denbighshire (Wales) on Christmas Day 1645.

Thomas Goade (Chaplain to Archbishop George Abbot)

Thomas Goade (1576–1638) was educated at King's College, Cambridge, where in 1595 he became a fellow. Elizabeth Allen notes that he was "influenced by the strong Calvinism of his father and that of George Abbot (1562–1633) who became the Archbishop of Canterbury in 1611, he then proceeded to appoint Goade as his chaplain."[38] In 1619, Abbot took the initiative for Goade to replace the early departing Joseph Hall from the Synod. Allen writes that "Goade shared Abbot's Calvinist view that Christ died only for the elect."[39] It seems that the defining line of being a "true Calvinist," for Archbishop Abbot at least, was concerning the matter of particular redemption.

The work of Goade remained stable post-Dort, at least until his master died and was subsequently replaced by Archbishop Laud. Afterward Goade was moved to a new post—rural dean of Bocking in Essex. He is the one delegate sent to Dort under King James's patronage who suffered demotion and estrangement later in life on the basis of his commitment to Calvinism.

---

35. I prefer to avoid the use of the label "British delegates" to prevent a misunderstanding as to their scope of representation.

36. Coffey, "Walter Balcanquhall."

37. Coffey, "Walter Balcanquhall." *The Letters and Journals of Robert Baillie, 1637–1662,* ed. David Laing (n.p.: Nabu Press, 2011), 1:286.

38. Elizabeth Allen, "Thomas Goade," in *Oxford Dictionary of National Biography (Online)* (Oxford: Oxford University Press, 2008), https://doi.org/10.1093/ref:odnb/10848.

39. Allen, "Thomas Goade."

However, this happened under the watch not of James I but his son and successor, the controversial figure Charles I.

It is desired that these sketches of the king's delegates individually and collectively provide a landscape of their contribution upon this historic synod. While they were episcopal in church governance, the crucial issue was Calvinism. It is evident that the "pupil in the eye" of Calvinism was particular redemption, as against universalism. The English voice, notably Davenant, in contending with the Counter-Remonstrance moderator Johan Bogerman, sought to soften or modify the final written Canons of Dort on "the infinite value of the death of Christ." The second head of doctrine is called "The Death of Christ and the Redemption of Man by It." Article 3 reads: "This death of the Son of God is the only and most perfect sacrifice and satisfaction for sins, of infinite value and worth, abundantly sufficient to expiate the sins of the whole world."

While this article pleased all parties, at least so that the Church of England delegates signed off on all the Canons, arguably there is insufficient precision and clarity here, which left the door open for a variety of positions to be maintained on the extent of the atonement. Positively, Milton is right to assert that there was a "distinctiveness of the contribution of the English delegates"[40] and their presence buttressed the international reputation of that synod.

So how significant were the Canons of Dort upon the life of the Church of England upon the return of the delegates? Was it viewed merely as a Dutch affair, one of little consequence for the British church? While the Synod enjoyed a favorable viewing due to James's involvement and by his support of the Dutch Calvinists, practically the Canons never held significant influence in England. Milton observes that divines such as William Laud and others "did what they could to undermine the authority and reputation of the Synod, but only came out fully against it after the death of King James."[41] More specifically, Milton claims that "just six years after the return" of the delegates, that "William Laud and his colleagues were already condemning the deeds of the Synod and were hinting darkly that such a non-Episcopalian assembly posed a threat to the established Church of England."[42] Laud used his vast ecclesiastical power to undermine the effects of Calvinism, Reformation, and the Synod of Dort in England.[43]

---

40. Milton, *The British Delegation and the Synod of Dort (1618–19)*, xxxvi–il.
41. Milton, *The British Delegation and the Synod of Dort (1618–19)*, xxx.
42. Milton, *The British Delegation and the Synod of Dort (1618–19)*, xix.
43. Milton, *The British Delegation and the Synod of Dort (1618–19)*, xix.

The Church in England would have to wait until the removal of Laud and the gathering of the Westminster Assembly for the topic of the death of Christ to be debated and further clarified in the Westminster Confession and Catechisms.

Conclusion

Nothing is ever truly and finally settled in this sinful world. The ever-active role of the leaven of sin ensures that final resolution will not be met in a fallen world. At different moments in history, doctrine emerges to challenge the church's understanding of Holy Scripture. It is Scripture alone that is the final bar of theological judgment, and not history or even the convictions of a famous theologian. Though the Synod of Dort achieved a magisterial settlement in the seventeenth century, there is much work to be done in the twenty-first century to teach, promote, and recover those historic truths. In this celebration of the 400th anniversary of the Synod of Dort, may we who profess to be Calvinist and Reformed—whether subscribing to the Three Forms of Unity or the Westminster Standards—endeavor to promote a biblical soteriology, thus magnifying the unspeakable glory of our sovereign God.

CHAPTER 4

The Everlasting Love of God: Election and Predestination

John V. Fesko

The doctrine of predestination and the Canons of Dort (CD) are irrefragably linked together. Many in the Reformed world look fondly upon the Synod's pronouncements on this topic, but others look upon it as a great doctrinal tragedy.[1] In terms of the popular nineteenth-century acrostic TULIP, people object to the U, unconditional election. While the merits of the TULIP acrostic are debatable, we can nevertheless ask, What does the Synod mean by "unconditional election"? Far from a loveless act from a distant God, the Synod's doctrine of predestination, even unconditional election, is ultimately a manifestation of the eternal and everlasting love of the triune God.[2] God bases His decision of election on His will and not the will of the sinner; in this manner the decree is unconditional.

In order to demonstrate this claim, this chapter begins with a brief survey of the views of Jacob Arminius (1560–1609). The historical background of Arminius's rejection of the common early modern Reformed doctrine of predestination sets the stage for a better understanding of the Synod's pronouncements.[3] Arminius was the doctrinal impetus for the formal

---

1. See, e.g., Nicolaus Hunnius, *Diaskepsis Theologica: A Theological Examination of the Fundamental Difference between Evangelical Lutheran Doctrine and Calvinist or Reformed Teaching,* trans. Richard J. Dina and Elmer Hohle (1626; repr., Malone, Tex.: Repristination Press, 2001).

2. This chapter focuses on the positive side of predestination—namely, election. For a historical treatment of reprobation, see Donald W. Sinnema, "The Issue of Reprobation at the Synod of Dort (1618–19) in Light of the History of This Doctrine" (PhD diss., University of St. Michael's College, 1985). For two brief primary source treatments from one of the delegates to the Synod and a participant, see Johannes Maccovius, *Scholastic Discourse: Johannes Maccovius (1588–1644) on Theological and Philosophical Distinctions and Rules,* trans. Willem J. van Asselt et al. (Apeldoorn: Instituut voor Reformatieonderzoek, 2009), 7:155–66; and William Ames, *The Marrow of Theology,* trans. John Dykstra Eusden (Grand Rapids: Baker, 1968), I.xxv. 152–56.

3. For an overview of the early modern Reformed doctrine of predestination, see Pieter

Remonstrance, and thus his views are essential for setting the context of the Synod's doctrine. Second, this chapter then explores the Synod's response to the Remonstrance, as well as its positive statements on the doctrine of predestination. It both surveys the Canons of Dort but also provides contextual information from theologians of the period who were either contemporaneous with or participants at the Synod. In the third and final section, the chapter presents a summary analysis of where, precisely, the Remonstrant and Reformed doctrines differ. The chapter concludes with some final observations about the Synod's doctrine of predestination.

Arminius and the Remonstrance

Arminius on Predestination

What drove Arminius to reject the common early modern Reformed doctrine of predestination? Some have posited that while Arminius was a student at Geneva he encountered the strict supralapsarian views of Theodore Beza (1519–1605) and thus reacted negatively to them.[4] But the truth of the matter is that Arminius was dissatisfied with Reformed views, whether of the supra- or infralapsarian varieties.[5] Stated briefly, Beza initially posed the question to John Calvin (1509–1564) regarding the status of the lump in Romans 9:21: "Hath not the potter power over the clay, of the same lump to make one vessel unto honour, and another unto dishonour?" Is the lump of which Paul writes pure and sinless or sinful and corrupt? In other words, is the object of predestination *homo creabilis et labilis* ("man creatable and liable to fall") or *homo creatus et lapsus* ("man created and fallen")?[6] A simpler way to formulate

---

Rouwendal, "The Doctrine of Predestination in Reformed Orthodoxy," in *A Companion to Reformed Orthodoxy*, ed. Herman J. Selderhuis (Leiden: Brill, 2013), 553–90; Cornelis Venema, *Chosen in Christ: Revisiting the Contours of Predestination* (Fearn: Mentor, 2019), chaps. 5–6; Richard A. Muller, *Christ and the Decree: Christology and Predestination in Reformed Theology from Calvin to Perkins* (1986; repr., Grand Rapids: Baker Academic, 2008).

4. Carl Bangs, *Arminius: A Study in the Dutch Reformation* (Eugene, Ore.: Wipf and Stock, 1998), 71–72.

5. For Arminius's interaction with William Perkins (1558–1602), Francis Junius (1545–1602), and Franciscus Gomarus (1563–1641) on predestination, see "Friendly Conference with Dr. F. Junius," "Modest Examination of Dr. Perkins's Pamphlet," and "Examination of the Theses of Dr. F. Gomarus Respecting Predestination," in *The Works of James Arminius*, trans. James Nichols and William Nichols (1825; repr., Grand Rapids: Baker, 1996), 3:1–484, 521–658.

6. Theodore Beza, "Beza to Calvin, 21 January 1552," and "Beza to Calvin, 29 July 1555," in Philip C. Holtrop, *The Bolsec Controversy on Predestination, from 1551–1555. The Statements of Jerome Bolsec and the Responses of John Calvin, Theodore Beza, and Other Reformed Theologians*, (Lewiston, N.Y.: The Edwin Mellen Press, 1993), 1/2:731–40; and *Correspondance de Théodore de Bèze*, vol. 1, 1539–1555, ed. Hippolyte Aubert (Geneva: Droz, 1960), 81–83, 169–72.

this question is, Does God take sin into account when He predestines some to everlasting life and rejects others? There were two major schools of thought on this question, although there were a number of subvariants on these two formulations.[7] Supra- and infralapsarians both recognized that God's decree is one and indivisible, but given our finitude, humans must conceive of the logical priorities in God's one decree according to various distinct decrees. Therefore, supra- and infralapsarians conceive of the order of decrees (*ordo decretorum*) in the following distinct manners:

Infralapsarianism	**Supralapsarianism**
1. Create	1. Predestine some individuals to salvation and others to damnation
2. Permit the fall	
3. Predestine the elect and pass by or reprobate the rest of fallen sinners	2. Create
	3. Permit the fall
4. Appoint Christ as savior to redeem the elect	4. Appoint Christ as savior to redeem the elect
5. Provide the means of salvation— i.e., the Holy Spirit and the means of grace	5. Provide the means of salvation— i.e., the Holy Spirit and the means of grace

We must note that both of these orderings are not chronological or temporal, but are part of God's pretemporal eternal decree prior to the creation of the world. Arminius rejected both of these.[8]

Arminius posits his own order of the decrees, which immediately reveals that his objection was neither to the scholastic nature of the views nor to the doctrine of predestination per se, but to common Reformed views.[9] According to Arminius, God

---

7. Note, the infra- and supralapsarian positions presented here are basic views, but there are several other variants. See Richard A. Muller, "Revisiting the Predestination Paradigm: An Alternative to Supralapsarianism, Infralapsarianism, and Hypothetical Universalism" (Mid-America Fall Lecture Series, Dyer, Ind., Fall 2008). Cf. with the taxonomy presented in Edward Leigh, *A Systeme or Body of Divinity: Consisting of Ten Books* (London: William Lee, 1654), III.i (220). Also see Maccovius, *Scholastic Discourse*, VII.iv (157).

8. Keith D. Stanglin and Thomas H. McCall, *Jacob Arminius: Theologian of Grace* (Oxford: Oxford University Press, 2012), 106–40, esp. 140 for the infra- and supralapsarian order of the decrees.

9. On Arminius's positive relationship to scholasticism, see Richard A. Muller, "Arminius and the Scholastic Tradition," *Calvin Theological Journal* 24 (1989): 263–77.

1. Makes an absolute decree concerning the salvation of sinful humans and appoints Jesus as savior.

2. Decrees to receive into His favor those who repent and believe in Christ and who persevere to the end, but conversely leaves all unrepentant sinners in a state of condemnation and ultimately damnation.

3. Administers the necessary means for repentance and faith in a sufficient and efficacious manner according to God's wisdom.

4. Decrees to save and damn certain particular persons, which has a foundation in the foreknowledge of God, by which He knew from eternity who would through His grace believe and persevere, and who, according to His foreknowledge, would not believe or persevere.[10]

The first three decrees do not necessarily seem all that different from the infra- and supralapsarian orders, but the fourth and final decree reveals the nature of Arminius's view. Unlike common Reformed views, Arminius bases God's predestination and rejection of individuals upon His foreknowledge— the foreseen belief and unbelief of different individuals. This fourth point sheds light on the previous three decrees and reveals that Arminius begins with two absolute decrees and the predestination of a class of people, not individuals. In the third, God decrees the necessary means for the class of repentant people but still has not, as of yet, determined who specifically is elected or rejected. Only by God's foreknowledge of foreseen unbelief and repentance, then, do the previous three decrees make sense.[11]

A simple contrast distinguishes Arminius from his Reformed peers: Arminius believes that God looks into the future to see what free choices people will make to believe or not believe, whereas Reformed theologians believe that God elects apart from a consideration of future free choices. On the whole, this is a fair general statement of the differences, but there are two theological characteristics in Arminius's order of the decrees that set his view apart: (1) his use of the *antecedent* and *consequent* will of God; and (2) his advocacy of *middle knowledge*. First, Reformed theologians were willing to employ the distinction between the antecedent and consequent will of God (*voluntas Dei antecedens vel consequens*). Theologians used this set of terms to distinguish between the absolute antecedent will of God, such as in the decree of election, and the consequent will of God, which is how He orders proximate causes

---

10. Jacob Arminius, *Declaration of Sentiments*, V, in *Works*, 1:653–54.
11. Richard A. Muller, "Grace, Election, and Contingent Choice: Arminius's Gambit and the Reformed Response," in *The Grace of God and the Bondage of the Will*, ed. Thomas R. Schreiner and Bruce A. Ware (Grand Rapids: Baker, 1995), 2:251–78, esp. 257–59.

and effects as they relate to the universal order and its laws that arise out of contingent events brought about by creaturely free wills.[12] An example of the consequent will of God is when He antecedently wills to punish unremitted sins and then consequently wills the damnation of a particular individual because of his sins. In other words, the consequent will of God is a byproduct of His antecedent will.[13] The Reformed place the decree of election in the antecedent will of God and the elect's subsequent salvation in His consequent will. Arminius inverts this pattern by placing the salvation of the general class of believers in the antecedent will of God and then their election in His consequent will. But Arminius's construction of God's consequent will does not rest in God's antecedent will but in the will of those who choose to believe in Jesus. In this form, the distinction assumes two contradictory wills in God, makes God reactive to human decisions, constitutes a denial of divine freedom of the will, and suggests contingency in God Himself.[14]

Second, Arminius advocated the doctrine of *middle knowledge* to undergird his doctrine of predestination.[15] In historic Reformed understandings of the knowledge of God (*scientia Dei*), theologians distinguished between *scientia necessaria* (necessary knowledge) and the *scientia visionis* (knowledge of vision). God's necessary knowledge is what He knows by virtue of His nature as God: His unqualified, absolute, and unbounded knowledge. By way of contrast, the knowledge of vision, or *scientia voluntaria* (knowledge of will), is God's knowledge as a consequence of His will; He knows all that He has decreed to come to pass.[16] In between the necessary and visionary (or voluntary) knowledge of God, Arminius followed Roman Catholic theologians Luis de Molina (1535–1600) and Francisco Suarez (1548–1617) in positing *scientia media* (middle knowledge). It was called middle knowledge because it supposedly sat in the middle of God's necessary and visionary knowledge thus: necessary knowledge, middle knowledge, and visionary (or voluntary) knowledge.[17] God's middle knowledge rests upon His knowledge of future contingents because of an event's occurrence. Middle knowledge is hence causally independent

12. Richard A. Muller, *Dictionary of Latin and Greek Theological Terms: Drawn Principally from Protestant Scholastic Theology*, 2nd ed. (1985; repr., Grand Rapids: Baker Academic, 2017), 400.

13. Muller, *Dictionary*, 401.

14. Muller, *Dictionary*, 400.

15. Richard A. Muller, *God, Creation, and Providence in the Thought of Jacob Arminius: Sources and Directions of Scholastic Protestantism in the Era of Early Orthodoxy* (Grand Rapids: Baker, 1991), 163–66; Muller, "Grace, Election, and Contingent Choice," 259–68; and Eef Dekker, "Was Arminius a Molinist?," *Sixteenth Century Journal* 27/2 (1996): 337–52.

16. Muller, *Dictionary*, 324–25.

17. Muller, *Dictionary*, 324.

of and consequent to events in time. Arminius employed middle knowledge in his third and fourth decrees to create an arena where human beings could presumably freely choose to believe in Christ.[18] God did not cause but only observed human free choices to believe or not believe. Arminius chose this route because he believed it freed God from the potential accusation that He was the author of sin, which was in his mind a legitimate if even undesired consequence of both the supra- and infralapsarian positions.[19]

The Remonstrance on Predestination

Arminius struck a chord with a number of Dutch Reformed pastors and theologians with his divergent views on predestination. A year after his death, Arminius's friend Johannes Uitenbogaert (1557–1644) and more than forty other ministers of the Reformed church in the Netherlands presented their Remonstrance, otherwise known as the Arminian Articles, in 1610. They formally requested of the Dutch government a national synod in order to revise the Belgic Confession and Heidelberg Catechism. They challenged the prevailing theology of the day on five major issues: (1) instead of humanity's total inability, they argued that there was some degree of human freedom that allowed sinners to repent; (2) instead of unconditional election, they believed that God chose the elect on the basis of His foreknowledge of their decision to believe; (3) they claimed that Christ's satisfaction extended to all people even though only those who believed in Jesus would be saved; (4) they promoted the idea that sinners could resist the saving grace of God; and (5) instead of an indefectible perseverance, they argued that it was possible for a person to lose his salvation.[20] The Remonstrance met with some initial success, as the government initially determined that the Remonstrants were allowed to continue their ministries free from censure; moreover, Remonstrant views were tolerated among newly examined ministers. Despite this decision, Remonstrants and anti-Remonstrants failed to reach a theological compromise on the disputed issues and engaged in a pamphlet war; thus the anti-Remonstrants convened an international synod in 1618–1619 to deal with the Remonstrance.[21]

---

18. Muller, *Dictionary*, 325.

19. Stanglin and McCall, *Jacob Arminius*, 112–13, 129–32.

20. The Remonstrance, or the Arminian Articles (1610), in Jaroslav Pelikan and Valerie Hotchkiss, eds., *Creeds and Confessions of Faith in the Christian Tradition* (New Haven, Conn.: Yale University Press, 2003), II:547. Hereafter all subsequent references to Pelikan and Hotchkiss will appear as *Creeds*.

21. The Remonstrance, in *Creeds*, II:547.

The first point of the Remonstrance deals with the doctrine of predestination and echoes Arminius's teaching on the subject. The Remonstrance states

> that God, by an eternal and unchangeable purpose in Jesus Christ His Son, before the foundations of the world were laid, determined to save, out of the human race which had fallen into sin, in Christ, for Christ's sake, and through Christ, those who through the grace of the Holy Spirit shall believe on the same His Son and shall through the same grace persevere in this same faith and obedience of faith even to the end; and on the other hand to leave under sin and wrath the contumacious and unbelieving and to condemn them as aliens from Christ, according to the word of the Gospel of John 3.36: "He who believes in the Son has eternal life; he who does not obey the Son shall not see life, but the wrath of God rests upon him," and other passages of Scripture.[22]

This first article addresses the doctrine of predestination but does so in a general way. The article neither addresses the technical lapsarian question nor invokes the word *foreknowledge*. Nevertheless, the article bears Arminius's fingerprints. Comparing this article with other common early modern Reformed confessions easily demonstrates the differences between the Remonstrant and Reformed doctrines of predestination.

The Second Helvetic Confession (1566), which was written by Heinrich Bullinger (1504–1575) and was adopted among the Swiss Reformed churches, for example, states: "From eternity God has freely, and of His mere grace, *without any respect to men*, predestinated or elected the saints whom He wills to save in Christ."[23] The Thirty-Nine Articles (1571) of the Church of England likewise state: "Predestination to life is the everlasting purpose of God, whereby (before the foundations of the world were laid), He hath constantly decreed by His counsel secret to us, to deliver from curse and damnation those whom He hath chosen in Christ out of mankind, and to bring them by Christ to everlasting salvation as vessels made to honor."[24] The confession that bears the most relevance for comparison with the Remonstrance is, of course, the Belgic (1561), which states: "We believe that…God…in His eternal and unchangeable counsel, has elected and chosen in Jesus Christ our Lord by His pure goodness, *without any consideration of their works*."[25] All three examples emphasize that predestination is God's choice and do not give

---

22. The Remonstrance, art. I, in *Creeds*, II:549.
23. Second Helvetic Confession, X.i, in *Creeds*, II:473, emphasis added; see also 458–59.
24. Thirty-Nine Articles, XVII, in *Creeds*, II:532.
25. Belgic Confession, XVI, in *Creeds*, II:413, emphasis added.

the slightest hint that He takes into account human actions or works in His inscrutable decree of election. In fact, the Second Helvetic and Belgic Confessions both highlight this point when they respectively state, "without any respect to men" and "without any consideration of their works."

The Remonstrance stands in stark contrast to these three Reformed confessions. The Remonstrance does not place emphasis on God's choice but rather on the choices of those who either believe or disbelieve the gospel: "God...determined to save...those who through the grace of the Holy Spirit shall believe on the same His Son and shall through the same grace persevere in the same faith and obedience of faith even to the end."[26] The Remonstrance does not mention the word *foreknowledge*, but it nevertheless introduces faith in Christ, obedience, and final perseverance as the underlying factors for God's decision to elect and conversely to reject. Arminius serves as the doctrinal impetus behind the Remonstrance's doctrine of predestination, and together they both set the stage for a thicker understanding of the Canons.

The Synod's Response

Prior to the convening of the Synod, other Reformed theologians expressed concern about Arminius's doctrine. Archbishop James Ussher (1581–1656), for example, was the chief architect of the Irish Articles (1615), which contributed to the first formal ecclesiastical rejection of Remonstrant doctrine.[27] The Irish Articles define predestination as God's sovereign choice and thus echo earlier Reformed confessions. But they arguably place a greater degree of emphasis upon the rejection of errors when they state: "The cause moving God to predestinate unto life is not the foreseeing of faith, or perseverance, or good works, or of any thing, which is in the person predestinated, but only the good pleasure of God Himself."[28] The Articles do not invoke the names of Arminius or the Remonstrance, but with this threefold rejection of grounds (foreseen faith, good works, and perseverance), they address the doctrine of predestination. Thus, the Synod's own convocation and efforts to address the Remonstrance were part of a larger European effort to deal with this doctrinal error.[29]

---

26. The Remonstrance, art. I, in *Creeds*, II:549.

27. Alan Ford, *James Ussher: Theology, History, and Politics in Early-Modern Ireland and England* (Oxford: Oxford University Press, 2007), 162–63.

28. Irish Articles, XIV, in *Creeds*, II:555.

29. Jonathan D. Moore, "James Ussher's Influence on the Synod of Dordt," in *Revisiting the Synod of Dordt (1618–19)*, ed. Aza Goudriaan and Fred van Lieburg (Leiden: Brill, 2011), 163–80.

The Synod convened in 1618 with Johannes Bogerman (1576–1637) presiding over a body of roughly eighty Dutch ministers and theologians and twenty-six representatives from the churches in England, Scotland, Germany, and Switzerland. Led by Simon Episcopius (1583–1643), thirteen Remonstrants were in attendance to participate in the Synod's deliberations. The Remonstrants were eventually dismissed and their views condemned by the Synod.[30] The Canons, of course, address the five points of the Remonstrance, but this chapter's concern lies with the first article, which treats the doctrine of predestination. Each section of the Canons first positively sets forth the doctrine and then presents a rejection of errors. Under the Canon's positive treatment of doctrine, the Synod presents eighteen articles that address the following topics:

1. God's right to condemn all people
2. The manifestation of God's love
3. The preaching of the gospel
4. The twofold response of the gospel
5. The sources of unbelief and of faith
6. God's eternal decision
7. Election
8. A single decision of election
9. Election not based on foreseen faith
10. Election based on God's good pleasure
11. Election unchangeable
12. The assurance of election
13. The fruit of this assurance
14. Teaching election properly
15. Reprobation
16. Response to the teaching of reprobation
17. The salvation of the infants of believers
18. The proper attitude toward election and reprobation

The first thing that likely strikes the reader is that the Synod's treatment of the doctrine is far more expansive than the solitary paragraph in the Remonstrance. The Synod wanted to provide a comprehensive response to the Remonstrant challenge.

---

30. *Creeds*, II:569.

That being said, articles 7, 9, and 10 are the most immediately relevant because they deal directly with the unique features of the Remonstrant doctrine. Article 7 is an extended statement that echoes earlier Reformed confessions when it highlights God's prerogative in predestination: "Before the foundation of the world, by sheer grace, according to the free good pleasure of His will, He chose in Christ to salvation a definite number of particular people out of the entire human race, which had fallen by its own fault from its original innocence into sin and ruin. Those chosen were neither better nor more deserving than others, but lay with them in the common misery."[31] The Synod explains election is by God's "sheer grace" and rests entirely with the divine will rather than with any consideration of human actions. Those whom God chooses are no better than others but are simply those whom God has predestined for salvation.

The seventh article expands upon earlier Reformed confessions when it explains that predestination is not on the basis of foreseen faith:

> This same election took place, not on the basis of foreseen faith, of the obedience of faith, of holiness, or of any other good quality and disposition, as though it were based on a prerequisite cause or condition in the person to be chosen, but rather for the purpose of faith, or the obedience of faith, of holiness, and so on. Accordingly, election is the source of each of the benefits of salvation. Faith, holiness, and the other saving gifts, and at last eternal life itself, flow forth from election as its fruits and effects. As the apostle says, "He chose us [not because we were, but] so that we should be holy and blameless before him in love."[32]

Like the earlier Irish Articles, this article rejects foreseen faith, obedience, holiness, or any other human quality as the motivating cause for election. But unlike earlier confessions, this article takes a step in a positive direction to explain the proper role of faith, obedience, and holiness. Rather than simply dismiss these human actions, the article explains that they have a proper soteriological place. But they do not have an antecedent but consequent role in predestination. That is, Arminius argued that God foresaw a person's faith and perseverance and on the basis of this foreknowledge chose people unto salvation. Dort, on the other hand, does not dismiss faith, obedience, and holiness but rather explains that they are the consequence, or effect, of divine

---

31. CD I, 7, in *Creeds*, II:572.
32. CD I, 9, in *Creeds*, II:573.

election rather than its antecedent cause. The next article then specifies what the true cause of divine election is when it states:

> But the cause of this undeserved election is exclusively the good pleasure of God. This does not involve His choosing certain human qualities or actions from among all those possible as a condition of salvation, but rather involves His adopting certain particular persons from among the common mass of sinners as His own possession. As Scripture says, "When the children were not yet born, and had done nothing either good or bad…, she [Rebecca] was told, 'The older will serve the younger.' As it is written, 'Jacob I loved, but Esau I hated'" [Rom. 9:11–13]. Also, "All who were appointed for eternal life believed" [Acts 13:48].

In contrast to the Remonstrants and Arminius but in line with earlier Reformed confessions, the Synod locates the motivating cause of election strictly in the divine will.

Analysis

While a simple juxtaposition of the Remonstrant and Reformed views on predestination reveals their differences, further analysis uncovers the specific exegetical and theological rationales for the Synod's rejection of the Remonstrant doctrine. In this analysis, explanations of theologians who were present at the Synod serve as the best sources of illuminating the Canon's doctrine of predestination. The following topics provide useful rubrics to delve into the exegetical and theological differences between the two positions: the good pleasure of God, the viability of middle knowledge, and the pastoral importance of predestination.

The Good Pleasure of God

Reformed theologians were well aware of the differences between common early modern Reformed versus Remonstrant views on predestination. As the seventh article above maintains, God did not base predestination on foreseen faith or works. This conviction marks Reformed theology before, during, and after the Synod of Dort. The *Leiden Synopsis* was a series of theological disputations that traced most of the major loci of theology and was written by four professors, three of whom were present at the Synod of Dort: Antonius Walaeus (1572–1639), Antonius Thysius (1565–1640), and Johannes Polyander

(1568–1646).[33] Nevertheless, the purpose of the *Leiden Synopsis* was to capture a purer form of theology in the wake of the Remonstrant controversy.[34] The *Synopsis*, therefore, provides an excellent window into the theological and exegetical rationales for rejecting the Remonstrant view, both because its authors were participants in the Synod and because it was written with the express purpose of refuting Remonstrant doctrine.

In his disputation on predestination, Walaeus identifies two different groups who try to locate the impelling cause of election in foreseen good works: the Pelagians and Remonstrants.[35] Pelagians maintained that God foresaw future good works that the elect would either do or would have done if they remained alive. But the Pelagian theory of election was rejected as heresy by the ancient church because it contradicted the clear witness of Scripture: "For the children being not yet born, neither having done any good or evil, that the purpose of God according to election might stand, not of works, but of him that calleth" (Rom. 9:11)."[36] Walaeus also appeals to Romans 11:5–6: "Even so then at this present time also there is a remnant according to the election of grace. And if by grace, then is it no more of works: otherwise grace is no more grace."[37] In Romans 9:11 Paul precludes good works as an impelling cause of election, and in Romans 11:5 he juxtaposes grace and works. Salvation cannot consist of a mixture of divine grace and human effort—such an attempted alchemy will not produce the gold of salvation. Rather, Paul presents an either/or argument when he contrasts grace and works. Walaeus opines, "If neither calling nor justification is based on works—as Scripture everywhere testifies—then indeed also election itself, which pertains to all things, cannot be based on works."[38] Walaeus notes that this Pelagian position was uncommon among the Reformed churches and thus does not offer further comments.

---

33. Antonius Walaeus, Antonius Thysius, Johannes Polyander, and Andreas Rivetus, Synopsis Purioris Theologiae/*Synopsis of a Purer Theology: Latin Text and English Translation*, vol. 2, Disputations 24–42, ed. Henk van den Belt, trans. Reimer A. Faber (Leiden: Brill, 2016).

34. Cf. Keith D. Stanglin, "How Much Purer is the *Synopsis Purioris Theologiae* (1625)? A Comparison of Leiden Disputations Before and After Dordt," *Church History and Religious Culture* 98/2 (2018): 195–224.

35. *Synopsis*, XXIV.xxxii: 44.

36. Cf. Pelagius, *Pelagius's Commentary on St. Paul's Epistle to the Romans*, trans. Theodore de Bruyn (Oxford: Oxford University Press, 2002), 115–20; Synod of Orange (529), in *Creeds*, I:693–98; CD I, rej. 5, in *Creeds*, II:578.

37. *Synopsis*, XXIV.xxxiii (44).

38. *Synopsis*, XXIV.xxxiii (44).

Walaeus spills a greater amount of ink in his refutation of the Remonstrant position, which "finds more supporters from among those who want to be members of the Reformed church."[39] Walaeus distinguishes between the Pelagian and Remonstrant positions.[40] According to Walaeus, Remonstrants believed "God decisively elected only those whose faith and perseverance He foresaw, at least as a prerequisite quality, and as a cause *sine qua non*."[41] Walaeus reflects the officially stated position of the Remonstrance.[42] If the Remonstrant position argued that faith and perseverance were granted purely by divine grace, then the difference between the two Reformed and Remonstrant views would be one of the logical order of the decrees and not one over the motivating cause of election.[43] But because the Remonstrants believed that faith and perseverance were antecedent prerequisites to election, Walaeus concludes that the Pelagian label was warranted even though they acknowledged that faith and perseverance rested partly in the gift of God and partly in human free will. In this conclusion Walaeus echoes the Synod's similar verdict in its rejection of errors.[44] To claim that faith and perseverance were prerequisites to election conflicts with Romans 9:16, which states that election does not depend upon man's will or effort but upon God's mercy. Other relevant passages include Romans 11:35, where Paul reminds the church, "Who hath first given to him, and it shall be recompensed unto him again?" The Scriptures attribute salvation entirely to God and remove everything from humanity in order that the redeemed boast solely in God.[45] Walaeus is fully aware that Remonstrants rejected the charge of Pelagianism. Arminius claimed true faith was ultimately given by God and by grace. Nevertheless, if God chose the elect on the basis of foreseen faith and perseverance, then one also had to factor foreseen works, even if they were partly by grace and partly by human free will.[46]

The Viability of Middle Knowledge
A second reason for the rejection of the Remonstrant view lies in the theological flaws inherent in the concept of middle knowledge. Gisbert Voetius (1589–1676) was one of the delegates to the Synod and wrote a number of theological

39. *Synopsis*, XXIV.xxxiv (44).
40. *Synopsis*, 44n25.
41. *Synopsis*, XXIV.xxxiv (44); cf. CD I, rej. 6, in *Creeds*, II:577.
42. Cf. The Remonstrance, art. I, in *Creeds*, II:549.
43. *Synopsis*, XXIV.xxxv (44–45).
44. CD I, rej. 4, in *Creeds*, II:577.
45. *Synopsis*, XXIV.xxxv (45).
46. *Synopsis*, XXIV.xxxvi (45), also n. 28; cf. e.g., Arminius, *Works*, 2:19.

disputations against the concept. Voetius and other Reformed theologians were well aware of the recent origins of the concept and the debates among Roman Catholic theologians who rejected the views of Augustine (354–430) and Thomas Aquinas (1225–1274). Debate broke out among the Jesuits and Dominicans over the views of Louis de Molina and Francisco Suarez.[47] The Reformed were also aware that the Remonstrants found the Jesuit doctrine of middle knowledge useful for their own doctrine of predestination.[48] Voetius and other Reformed theologians did not reject middle knowledge because of its Roman Catholic origins; such an objection would rest in the genetic fallacy. There were many aspects of medieval theology that the Reformed willingly employed because they were true.[49] Nevertheless, Voetius and others rejected middle knowledge because it was exegetically and theologically untenable.

Voetius offers a number of reasons why he rejects middle knowledge, but four stand out. First, "the division of divine knowledge into knowledge of single intelligence and that of vision exhausts the entire nature of the knowable object."[50] Recall the traditional distinction between God's necessary versus visionary (or voluntary) knowledge. On the one hand, God's necessary knowledge is what He knows by virtue of His nature as God; this knowledge is unqualified, absolute, and unbounded. Knowledge of vision, or *scientia voluntaria* (knowledge of will), on the other hand, is God's knowledge as a consequence of His will; He knows all that He has decreed to come to pass. According to Voetius there is no need for middle knowledge because His necessary and visionary knowledge exhaust all possibilities. By His necessary knowledge God knows all potential variables and possibilities. Conversely, God knows all that will come to pass by virtue of His knowledge

---

47. R. J. Matava, *Divine Causality and Human Free Choice: Domingo Bañez, Physical Premotion and the Controversy* De Auxiliis *Revisited* (Leiden: Brill, 2016).

48. Gisbert Voetius, *De Scientia Dei*, in *Selectarum Disputationum Theologicarum*, vol. 1 (Utrecht: Joannes à Waesberge, 1648), 1:254–57, in Heinrich Heppe, *Reformed Dogmatics: Set Out and Illustrated from the Sources*, ed. Ernst Bizer, trans. G. T. Thomson (London: George Allen & Unwin Ltd., 1950), 77–78.

49. See, e.g., William Perkins, *A Reformed Catholike, or a Declaration Shewing How Neere We May Come to the Present Church of Rome in Sundrie Points of Religion and Wherein We Must For Ever Depart From Them With an Advertisement to All Favorers of the Romane Religion, Shewing That the Said Religion Is Against the Cathoike Principles and Grounds of the Catechisme* (Cambridge: John Legat, 1598); and Willem J. van Asselt et al., *Introduction to Reformed Scholasticism* (Grand Rapids: Reformation Heritage Books, 2013).

50. Gisbert Voetius, *De Conditionata seu Media in Deo Scientia*, sect. III, in *Selectarum Disputationum Theologicarum* (Utrecht: Joannes à Waesberge, 1648), 1:309, in Heppe, *Reformed Dogmatics*, 79.

of vision (or voluntary knowledge) because He has decreed that it would come to pass.

Second, Voetius explains: "Whatever object is not knowable, there is no knowledge of it with God. But a conditioned future, one prior to any *actus* of the divine will is not knowable. Therefore there is no knowledge of it with God."[51] The Reformed believed that only things that God decreed could actually exist; if God did not decree that an event come to pass, then it would not exist in the decree, in His consequent visionary (or voluntary) knowledge, or in time. Reformed theologians such as James Ussher codified this conviction in the Irish Articles, which were written a few years before the Canons: "God from all eternity did, by His unchangeable counsel, ordain whatsoever in time should come to pass; yet so, as thereby no violence is offered to the wills of the reasonable creatures, and neither the liberty nor the contingency of the second causes is taken away, but established rather."[52] The only way for something to exist is if God decrees it. Yet, according to the proponents of middle knowledge, God observes the free acts of people apart from decreeing them. Voetius avers, "Could free conditioned things, from eternity indifferent by nature to futurition or non-futurition, have passed over into the state of a future event otherwise than by the divine decree?"[53] Hence, according to Voetius, "the object of middle knowledge is simply not-being and nothing. Therefore the knowledge itself is not knowledge."[54] That is, nothing can exist apart from God's decree, and thus undecreed human actions technically have no existence, and if they have no existence, then God can have no knowledge of them.

Third, according to Voetius, advocates of middle knowledge did not truly advocate a doctrine of *predestination*. God did not determine according to His own divine good pleasure who would and would not be chosen: "Pre-destination as regards this knowledge will have to be called postdestination rather than predestination, as regards the temporary object."[55] In other words, in Remonstrant formulations, predestination was not truly God's choice but merely the divine ratification of a foreseen human choice.

Fourth, and finally, Voetius believed that middle knowledge meant that God had to wait on the creature to act before He could decree events:

51. Voetius, *Selectarum Disputationum*, 1:310, in Heppe, *Reformed Dogmatics*, 79.
52. Irish Articles, XI, in *Creeds*, II:555.
53. Voetius, *Selectarum Disputationum*, 1:336, in Heppe, *Reformed Dogmatics*, 80.
54. Voetius, *Selectarum Disputationum*, 1:318, in Heppe, *Reformed Dogmatics*, 79.
55. Voetius, *Selectarum Disputationum*, 1:320, in Heppe, *Reformed Dogmatics*, 80.

> This is the center from which are drawn the shapeless and absurd hypotheses with which these hypothetical D. D.s wretchedly spatter both philosophy and also sacred theology, viz., that God's will were a blind potency in making decrees, but for the previous shining light of middle knowledge. Middle knowledge is effective and congruous for any end by its nature. Upon it God is forced to wait in the wise framing of His decrees, which are bound to have a fixed result. The truth or falsity of future conditioned free ones is not known from their causes or from the divine decree, but from the actual occurrence of the thing. Before every act of His will God can see certainty in things quite uncertain by their nature. In short, there is an *ens* independent of the supreme *ens*.[56]

In other words, God must await the outcome of human actions before He can decree future events (note, by "await," Voetius does not mean that God cannot decree events until the creation exists and history unfolds but rather in the eternal decree God must factor human decisions that He does not decree). This conclusion is not merely a matter of God reacting to human decisions but ultimately posits human agents as possessing some form of existence apart from God. In more technical terms, human agents become primary rather than secondary causes; or, correlatively, human agents possess some form of aseity (self-existence apart from God), something that only God possesses.

The Pastoral Importance of Predestination

Thus far the impression one might get is that the debate over predestination and the subsequent deliverances by the Synod yielded technical and seemingly speculative doctrinal conclusions. After all, the order of decrees and God's eternal knowledge may not immediately strike the reader as practical subjects; in fact, they might initially appear unwarranted and speculative. The delegates at the Synod of Dort were well aware of the possibility of misunderstanding and misusing the doctrine of predestination and thus insisted on addressing its pastoral aspects. The delegates were careful to explain three chief practical elements of the doctrine of predestination.

First, predestination was a source of the believer's assurance. The Canons explain that believers are not supposed to search "into the hidden and deep things of God," but rather were to look for the "unmistakable fruits of election pointed out in God's word—such as true faith in Christ,

---

56. Voetius, *Selectarum Disputationum*, 1:336, in Heppe, *Reformed Dogmatics*, 80–81; see also Maccovius, *Scholastic Discourse*, VII.iii, xiv, xix (155–57, 161, 165); Ames, *Marrow of Theology*, I.xxv.9, 12–14 (153–54); and CD I, rej. 1, 3, in *Creeds*, 2:576.

a childlike fear of God, a godly sorrow for their sins," and "a hunger and thirst for righteousness."[57] In other words, Christians should not speculate about what goes beyond Scripture and their ability to know. Instead, they must engage the doctrine of predestination through Scripture and its concrete Spirit-produced manifestations in the Christian life. Christians need to ask whether they truly believe in Christ, mourn over their sin, and hunger for righteousness. Such actions were sure signs that a person was elected by God.[58] This struggle in the Christian life was not supposed to be a source of unrest but comfort and assurance because, in spite of one's sin, the struggle was the evidence that God's decree of election and its fruit was manifest in a person's life. The realization that one was a benefactor of God's election was a spur to greater love and devotion. Believers were "to adore the fathomless depth of His mercies, to cleanse themselves, and to give fervent love in return to Him who first greatly loved them." Predestination, therefore, was not a license for a lax observation of God's commandments or a carnal self-assurance, but the sacred ground of love between God and His elect.[59]

Second, because predestination was taught throughout the Scriptures, pastors should preach and teach it in an edifying manner. True, the delegates at Dort believed that predestination was imminently practical, a fountain of assurance for believers and a motivating factor in their love for God, but at the same time they knew that it was challenging. Thus, the delegates opined, "This teaching must be set forth—with a spirit of discretion, in a godly and holy manner, at the appropriate time and place, without inquisitive searching into the ways of the Most High." Vain speculation was supposed to be far from the hearts and minds of pastors and theologians in the exploration of this doctrine. Instead, ministers were supposed to teach the doctrine "for the glory of God's most holy name, and for the lively comfort of His people."[60] The Canons do not mention him by name, but likely targets are Arminius and the speculative doctrine of middle knowledge—supposing that God

---

57. CD I, 12. Also see rej. 7, in *Creeds*, 1:573, 578.

58. Cf. Theodore Beza, *A Briefe Declaration of the Cheife Poyntes of Christian Religion Set Forth in a Table* (London: David Moptid and John Mather, 1575); Richard A. Muller, "The Use and Abuse of a Document: Beza's *Tabula Praedestinationis*, the Bolsec Controversy, and the Origins of Reformed Orthodoxy," in *Protestant Scholasticism: Essays in Reassessment*, ed. R. Scott Clark and Carl R. Trueman (Milton Keynes: Paternoster, 2005), 33–61; and Richard A. Muller, *Calvin and the Reformed Tradition: On the Work of Christ and the Order of Salvation* (Grand Rapids: Baker Academic, 2012), 244–76.

59. CD I, 13, in *Creeds*, II:574.

60. CD I, 12, and rej. 3, in *Creeds*, II:574, 576–77.

observes undecreed human decisions and then bases His own decrees upon such supposed observations.[61]

Third, the church needed to have a proper attitude regarding the doctrine of predestination. Echoing the apostle Paul, the delegates at Dort recognize that some within the church might have questions about the equity of God's election and reprobation. A censorious attitude has no place in the Christian's heart: "Nay but, O man, who art thou that repliest against God?" (Rom. 9:20). "For who hath known the mind of the Lord? or who hath been his counsellor?" (Rom. 11:33–36).[62] In other words, far from arrogance, the doctrine of predestination was a reminder of the need for humility and recognition that we are but creatures and the triune God alone is creator.

Conclusion

In summary, while some have vilified the Synod's doctrine of predestination, in truth, the delegates were jealous to preserve the integrity of God's sovereign, eternal love. Walaeus observes that because the Remonstrants based God's election on foreseen faith and works, these things precede God's election. Thus, in the Remonstrant view the doctrine of election cannot be a source of assurance for the believer because he never knows if he will persevere; God only elected those who persevere to the end. This conflicts with numerous passages of Scripture that state that faith, holiness, and perseverance stem from election (Matt. 24:24; Acts 13:48; Rom. 8:29; 11:24; Eph. 1:4). The moving cause of God's election, therefore, is His own good pleasure.[63] The simplest way to understand this truth is by asking, Do we first love God or does He first love us? Does our love of God commend us to God in His decree, or does His decree create in us the ability to love Him? The answer to these questions is simple: "We love him, because he first loved us" (1 John 4:19). The delegates at Dort sought to preserve this simple but nevertheless profound truth and thus defend the everlasting love of God in His sovereign decree of election.

---

61. Another potential target might be Johannes Maccovius, who was brought up on charges before the Synod for supposedly teaching that God was the author of sin, a charge he rejected. See Willem J. van Asselt, "On the Maccovius Affair," in *Revisiting the Synod of Dordt (1618–19)*, ed. Aza Goudriaan and Fred van Lieburg (Leiden: Brill, 2011), 217–42.

62. CD I, 18, in *Creeds*, II:575.

63. *Synopsis*, XXIV.xxxv–xli (45–49).

CHAPTER 5

Dead in Sin: The Utter Depravity of Mankind

Christopher J. Gordon

It was an awkward moment on the floor at the Synod of Dordrecht when Franciscus Gomarus (1563–1641) challenged Martinius of Bremen (1572–1630) to a duel. Martinius was known to be tolerant of Remonstrant teachings and was attempting to bring a moderating position to the Synod of Dort on the points in question.[1] Gomarus's challenge, albeit ill-tempered, exhibited to the Synod the great question that needed clarification in Reformed churches: Is there a middle way between God's absolute sovereignty in salvation and a sinner's ability to exercise free will in regard to his salvation? This struggle over Remonstrant teachings demonstrated how necessary it was for the Reformed churches to compose a confessional statement on salvation.

What became known as the five points of Calvinism is the fruit of the work that took place at the Synod of Dort in 1618–1619. These points provide Reformed churches with an explanation of doctrine aimed at helping the believer to understand the role of God's sovereign grace in salvation. Each point builds on the other, mutually explaining the whole work of salvation through the person and work of Jesus Christ.

The Canons of Dort (CD) purposely linked the Third and Fourth Points on sin and grace in response to the Remonstrant position that the human will has the ability to choose good over evil in spiritual matters.[2] The Synod desired to make clear the Reformed doctrine of sin and how that directly affects our understanding of grace. In this chapter, we will evaluate the doctrine of total or utter depravity. But before we look at the biblical and

---

1. John Hales, "Mr. Hales Letters from the Synod of Dort," in *Golden Remains of the Ever Memorable Mr. John Hales* (London: Newcomb, 1673), 87.

2. See David N. Steele and Curtis C. Thomas, "The Five Points of Calvinism: Defined, Defended, and Documented," in *International Library of Philosophy and Theology: Biblical and Theological Studies,* ed. J. Marcellus Kik (Philadelphia: P&R, 1967), 16.

confessional testimony of the doctrine, we will first consider the conflict that took place at the Synod of Dort over Remonstrant teachings on sin and grace.

The Arminian Controversy over Sin and Grace

Though there were many precursors to the Arminian controversy, problems surfaced when Jacob Arminius (1560–1609) preached a series of sermons on Romans in Amsterdam. According to Jacobus Triglandius (1583–1654), Arminius said "his hearers would have done better to remain in the Roman Catholic Church because then at least they would be doing good works in the hope of eternal reward while now they did none at all."[3] Further, Arminius advanced the idea of the participation of man's free will in obtaining salvation, greatly disturbing his congregation.[4] There were other isolated ministers teaching similar things.

A year following Arminius's death, many of his students produced a summary of his teachings known as the Remonstrance of 1610. A series of counter-remonstrance would follow, signaling to the Reformed churches that a major theological conflict was upon them. In response to the Remonstrance, the famous Synod at Dordrecht was called and met in 1618–1619 to address the tenants of Arminianism.

The delegates to the Synod of Dort faced the challenge of understanding the Arminian system and the consequences of the views of those who supported it. The frustration of Gomarus and other delegates at Dort had to do with the Remonstrants' effort to mingle Reformation doctrines of sovereign grace with what appeared to be a form of Pelagianism.

The first challenge for the Synod was to address the Remonstrants' obfuscation and belligerency. The Synod required the Remonstrants to write out their express views on the five points as affirmatives,[5] but the Remonstrants responded by questioning the legitimacy of the Synod of Dort, labeling the Synod itself an adverse party and schismatic. They also attempted to establish what English observer and Synod historian John Hales (1584–1656)

3. Louis Praamsma, "The Background of the Arminians Controversy (1586–1618)," in *Crisis in the Reformed Churches: Essays in Commemoration of the Great Synod of Dort, 1618–1619,* ed. Peter Y. DeJong (Grand Rapids: Reformed Fellowship, 1968), 27.

4. Richard Muller writes, "He first directed his attention to Romans 7 and the problem of the will. He moved away from the traditional Augustinian pattern of the Reformers and argued that the inward struggle of Paul was pre-conversion, not a post-conversion, struggle. Here already are hints of a synergism in which the human will takes the first step towards grace." Richard A. Muller, "Arminius and Arminianism," in *The Dictionary of Historical Theology,* ed. Trevor A. Hart (Grand Rapids: Eerdmans, 2000), 33.

5. Hales, *Golden Remains,* 41.

designated as an anti-Synod, moving to elect pro-Remonstrant officers in an effort to become their own judges over the points in question.[6] When these attempts failed, the Remonstrants became obstinate, refusing to answer the Synod's questions.

According to Hales, the Remonstrants produced their thoughts in a "distracting, confusing, and obscure" manner.[7] Their statements were full of negatives and ambiguous in their affirmatives so as to *appear* clear in what they believed while only stating what they were against.[8] This problem was evident in the preface to the Counter-Remonstrance of 1611. Here the authors complained that the Remonstrants did not argue "honestly and in good faith" and that their articles were "set forth in an ambiguous and dubious manner of speaking, in part conflicting with God's Word."[9]

The Remonstrant obfuscation on the points in question caused many problems for the Synod, especially when it came to addressing the issues of sin and grace. The Remonstrance theology of sin is stated in article 3:

> That man does not posses saving grace of himself, nor of the energy of his free will, inasmuch as in his state of apostasy and sin he can of and by himself neither think, will, nor do any thing that is truly good (such as saving Faith eminently is); but that it is necessary that he be born again of God in Christ, through His Holy Spirit, and renewed in understanding, inclination, and will, and all his faculties, in order that he may rightly understand, think, will, and effect what is truly good, according to the Word of Christ, John 15:5, "Without me you can do nothing."[10]

As far as the statement goes there is nothing that stands in opposition to the Reformed confessions, but read in isolation, the statement lacks an explanation of the consequence of sin and its effect on human nature. When the Synod pressed the Remonstrants for further clarity, the Remonstrants submitted their Opinions (*Sententiae*) in response, affirming that man does not have saving faith in himself and that "the will in the fallen state, before calling, does not have the power and the freedom to will any saving good."[11] They also believed that fallen human beings are born with a corrupt human nature and that sin rendered all people guilty before God, deserving His

---

6. Hales, *Golden Remains*, 41.
7. Hales, *Golden Remains*, 41.
8. Hales, *Golden Remains*, 41.
9. "Appendix D: The Counter Remonstrance of 1611," in *Crisis in the Reformed Churches*, 207.
10. "Appendix C: The Remonstrance of 1610," in *Crisis in the Reformed Churches*, 208.
11. "Appendix H : The Opinions of the Remonstrants, 3.4," in *Crisis in the Reformed Churches,* 225.

wrath. It is important to note that the Remonstrants believed that the grace of God was absolutely necessary for any response to the gospel. Their inconsistencies, however, became apparent in the way they spoke confusingly of grace and conversion.

The Remonstrants affirmed that every good work performed is a result of the grace of God, but the Remonstrance of 1611 and their Opinions referenced different kinds of grace: prevenient, cooperative, and sufficient. Together these were referenced as the "grace of God."[12] When the Remonstrants affirmed that man could do nothing without the grace of God, it was unclear how they were using the word "grace" since they attributed cooperative abilities to the human will.[13]

The inconsistencies present in the Remonstrant's Opinions and other writings were enough to judge that their understanding of grace and nature differed from Reformed orthodoxy as is evident in 3.2 of their Opinions:

> We hold, however, that the grace of God is not only the beginning but also the progression and the completion of every good, so much so that even the regenerate himself is unable to think, will, or do the good, nor to resist any temptations to evil, apart from that preceding or prevenient, awakening, following and cooperating grace.[14]

The real cause for concern was their use of the term "prevenient" in reference to grace. Prevenient grace, in the Arminian system, is a preceding grace that is given by God before any positive action of the human will is exercised. While this term was not unfamiliar to the Reformed, the Arminians were using it in a way foreign to a biblical understanding of grace. This kind of grace removes the obstacles sin wrought in human nature and places human beings in the position of autonomy, of being able to choose or reject God.

With this in mind, it would be unfair to say the Remonstrants were *openly* Pelagian or semi-Pelagian since they were willing to affirm that the first

---

12. "Appendix H: The Opinions of the Remonstrants, 3.2," in *Crisis in the Reformed Churches,* 225.

13. Fred Klooster writes, "The chief point of difference concerned the effect of the fall upon man and the extent of his corruption. And this affected their view of how grace operates in man's conversion. Over against the Arminian view of man's partial depravity and retention of the will's cooperative ability, the Synod of Dort affirmed what it believed to be the biblical doctrine of man's total depravity and his loss of free will." Fred Klooster, "The Doctrinal Deliverances of Dort," in *Crisis in the Reformed Churches,* 60.

14. "Appendix H: The Opinions of the Remonstrants, 3.2," in *Crisis in the Reformed Churches,* 225.

conferring of grace belongs to God. As section 3.1 of their Opinions states, "Man does not have saving faith of himself, not out of the powers of his free will, since in the state of sin he is able of himself and by himself neither to think, will, or do any good."[15] The Remonstrants recognize that man has no ability "in the state of sin" to will any good. The question is what prevenient grace accomplishes in bringing man out of the state of sin. Article 3.1 says the sinner's faculties are renewed to "carry out the good things which pertain to salvation."[16] What does this mean? Is it the Holy Spirit who generates a renewal to make salvation possible by the performance of these good things?

When read carefully, the answer becomes apparent in section 3.3 of the Opinions where they speak of certain spiritual qualities that are necessary for the "obtaining of salvation."[17] These qualities, such as zeal, care, diligence, hearing the Word, and sorrow for sin are "necessary for the obtaining of faith and of the Spirit of renewal."[18] The Remonstrants believed that the unregenerate not only could perform certain spiritual good works but that these good works are necessary for the "obtaining of salvation *before* faith itself and the Spirit of renewal comes."[19] As will be demonstrated below, this was a clear departure from Reformed orthodoxy's teaching on sin and grace.

The Arminian understanding of prevenient grace is crucial to their system of doctrine as presented at Dort.[20] Prevenient grace is not a grace that *actually rescues* human beings from the power of darkness since it is not effectual in its intention. Prevenient grace, instead, moves someone out of their state of sin and into a position of autonomy, giving one the power and freedom to will saving good.

---

15. "Appendix H: The Opinions of the Remonstrants, 3.1," in *Crisis in the Reformed Churches,* 225.

16. "Appendix H: The Opinions of the Remonstrants, 3.1," in *Crisis in the Reformed Churches,* 225.

17. "Appendix H: The Opinions of the Remonstrants, 3.3," in *Crisis in the Reformed Churches,* 225.

18. "Appendix H: The Opinions of the Remonstrants, 3.3," in *Crisis in the Reformed Churches,* 225 (emphasis added).

19. 3.3 of the Opinions states, "Yet we do not believe that all zeal, care, and diligence applied to the obtaining of salvation before faith itself and the Spirit of renewal are vain and ineffectual—indeed, rather harmful to man that useful and fruitful. On the contrary, we hold that to hear the Word of God, to be sorry for sins committed, to desire saving grace and the Spirit of renewal (none of which things man is able to do without grace) are not only not harmful and useless, but rather most useful and most necessary for the obtaining of faith and of the Spirit of renewal." "Appendix H: The Opinions of the Remonstrants, 3.3," in *Crisis in the Reformed Churches,* 225.

20. Prevenient grace was employed more by Rome than by Protestants and is not found in Scripture or the Reformed confessions.

It is important to note the Canons of Dort's emphasis that salvation "must be credited to God" and that God renews our heart, making us alive "without our help."[21] This is not the Arminian position. Prevenient grace, in contrast, places man in a neutral state by which he then cooperates—first accepting or rejecting Christ, then receiving the sufficient grace of the Holy Spirit and faith.

Additionally, because the Arminians maintained that after the fall humans retain an ability to cooperate with grace, they were able to affirm that "the efficacious grace by which anyone is converted is not irresistible.... Man is able of himself to despise that grace and not to believe."[22]

To the Synod, this was akin to the Roman medieval scheme of Gabriel Biel (d. 1495), which had promised "to those who do what lies within themselves (toward saving good), God will not deny grace." The problem was evident: the line between nature and grace was blurred, as it was in Pelagius, Ockham, and Biel. If man is able to resist this grace over against the sovereign action of God, then man is able to accept this grace by his own power. If there are cooperative abilities in the human will before the Spirit's work of regeneration, then the nature of man, before regeneration, has some ability to take steps toward his own conversion. This would make salvation a joint work of God's grace and human effort.

The Arminian doctrine of prevenient and cooperative grace was clearly seen as a fundamental threat to the doctrine of salvation by sovereign grace alone. In the final analysis, there is no way of avoiding errors of Pelagianism that leave in the human will the ability to cooperate or not with God's grace. As Matthew Barrett observes, "To conclude, for the Remonstrants, while

grace is necessary it is not effectual. While God initiates grace, man can thwart the Spirit's purpose to save."[23]

---

21. CD III/IV, 10 states, "The fact that others who are called through the ministry of the gospel do come and are brought to conversion must not be credited to man, as though one distinguishes himself by free choice from others who are furnished with equal or sufficient grace for faith and conversion (as the proud heresy of Pelagius maintains). No, it must be credited to God: just as from eternity He chose His own in Christ." CD III/IV, 12 states, "And this is the regeneration, the new creation, the raising from the dead, and the making alive so clearly proclaimed in the Scriptures, which God works in us without our help." "Canons of Dort," in *Forms and Prayers of the United Reformed Churches Together with the Doctrinal Standards of the URCNA* (Wellandport: United Reformed Churches of North America, 2018), 272–73.

22. "Appendix H: The Opinions of the Remonstrants, 3.5," in *Crisis in the Reformed Churches*, 225.

23. Matthew Barrett, *The Grace of Godliness: An Introduction to Doctrine and Piety in the Canons of Dort* (Kitchener: Joshua Press, 2013), 81.

The Reformed Doctrine of Total Depravity

With this struggle in mind, we can appreciate why the Synod linked the third and fourth heads of doctrine—namely, total depravity and irresistible grace.[24] Since the early twentieth century, the "five points of Calvinism" have been summarized in the acronym TULIP, the first point in priority being total depravity. One's view of sin is the logical starting point in any discussion of salvation, but the Synod was purposeful in juxtaposing the doctrine of sin and grace in response to Arminian obfuscation on grace and human nature. The position one holds regarding sin and the extent of its corruption of human nature will largely determine the view one takes regarding salvation as monergistic or synergistic, as by grace, works, or both.

The Fall

Any treatment of sin must begin with creation and Adam's rebellion in the garden of Eden.[25] The Canons of Dort emphasize the goodness of God's creative work and the adornments God bestowed on Adam at creation:

> Man was originally created in the image of God and was furnished in his mind with a true and salutary knowledge of his Creator and things spiritual, in his will and heart with righteousness, and in all his emotions with purity; indeed, the whole man was holy. However, rebelling against God at the devil's instigation and by his own free will, he deprived himself of these outstanding gifts. (III/IV, 1)

When God created Adam, He created him good and in His image (Gen. 1:27). The image of God has been understood in Reformed theology to have a broader and narrower sense. In the broader sense, human beings image God as rational creatures with moral qualities, enabling them to rule over the lower creation. In the more restricted sense, human beings image God with the spiritual qualities of true righteousness and holiness (Eph. 4:24). In the fall of Adam, the former was marred and the latter lost.

Dort recognizes the absolute purity of Adam in his state of innocence. Adam enjoyed a freedom not to sin (*posse non peccare*). He could exercise

---

24. Hales observes that the Synod required the Arminians to deliver their opinions all at once, since it was difficult to understand one point without the others as they were mutually connected." Hales, *Golden Remains*, 42.

25. Herman Bavinck observes, "When reading the early chapters of Genesis without bias, one gets the impression of profound unity and of its obvious aim to tell us not about progress and development but about the fall of humankind." Herman Bavinck, *Reformed Dogmatics: Abridged in One Volume,* ed. John Bolt (Grand Rapids: Baker Academic, 2011), 341.

"salutary knowledge" of all "things spiritual" and freely choose obedience not to eat of the tree of the knowledge of good and evil; but instead, Adam chose the lie of the serpent and ate of the tree (CD III/IV, 1).

God warned Adam that in the day he ate of it, he would experience death as the curse of breaking His commandment (Gen. 2:17).[26] As Herman Bavinck states, "They would make themselves like God in the sense that they would position themselves outside and above the law and, like God, determine and judge for themselves what good and evil was."[27] Satan offered Adam emancipation from God. As soon as Adam ate, he began to experience the guilt, pollution, suffering, and death that sin brings. God's creative masterpiece and image bearer became guilty, desperately trying to cover his shame before his Creator. As Heidelberg Catechism 9, summarizes, "Man, however, at the instigation of the devil, in a willful disobedience, robbed himself and all his descendants of these gifts."

The Spread of Sin

Of crucial importance to the Arminian controversy is the question of what happened to man's nature after the fall. The Canons testify to the biblical teaching of the total corruption of human nature:

> However, rebelling against God at the devil's instigation and by his own free will, he deprived himself of these outstanding gifts. Rather, in their place he brought upon himself blindness, terrible darkness, futility, and distortion of judgment in his mind; perversity, defiance, and hardness in his heart and will; and finally impurity in all his emotions. (III/IV, 1)

Human nature is sinful, poisoned, and corrupt throughout. Using the word "total" or "utter" to describe human depravity is not to say that every sinner is as completely corrupt in his actions as he possibly could be. The Canons acknowledge this in head III/IV, 4:

> There is, to be sure, a certain light of nature remaining in man after the fall, by virtue of which he retains some notions about God, natural things, and the difference between what is moral and immoral, and demonstrates a certain eagerness for virtue and for good outward behavior.

---

26. Satan said to Eve, "You will not surely die. For God knows that in the day you eat of it your eyes will be opened, and you will be like God, knowing good and evil" (Gen. 3:4–5 NJKV).

27. Herman Bavinck, *Reformed Dogmatics* (Grand Rapids: Baker Academic, 2006), 3:33.

As previously mentioned, the image of God understood narrowly as true righteousness and holiness was completely lost in the fall. The fall not only conveyed the loss of original righteousness but also a corruption of the human heart from which every kind of evil springs forth. The human heart of Adam is the seat of emotions, passions, urges, inclinations, attachments, desires, and decisions of the will. After the fall, it is utterly corrupt.[28] Not only was Adam's mind given over to all kinds of debased thoughts but his will too lost all desire and ability for good. As Calvin observes, "The heavenly image was obliterated in him, in the place of wisdom, virtue, holiness, truth, and justice, with which adornments he had been clad, there came forth the most filthy plagues, blindness, impotence, impurity, vanity, and injustice."[29]

The scriptural witness to this point is so abundant it is difficult to know what to include. In Genesis 6:5, before the flood event, God assessed the human heart as wicked: "The LORD saw that the wickedness of man was great in the earth, and that every intent of the thoughts of his heart was only evil continually" (Gen. 6:5 NKJV). The flood itself did not eradicate the problem of the sinful heart, for shortly after the flood the Lord told Noah that the "the imagination of man's heart is evil from his youth" (Gen. 8:21). Jeremiah preached, "The heart is deceitful above all things, and desperately wicked: who can know it?" (Jer. 17:9). Jesus's assessment was even more comprehensive when He told His hearers that out of the heart come evil thoughts, murder, adultery, sexual immorality, theft, false witness, and slander (Matt. 15:19).

So radical a solution was needed to resolve corruption in the human heart that Jesus told Nicodemus he needed a rebirth (John 3:3). There is an absolute necessity for the Spirit to implant life in the completely dead human heart. It is the truth of our absolute spiritual deadness that leads the apostle to his grand gospel declaration:

> When we were dead in trespasses, [God] made us alive together with Christ.... For by grace you have been saved through faith, and that not of yourselves; it is the gift of God, not of works, lest anyone should boast (Eph. 2:5, 8–9).

The position on sin adopted at Dort followed Augustine. Before the fall, man was *posse non pecarre* (able to sin). Postfall, man in his human nature is *non*

---

28. Bavinck, *Reformed Dogmatics: Abridged in One Volume*, 326.

29. John Calvin, *Institutes of the Christian Religion*, ed. John T. McNeill, trans. Ford Lewis Battles (Philadelphia: Westminster Press, 1960), II.1.

posse non peccare (not able not to sin). Bavinck provides a helpful summary of the Reformed position on total depravity: "This corruption of human nature is so total that humans are by nature incapable of any spiritual good, inclined to all evil, and on account of it alone, deserving of of eternal punishment."[30]

Original Sin

The Synod recognized the radical corruption of human nature by the fall in reaffirming the Reformed doctrine of original sin:

> Man brought forth children of the same nature as himself after the fall. That is to say, being corrupt he brought forth corrupt children. The corruption spread, by God's just judgment, from Adam to all his descendants—except for Christ alone—not by way of imitation (as in former times the Pelagians would have it) but by way of the propagation of his perverted nature. (CD III/IV, 2)

Though great efforts have been made to distance Arminian teachings from the errors of Pelagianism and semi-Pelagianism, it is important to note that the Synod did not hesitate, when evaluating the Remonstrant aberrations, to describe the Arminian view as Pelagian.

Pelagianism created a sharp dichotomy between Adam's sin and that of his posterity. Adam was viewed as standing alone in his choice to sin. According to Pelagius, sin was transmitted through imitation due to outside influences, not the propagation of a sinful nature. Semi-Pelagianism also denied the doctrine of original sin in the sense of inheriting Adam's guilt, but moderated their view by accepting "hereditary sickness"—human nature and moral abilities are weakened proponents leaving humans with only an inclination toward evil.

The Arminians, though recognizing the need for prevenient grace, did not end in a better place than the Pelagians and semi-Pelagians. They still believed there were enough positive qualities in the human will that every descendent of Adam retains the ability to cooperate or not cooperate, aided by prevenient grace. To Dort, this was clearly a form of the old Pelagian error.

Unlike the ambiguity and confusion in the Arminian system, the Canons are clear in affirming the biblical doctrine of original sin. Sin is not merely something learned by imitation, but rather it is a propagation from Adam of a perverted nature (CD III/IV, 2). The very same corrupt nature is propagated to Adam's posterity as a just judgment of God. The Canons affirmed the

---

30. Bavinck, *Reformed Dogmatics*, 3:98.

Augustinian truth that we bear the inborn defect from our mother's womb. Adam is presented in the Scriptures as the federal head of the human race and the root of human nature. As Romans 5:19 (NJKV) states, "For as by one man's disobedience many were made sinners, so also by one Man's obedience many will be made righteous."

In the Scriptures, Adam is presented as plunging human nature into ruin. David testifies to sin's presence from conception in Psalm 51:5. Heidelberg Catechism 10 follows Scripture's testimony that "God is terribly angry with the sin we are born with as well as our actual sins." Scripture is not reserved in its description of the depravity of infants, for "the wicked are estranged from the womb; they go astray as soon as they be born, speaking lies. Their poison is like the poison of a serpent" (Ps. 58:3–4). The perverted human nature that we are born with is both a hereditary depravity and a corruption of our nature, diffused, as Calvin observes, "into all parts of the soul bringing forth all kind of works of the flesh."[31]

The Synod thought it very important to combat any error that somehow would neutralize and separate Adam's descendants from the immediate imputation of his sin to his posterity. By contrast, the Arminians believed that prevenient grace restored people to a position of being able to cooperate with God's saving grace. This cooperation could be accomplished apart from the regenerating grace of God. The Synod saw this as undermining the entire doctrine of salvation by grace alone:

> Therefore, all people are conceived in sin and are born children of wrath, unfit for any saving good, inclined to evil, dead in their sins, and slaves to sin. Without the grace of the regenerating Holy Spirit they are neither willing nor able to return to God, to reform their distorted nature, or even to dispose themselves to such reform. (CD III/IV, 3)

This canon was clearly the strongest blow to the Arminian system. The human will, along with all other faculties, is completely fallen, corrupt, and driven by its slavery to sin. As was demonstrated, prevenient grace has only made salvation possible insofar as the human will acts upon the grace offered.

To combat the Arminian errors of prevenient and cooperating grace, the Canons purposely use the phrase "regenerating grace" of the Holy Spirit. Unless someone is born again by the Spirit and life is implanted in the heart, it is absolutely impossible for human beings to "will their return to God, or to reform their distorted nature" (CD III/IV, 3):

---

31. Calvin, *Institutes of the Christian Religion*, II.1.

> Moreover, when God carries out this good pleasure in His chosen ones, or works true conversion in them, He not only sees to it that the gospel is proclaimed to them outwardly, and enlightens their minds powerfully by the Holy Spirit so that they may rightly understand and discern the things of the Spirit of God, but, by the effective operation of the same regenerating Spirit, He also penetrates into the inmost being of man, opens the closed heart, softens the hard heart, and circumcises the heart that is uncircumcised. He infuses new qualities into the will, making the dead will alive, the evil one good, the unwilling one willing, and the stubborn one compliant; He activates and strengthens the will so that, like a good tree, it may be enabled to produce the fruits of good deeds. (CD III/IV, 11)

The will must be activated and renewed by God before man can ever repent and believe. The Holy Spirit not only causes the gospel to be preached, but He also powerfully illuminates the mind to understand and discern spiritual things (CD III/IV, 11). Only then is the will renewed and becomes active so that "man himself is rightly said to believe and repent by virtue of the grace received" (CD III/IV, 3).

The grace of regeneration, as the Canons state, "does not act in people as if they were blocks and stones; nor does it abolish the will and its properties or coerce a reluctant will by force, but spiritually revives, heals, reforms and—in a manner at once pleasing and powerful—bends it back" (CD III/IV, 3). However, with regard to any saving good, the corruption of the will is so pervasive that human beings are totally unable to exercise their wills in the direction of God.

If unregenerate man is utterly dead in sin, he is incapable of using his will properly. In the fall of Adam, human beings lost the ability to use their wills to accomplish any saving good.[32] Human beings are completely cast upon the mercies of God to sovereignly regenerate their hearts. This removes from the sinner any boasting through the exercise of his own abilities to obtain salvation and gives all glory to God.

We have great reason to celebrate what took place at the Synod of Dort in 1618–1619. In the face of serious challenges to a system of doctrine confessed and believed by Reformed Christians, the Synod fought for what they believed was the heart of the gospel of Jesus Christ. If our starting point is wrong and we attempt to downgrade Scripture's serious diagnosis of human nature, it will have a direct consequence on how we understand the nature of

---

32. Bavinck, *Reformed Dogmatics*, 3:121.

grace in the gospel of Jesus Christ. The cure is only as radical as the disease. If Christ is to be exalted for His sacrificial love for sinners, sinners will first have to confess how much they need that love.

To downplay sin is to downplay the need for grace. To downplay grace is to downplay the sufficiency of Christ's work to save. In the words of Belgic Confession 22, "To say that Christ is not enough but that something else is needed as well is a most enormous blasphemy against God—for it then would follow that Jesus Christ is only half a Savior." The Synod of Dort was faithful in showing Jesus not as half a savior, but wholly capable to save totally depraved sinners.

CHAPTER 6

The Promise of the Gospel:
Redemption in Christ

Michael Horton

Composed in AD 130, this early gospel summary—the Epistle of Mathetes to Diognetus—provides an apt point of departure for this chapter:

> When our wickedness had reached its height, and it had been clearly shown that its reward, punishment and death, was impending over us…and when the time had come which God had before appointed for manifesting His own kindness and power, how the one love of God, through exceeding regard for men, did not regard us with hatred, nor thrust us away, nor remember our iniquity against us, but showed great long-suffering, and bore with us…He Himself took on Him the burden of our iniquities! He gave His own Son as a ransom for us,
>
> > the holy One for transgressors,
> > the blameless One for the wicked,
> > the righteous One for the unrighteous,
> > the incorruptible One for the corruptible,
> > the immortal One for them that are mortal.
>
> For what other thing was capable of covering our sins than His righteousness? By what other one was it possible that we, the wicked and ungodly, could be justified, than by the only Son of God?
>
> > O sweet exchange! O unsearchable operation! O benefits surpassing all expectation! that the wickedness of many should be hid in a single righteous One, and that the righteousness of One should justify many transgressors!

It was the conviction of the Reformers and of the delegates at the Synod of Dort that this "great exchange" was the heart of the gospel.

It is a simple gospel—so simple that a child can understand it. Yet it is alien to our fallen hearts. Even more than external threats to the gospel, it is dangers within the church that seem most serious and perennial. Just as "savage wolves" sought to lead many astray in Ephesus, as Paul warned the church's elders in Acts 20, Timothy found the apostle's warning to guard the gospel a challenging task (e.g., 2 Tim. 1:14).

Is Dort Still Relevant?

In our day, this gospel of God's saving grace toward sinners in Jesus Christ is under threat in a variety of ways. First, there is *presumption*. Many who are raised in conservative churches (including Reformed ones) assume that everyone understands the gospel. In many churches, the gospel is something one hears to "get saved"; it's for unbelievers. But once one is converted, the focus is on "Christian living"—in other words, what we are called *to do* as God's people. There is a certain appropriateness to this phenomenon. The Heidelberg Catechism itself suggests such a pattern, moving from guilt to grace and then from grace to gratitude. Nevertheless, the gospel is always the basis and motivating factor for the Christian life. If we assume it, we will lose sight of it.

As individuals and churches, our natural tendency is to drift from the gospel, to look away from Christ. It begins by treating this saving message as something we already know and need not return to again and again. It becomes an "of course!" When one questions the emphasis on exhortations and programs for personal or collective activism by redirecting the conversation to Christ and His saving acts, the reply is often heard, "Well, of course! We all know that. But now it's time to focus on becoming a better 'you' or creating a better world." Yet the central message of the Bible, from Genesis to Revelation, is God's fulfillment of His promise to send His Son into the world to deliver us from the guilt and power of sin. As "the power of God for salvation" throughout the Christian life, not just at the beginning, the gospel proclaimed is the primary means through which the Holy Spirit creates and sustains the church and each member of it.

Second, there is *distraction*. Typically, when the gospel becomes an "of course," the *assumed* gospel, we become distracted by other things. Many of these things are good, even derived from scriptural commands. Yet forgetting the baseline of God's works in Jesus Christ, we shift our focus to our works as if they were more relevant to the immediate needs that surround us. Mainline Protestant denominations have been distracted for a long time by political and social agendas. Yet even in evangelical circles, there is a vast phenomenon of distraction as well. In more conservative contexts, distraction often takes the form of better behaviors, families, marriages, relationships, and right-wing politics, while the next generation often reacts by embracing a more progressive political agenda. Our messaging drifts away from God and His works in Christ to *us* and *our works* for God and the world. The language slips. Instead of proclaiming Christ as the Savior of sinners, we begin to preach ourselves. We even hear slogans about our "living the gospel" or even calls to "*be* the gospel," as if our lives and actions were the good news of saving deliverance. Nothing could be further from the biblical gospel, announcing the only One (namely, Jesus Christ) who *lived the law* so that He could *become the gospel*.

Third, there is outright *rejection*. Turning from the triune God to ourselves, it is not a far step to revise the message entirely, rejecting key elements. God is no longer holy, sovereign, righteous, and just, as well as loving and gracious. In fact, He need not be gracious and merciful at all, since we are not born in a condition of enmity and guilt. In the 1950s, Yale theologian H. Richard Niebuhr aptly described this moralistic message of liberal theology: "A God without wrath brought men without sin into a kingdom without judgment through a Christ without a cross."[1] In his powerful exposé *Christianity and Liberalism,* J. Gresham Machen argued persuasively that theological liberalism is not a different type of Christianity, but a different religion altogether.

Today the lines are not as clear. As sociologists like Christian Smith have documented, those raised even in conservative evangelical contexts today are as prone as the unchurched to embrace what Smith calls "moralistic, therapeutic deism."[2] Numerous studies in recent decades demonstrate that even evangelicals are "stunningly inarticulate" about Christian teaching in general and the gospel in particular.[3] Most believe that salvation is something that we attain with God's help. Although this widespread phenomenon reflects ignorance more than explicit rejection, there is a long line from evangelist Charles Finney in the nineteenth century to current "progressive evangelical" theologians who reject the doctrines of original sin, substitutionary atonement, justification through faith alone in Christ alone, and the need for a supernatural gift of new birth. Increasingly, salvation is seen less as a radical rescue operation by the triune God than as a process of personal or social recovery through the proper therapeutic and political management.

---

1. H. Richard Niebuhr, *The Kingdom of God in America* (New York: Harper & Row, 1959), 193.

2. Christian Smith and Melinda Lundquist Denton, *Soul Searching: The Religious and Spiritual Lives of America's Teenagers* (Oxford: Oxford University Press, 2005), esp. 163–71.

3. Smith and Lundquist Denton, *Soul Searching,* 15. Several recent studies from the Pew Research Center support the authors' conclusions. In addition, see "The State of Theology 2018," commissioned by Ligonier Ministries at https://thestateoftheology.com.

This tragic and indeed alarming situation provides the backdrop for the tremendous opportunities before us of returning to the "solid joys and lasting treasures" found in the gospel as it was defended so clearly at the Synod of Dort. Dort's treatment of this central topic in the second head of doctrine— "The Death of Christ and Our Redemption by It"—cannot be separated from its prior delineation of election and reprobation and the seriousness of sin taken up in the third head. Nevertheless, since these topics are richly discussed in other essays, my focus here is on this marvelous core of Dort's teaching in the second head of doctrine.

Redemption in Christ Alone

It is of paramount importance that this second head begins with God. We do not properly understand the gospel unless we begin with the character of God—the unchangeable perfection of His essence. All errors begin here, with false assumptions about the nature of God. If one assumes, for example, that God is only loving and that when push comes to shove, His love trumps His righteousness, then it will follow that He cannot express wrath. Consequently, there is no place for propitiation through Christ's sacrificial death. But if God's wrath against sin is denied, then one cannot maintain that God is holy, righteous and just, or even that He is loving, since a loving God could hardly allow injustice, oppression, wickedness, and hatred to have the last word over His creation.

The denial of God's wrath (and hence, propitiation) is not a sudden innovation (e.g., Rob Bell's *Love Wins*).[4] We find it all the way back in the third century with Origen, and it was a key tenet of the Socinians. Followers of Lelio Socinus and his nephew Fausto, the Socinians rejected the Trinity, the divinity of Christ, original sin, substitutionary atonement, justification by Christ's imputed righteousness through faith alone, and other crucial doctrines. In many respects, Socinianism represented a combination of Arian and Pelagian heresies that would become popular in the Enlightenment.

Arminius and his followers did not go quite so far. However, their attempt at a "middle way" only made them less consistent. Hugo Grotius lodged the significance of Christ's death in two effects. First, it demonstrated God's justice—His moral government of the world. Second, it made it possible for God justly to offer salvation on easier terms than perfect moral obedience. Instead, repentance and new obedience sufficed to justify sinners before

---

4. Rob Bell, *Love Wins: A Book about Heaven, Hell, and the Fate of Every Person Who Ever Lived* (San Francisco: HarperOne, 2011).

God. In effect, this meant that objective reconciliation and peace with God was effected by the believer's response rather than by Christ. But the divines at Dort begin with God's self-revelation:

> God is not only supremely merciful, but also supremely just. And His justice requires (as He has revealed Himself in His Word) that our sins committed against His infinite majesty should be punished, not only with temporal but with eternal punishments, both in body and soul; which we cannot escape, unless satisfaction be made to the justice of God.[5]

Not only the Socinian but also Remonstrant positions, like those of Grotius, assume that God's justice does not require full and complete satisfaction. Although Grotius's "moral government" view emphasizes divine justice, his theory undermines it by insisting that instead of requiring actual justice, all that is required is a public demonstration of God's serious offense at sin and the sinner's sincere effort at amendment of life.

The Dort delegates recognized, however, that divine justice is not something that can be relaxed. Like His other attributes, justice is intrinsic to God's simple being. Unlike us, God does not *possess* these attributes; He *is* love, justice, holiness, life, and all perfection. God never experiences inner turmoil, negotiating between love and justice. None of His attributes can be diminished or subordinated to others. He is love when He judges, and He loves justly. It is at the cross especially where we recognize this truth. If God is to save sinners, it cannot be by relaxing His law, but only because He has found a way to be "just and the justifier of the one who has faith in Jesus" (Rom. 3:26 NKJV). And this is precisely where the second article leads:

> Since, therefore, we are unable to make that satisfaction in our own persons, or to deliver ourselves from the wrath of God, He has been pleased of His infinite mercy to give His only-begotten Son for our Surety, who was made sin, and because a curse for us and in our stead, that He might make satisfaction to divine justice on our behalf.[6]

The Remonstrants were well aware that such a view (held by the church fathers and the better theologians of the Middle Ages) entailed *particular* redemption: that is, that Christ died to save the elect. After all, if Christ satisfied divine justice for every sin, then all for whom He died are objectively redeemed. In fact, medieval theologians recognized this entailment with the

---

5. Canons of Dort (CD) II, 1.
6. CD II, 2.

common formula, "Christ's death is sufficient for the world, efficient for the elect only." It is precisely this formula that Dort invokes in article 3: "The death of the Son of God is the only and most perfect sacrifice and satisfaction for sin, and is of infinite worth and value, abundantly sufficient to expiate the sins of the whole world."

Article 4 lodges the infinite sufficiency, worth, and value of Christ's death in the fact that He is "not only really man and perfectly holy, but also the only-begotten Son of God, of the same eternal and infinite essence with the Father and the Holy Spirit, which qualifications were necessary to constitute Him our Savior; and, moreover, because it was attended with a sense of the wrath and curse of God due to sin for us."

Articles 5–7 underscore the universal and free promise of the gospel, that all who believe will be saved. "This promise, together with the command to repent and believe, ought to be declared and published to all nations, and to all persons promiscuously and without distinction, to whom God of His own good pleasure sends the gospel" (art. 5). The fact that not all believe it is in no way due to any defect in Christ's work, but only to the one who rejects it (art. 6). "But as many as truly believe, and are delivered and saved from sin and destruction through the death of Christ, are indebted for this benefit solely to the grace of God given them in Christ from everlasting, and not to any merit of their own" (art. 7).

Unbelievers have only themselves to blame, while believers have only God in Christ to thank. Because Christ's death itself objectively saved sinners, rather than making redemption possible only if they fulfill certain conditions, those who do believe are assured that they can never come into judgment. It is not their repentance and new obedience that satisfies God's justice, but Christ's death alone. Precisely because Christ won for us all the gifts that the Father destined for His elect, repentance, faith, and new obedience will be given in due time as the elect hear and embrace this gospel. The death of Christ was effective for all the elect in

> bestowing the gift of justifying faith, thereby to bring them infallibly to salvation; that is, it was the will of God that Christ, by the blood of the cross, whereby He confirmed the new covenant, should effectually redeem out of every people, tribe, nation and language all these, and only these, who were from eternity chosen to salvation and given to Him by the Father, that He should confer on them faith, which, together with all the other saving gifts of the Holy Spirit, He purchased them by His death; should purge them of all sin, both original and actual, whether committed before or after believing; and having faithfully preserved

them even to the end, should at last bring them, free from every spot and blemish, to the enjoyment of glory in His presence forever.[7]

I recall, when in my freshman year in public high school, I sought permission to hold a Bible study on my church's campus, which was conveniently adjacent to the school. Several of my non-Christian friends even wanted to join in. Aware of my age, the pastor suitably wanted to know what I'd be teaching. "Romans!" I answered, assuming he would share in my excitement. "Romans? That is a very difficult book," he replied. As I explained *what* I found in Romans that was so revolutionary, he told me that I was a Calvinist and that he was unsure of my conversion. "Son, when were you saved?" Without intending to be provocative, the answer came to me: "Two thousand years ago." At the end of the conversation, the pastor not only declined permission but summarily dismissed me from the youth group as a negative influence. This was a disillusioning experience for me and especially for my parents, but it was also a wonderful realization on my part of the heart of the gospel.

And this is precisely the message of this article of Dort. Yes, we come to faith in Christ and are justified when we believe. Yet even this faith was purchased by Christ and given by the Holy Spirit on that basis. It is Christ and His work, not my faith, that saves and all that Christ accomplished *in the past, once and for all*, secures infallibly my entire salvation. This is the good news of grace. The good news is not, "Jesus did His part and the rest is up to you," but "Jesus paid it all!"

If Christ died for everyone, then everyone is saved. Of course, universal salvation is not taught in Scripture. On the contrary, it is everywhere refuted. Only those who believe are saved. Yet because Christ died effectually for all of the elect, they will all come to Christ through the gospel and will be justified, sanctified, and glorified forever. Consequently, all who come to Him are His sheep, the bride given to the Son by the Father from all eternity, and all of them are called and kept by the Holy Spirit. From beginning to end, "salvation is of the LORD" (Jonah 2:9).

It is not surprising, then, that Arminian theologians ever since have expressed a preference for Grotius's theory of moral government over substitution and satisfaction, even to the point of identifying substitutionary atonement as a "Calvinist doctrine."[8] They realize that if Christ's death fully

---

7. CD II, 8.
8. See, for instance, H. Orton Wiley, *Christian Theology* (Kansas City, Mo.: Beacon Hill Press, 1952), 2:245–46; John Miley, *The Atonement in Christ* (New York: Hunt & Eaton, 1879); and John Miley, *Systematic Theology* (New York: Hunt & Eaton), 2:145.

satisfied for all the sins of every person for whom He died, the only options are universal salvation or particular redemption.[9] Therefore, they conclude, Christ did not die for the sins of any actual person but only to make salvation *possible* on terms that are easier than perfect obedience to God's law.[10]

There are exceptions to this idea of justification through obedience to a relaxed law. For example, Charles Finney went beyond Arminianism (and even semi-Pelagianism) to a full Pelagian position, insisting that perfect, personal obedience to God's law was the *sine qua non* of justification.[11] Yet in their effort to defend a universal atonement whose efficacy is determined by human response, Arminians cannot—and do not—affirm the view that Christ actually saved—objectively and completely—every person for whom He died, such that each will be called and justified, gradually sanctified, and finally glorified by grace alone. Dort affirms that the purpose of the triune God has "to this day been powerfully accomplished," so that the church will always exist and ever prevail against the gates of hell (art. 9).

Rejection of Errors

Given this positive statement of the doctrine, it is not surprising that Dort rejects several errors, mostly of Remonstrant provenance. The first error (para. 1) is "that God the Father has ordained His Son to the death of the cross without a certain and definite decree to save any," as if Christ's death could be successful even if no one had actually been saved (in opposition to passages such as John 10:15, 27 and Isaiah 53:10). The second error (para. 2) targets directly the theory of Grotius described above—namely, that Christ died not to "confirm the new covenant of grace through His blood, but only that He should acquire for the Father the mere right to establish with man such a covenant as He might please, whether of grace or of works." Dort cites Hebrews 7:22 and 9:16–17, confirming that it is the new covenant, a covenant of grace, that is sealed by Christ's death; the atonement does not merely make it possible for God to institute another covenant with easier terms (but that is still based on works). Here neonomianism of every stripe, including that of Richard Baxter and John Goodwin, is excluded. The gospel is not a new law, as Rome and

---

9. Wiley, *Christian Theology*, 2:245–46; and Miley, *Systematic Theology*, 2:145.

10. In addition to the above works, for a summary of this view, see J. I. Packer, "Arminianisms," in *Through Christ's Word*, ed. W. Robert Godfrey and Jesse L. Boyd (Phillipsburg, N.J.: Presbyterian and Reformed, 1985), 121–148.

11. Charles G. Finney, *Finney's Systematic Theology* (Minneapolis, Minn.: Bethany, 1976), 206, 320, 372–73. See also R. C. Sproul, "The Pelagian Captivity of the Church," *Modern Reformation*, vol. 10, no. 3 (May/June 2001): 22–29.

the Arminians taught, but a gracious promise anchored in God's uncondi-tional election and fulfilled in Christ. Similarly, paragraph 3 rejects the view

> that Christ by His satisfaction merited neither salvation itself for anyone, nor faith, whereby this satisfaction of Christ unto salvation is effectually appropriated; but that He merited for the Father only the authority or the perfect will to deal again with man, and to prescribe new conditions as He might desire, obedience to which, however, depended on the free will of man, so that it therefore might have come to pass that either none or all should fulfill these conditions.

The Dort divines pull no punches here: "For these adjudge too contemp-tuously of the death of Christ, in no wise acknowledge the most important fruit or benefit thereby gained, and bring again out of hell the Pelagian error." This verdict, it must be recalled, was not that of a small cadre of hyper-Calvinists but was the position of mainstream Reformed churches, including the Church of England, whose leadership was at this time committed to the views summarized at Dort. King James I, in fact, deemed Arminian preach-ers "seditious and heretical," asserting that their teaching is a "corrupt seed which that Enemy of God has sown."[12]

At first this may strike us as an unfair judgment. After all, Arminius him-self and certainly evangelical Arminians like John Wesley affirmed original sin, Christ's substitutionary atonement, and the inability of human beings to repent and believe apart from God's prevenient grace. Pelagianism denies these doctrines, and semi-Pelagianism teaches that God gives His grace to those who, apart from it, show an interest of their own free will. But what leads the fathers at Dort to reach their severe conclusion is the essentially neonomian position that Christ's death merely makes it *possible* for God to offer salvation on terms other than Christ's actual sealing of the covenant of grace. Regardless of how much gracious assistance is given or offered, the *basis* of justification would seem to be located in the believer rather than in Christ. We are justified *through* faith but *on the basis of* (or because of, for the sake of) Christ—*propter Christum per fidei.* The Westminster divines would issue a similar rejection, confessing that sinners are justified

> not for anything wrought in them or done by them, but for Christ's sake alone; nor by imputing faith itself, the act of believing, or any other evangelical obedience to them as their righteousness; but by imputing

12. Peter White, *Predestination, Policy and Polemic: Conflict and Consensus in the English Church from the Reformation to the Civil War* (Cambridge: Cambridge University Press, 2002), 159.

the obedience and satisfaction of Christ unto them, they receiving and resting on Him and His righteousness by faith; which faith they have not of themselves, it is the gift of God (WCF 11.1).

The choice comes down to this: either Christ merited for all of His elect their whole salvation, including satisfaction, regeneration, faith, justification, sanctification, and glorification, or He made it possible for everyone generally to be saved if they complied (at least by purpose and intention) with His law.

This argument is continued in paragraph 4. According to the Remonstrant position, instead of upholding the law by fulfilling it and imputing His meritorious obedience and satisfaction to the elect, Christ somehow makes it possible for God to revoke the law's severe requirement and instead "regards faith itself and the obedience of faith, although imperfect, as [if it were] the perfect obedience of the law, and does esteem it worthy of the reward of eternal life through grace." This plainly contradicts Scripture (e.g., Rom. 3:24–25): "And these proclaim, as did the wicked Socinus, a new and strange justification of man before God, against the consensus of the whole Church." It is worth noting that Grotius felt obliged to write a defense of his position against the charge of Socinianism. Regardless of whether his view can be described as Socinian *simpliciter* (which the fathers of Dort do not claim here), Grotius himself saw it as a *via media*, as have many Arminian theologians ever since.[13] When the paragraph concludes, "against the consensus of the whole Church," they are not exaggerating. Whatever the errors of Rome, the medieval church taught clearly that Christ's death was a satisfaction for particular sins—that Christ died *in the place of* (as a substitute for) the elect. Again, "sufficient for the world, efficient for the elect only," was the common formula of the schools. The Remonstrants introduced a new view that, whatever its differences with Socinianism, shifted the basis of salvation from Christ to the believer.

Paragraph 5 rejects the error that all people, by virtue of Christ's death, are no longer liable to condemnation and that "all are free from the guilt of original sin," whereas Scripture "teaches that we are *by nature children of wrath* (Eph. 2:3)." Also rejected (para. 6) is the Remonstrant distinction "between meriting and appropriating," as if in God's view everyone is included in Christ's death, "but that, while some obtain the pardon of sin and eternal life, and others do not, this difference depends on their own free will, which joins itself to the grace that is offered without exception, and that it is not dependent on the special gift of mercy, which powerfully works in them...."

---

13. Hugo Grotius, *De satisfactione Christi adversus Faustum Socinum* (Leiden, 1617).

For these, while they feign that they present this distinction in a sound sense, seek to instill into the people the destructive poison of the Pelagian errors." In other words, although Christ *merited* salvation for every person, according to the Remonstrants, the real basis of their salvation is their own *appropriation* of Christ and His benefits by free will.

Arminians rebuffed the charge of Pelagianism—or even semi-Pelagianism—by insisting that God's grace is necessary for repentance and faith. It is true that all are born in sin, but it is also true (they argued) that God gives to all *sufficient* grace to believe if they exercise their free will. This runs counter to the teaching of Scripture, the Dort divines maintain, and even against the standard Augustinian view held by such teachers as Thomas Aquinas, who insisted that sinners required not only *sufficient* but *efficient* grace to believe. Since this involves God's giving particular grace to particular individuals (the elect), withholding it from others, Arminians must reject this teaching as they do particular redemption. As with Christ's death, so with the Spirit's application: the work of God makes our cooperation possible, but it does not actually redeem or secure the gifts of regeneration, faith, justification, sanctification, and glorification for anyone. At the end of the day, for the Arminian, it is the believer's "willing and running" that effects salvation.

The final paragraph of the second head rejects the error "that Christ neither could die, nor needed to die, and also did not die, for those whom God loved in the highest degree and elected to eternal life, since these do not need the death of Christ." Citing Galatians 2:20; Romans 8:33–34; John 10:15; and 15:12–13, the divines return to the point on which they launched this section: God's love and justice cannot be set in opposition. At the cross, we see that God found the way to be "just and the justifier of the one who has faith in Christ Jesus."

Ever since Dort, many theologians—including some in the Reformed tradition—have sought to ignore, revise, or reject the doctrine of particular redemption. Yet they always end up diminishing the glory of the meritorious obedience (both active and passive) and resurrection of Christ. Like Arminians, advocates of "hypothetical universalism" (known as "Amyraldians," rejected by the Consensus Helvetica after Dort) cannot say that Christ actually secured the salvation of anyone at the cross. They can say only that He made salvation possible, but that it becomes actual by the believer's appropriation. By contrast, Dort reminds us that Christ's work actually saves everyone for whom He died and rose again. It is not logical consistency that proves Dort's teaching but the explicit passages of Scripture that underpin every statement. And it is not a minor point, since it determines one's view not only of the extent but of the very nature of Christ's work.

Dort's position is truly *good news*! Christ has purchased redemption from sin, death, and hell; He has secured the gifts of effectual calling, justification, sanctification, and glorification, including the faith that receives Christ with all of His benefits. And it is truly good news *for everyone*. What is more blessed: To hear that Christ did His part and now we do our part in salvation? Or to hear that Christ accomplished everything for our salvation, to be applied by the Holy Spirit, and that everyone who believes in Christ alone for salvation is chosen, redeemed, justified, sealed for the day of final resurrection, and cannot come into condemnation? Jesus Christ is not the hypothetical Savior of all but the actual Savior of the elect, of all who trust in Him because of the grace that He won for them at Calvary.

CHAPTER 7

The Irresistible Spirit: The Work of the Holy Spirit

Sebastian Heck

In the spring of 1619, a highly influential letter was read to the gathered Synod of Dort by the famous Heidelberg theologian David Pareus (1548–1622). In the beginning of the letter, Pareus notes that the Remonstrants use much of the same language, even some of the same biblical proof texts as the Reformed orthodox theologians. However, they constantly engage in a kind of equivocation (*aequivocatio*), giving to the words multiple and different meanings from what the Reformed intended by them. They speak much of grace, but they mean something entirely different by it. They speak much of the work of the Holy Spirit, but they mean something entirely different by it than the Reformed do.

It is my goal in this chapter to argue that the most fundamental difference between the Remonstrants (or Arminians) and the Reformed, and therefore the most fundamental point of contention at the Synod of Dort, was and is their respective views of the work of the Holy Spirit.

It is interesting that when we think of the Canons of Dort (CD), we rarely think of them as providing anything like a theology of the Holy Spirit. Doctrines such as the nature and ability (or inability) of fallen man, the extent of the atonement of Christ on the cross, or the perseverance of faith immediately come to mind, but not primarily the work of the Holy Spirit. The popularized versions of the so called five points of Calvinism also do not lead one to suspect the importance and centrality of the person and work of the Holy Spirit in the application of redemption.

The sheer frequency, however, with which reference is made to the person and work of the Holy Spirit in the Canons at the very least suggests that one important way to understand the differences between the Reformed and Arminian views of salvation is by looking at the underlying doctrine(s) of the Holy Spirit.

As pointed out in other chapters, the Canons were not intended to be a full system of doctrine, but merely an explanation of the already established doctrines of grace and faith as outlined in the Belgic Confession (1561). Thus, the crux of the matter, as the Five Articles of Remonstrance rightly state it, was pinpointing the exact "mode of the operation of this grace" of God (art. 4), which is also "the grace of the Holy Ghost" (art. 1).

In order to determine the precise differences between the two systems of theology, we will look first at the doctrine of the *person* of the Holy Spirit, and then at the doctrine of the *work* of the Holy Spirit.

The Person and Power of the Holy Spirit

On the face of it, both the Remonstrants and the Reformed shared the same doctrine of the Holy Spirit. They both confessed the true and eternal divinity of the Holy Spirit as the third person of the holy Trinity (Belgic Confession 11; cf. also 8–9).[1] The bulk of the statements regarding the Holy Spirit in the Canons are concerned with His work. However, some of them reveal that the Remonstrant doctrine of grace also has possible ramifications for the doctrine of God—namely, the divinity and power of the Holy Spirit.

One such place is rejection 7 following head III/IV—"Of the Corruption of Man, His Conversion to God, and the Manner Thereof." What is rejected is the view "that the grace whereby we are converted to God is only a gentle advising." A similar statement can be found in rejection 8, where the Reformed reject that God "does not use such powers of His omnipotence." The Arminians did not deny that the Holy Spirit is all-powerful in His being, which would be clear heresy, but rather that He freely limits the exertion of His omnipotent power to a "gentle advising." Why? Because this supposedly respects the nature of man as a responsible creature. It is not out of lack of power that the Spirit does not simply take over and convert man forcefully, but out of respect for man's responsibility. According to the Remonstrants, "this is the noblest manner of working in the conversion of man" (CD III/IV, rej. 7).

The Reformed viewed it differently. They were concerned first that this "noble manner of working" of the Holy Spirit presupposed a heretical—namely Pelagian—view of the nature of man. "This is altogether Pelagian" (rej. 7). Second, they were concerned that this view of the Spirit restricting

---

1. This is not to deny that some Arminians were open to and became Socinian, not only with respect to the doctrine of election and foreknowledge but also with respect to the doctrine of the Trinity.

His influence to a kind of "gentle advising" also denied the true power of the Holy Spirit. They stated that it is "contrary to the whole Scripture which… teaches yet another and far more powerful and divine manner of the Holy Spirit's working in the conversion" (rej. 7). While the Reformed were very much aware that the Spirit sometimes does indeed limit the exertion of His power (e.g., in not keeping believers infallibly from sinning; CD V, 4), they simply confessed that Scripture never says that He does this with respect to regeneration. On the contrary, it is detrimental to His nature as a divine (i.e., almighty) being to claim that He does. And if the Scriptures do not witness to such self-restraint on the part of the Holy Spirit, the Arminian notions of grace would seem to render the Holy Spirit less than all-powerful.

A similar statement is made in head III/IV, rejection 8. There, the Orthodox reject that man may "resist God and the Holy Spirit when God intends man's regeneration and wills to regenerate him." Here, too, the problem is not merely that Scripture does not teach this but that this view effectively denies the divinity of the Holy Spirit. "This is nothing less than the denial of all the efficiency of God's grace in our conversion, and the subjecting of the working of the Almighty God to the will of man" (rej. 8). Ostensibly, the Holy Spirit would no longer be "Almighty God" if He nowhere exercised His omnipotence in the regeneration of sinners, His chief action. But indeed, regeneration is a divine miracle, called "a supernatural work, most powerful" (CD III/IV, 12). As the Belgic Confession so clearly states, "The Holy Ghost is the eternal power and might" (art. 8).

From these considerations of the person of the Holy Spirit as being omnipotent and divine and necessarily exercising these attributes in the salvation of man, we now turn to the actual work of the Holy Spirit.

The Work of the Holy Spirit

The Canons of Dort are a response to the Five Points of Remonstrance. Therefore, the five heads of doctrine are not organized as logically as they might otherwise have been. That does not mean, however, that there is no logic to them. Head I starts out with the presupposition of the fall, showing that only those who have faith in the gospel of Jesus Christ can be saved. It then goes on (beginning with article 6) to root the origin of faith in the electing purposes of God. Election in its different aspects is the main content of head I. Head II starts out with the presupposition of the justice of God (art. 1) and moves to the justice and graciousness of redemption in Christ, connecting it with the doctrine of election already established (arts. 8–9). Heads III and IV are about the way sinners can become beneficiaries of that redemption accomplished by Christ. Logically, head III/IV begins with the nature of fallen man, his total depravity, showing that only the miracle of regeneration can transform man's nature and will. Consequently, this enables him to believe in the redemption already established in head II. Finally, head V inquires into the problem of indwelling sin in the believer and answers with a strong affirmation of the doctrine of sanctification and of the final perseverance of the saints.

Given this order, it is clear why mention of the Holy Spirit is relatively rare under heads I and II and rather concentrated in heads III/IV and V. This does not mean, however, that the Holy Spirit plays no role whatsoever in heads I and II. Thus, we shall look briefly at each head and what it teaches concerning the work of the Holy Spirit.

The Work of the Holy Spirit in Creating Faith

Head I, article 1, summarizes the dark but realistic picture of man after the fall: sin, the curse, death, and condemnation. Article 2, however, immediately shines the light of the gospel on this terrible human predicament. This gospel must be believed, and for it to be believed, God sends human messengers with the free offer of the gospel. Some believe it and others do not, as it always has been and shall be until the end of the ages. The reason for this lies in the decree of God (art. 6). And with this, we are thrown into the middle of the controversy at Dort—namely, the question, What is faith? Is it a gift that we are given by God or is it something man is able to do? And if it is a gift from God, why do some receive it and others do not? At this point in the Canons, we find the first reference to the work of the Holy Spirit without His name being mentioned. Article 6 states that some receive the gift of faith, while others do not. And this is according to God's eternal decree, "according to which decree, He graciously softens the hearts of the elect, however obstinate, and inclines them to believe." Here, already, we find an explicit denial of the Arminian doctrine of the Holy Spirit's "gentle advising" (CD III/IV, rej. 7). The Holy Spirit is the one who acts in accordance with God's eternal decree. God does not simply advise, but He inclines the renewed hearts of the elect in such a way that they actually believe.

How does He do that? God draws them to Christ "by His Word and Spirit, to bestow upon them true faith." Here we have the basic tenet of the Reformation: the Spirit with the Word—the Word by the Spirit. In fact, by the combination of the Word and the Spirit, God effects the entire application of redemption. He bestows "upon them true faith, justification and sanctification; and having powerfully preserved them in the fellowship of His Son," He finally glorifies them "for the demonstration of His mercy and for the praise of His glorious grace" (art. 7). From the beginning then, the Holy Spirit is mentioned expressly as the agent of the application of salvation, and He does His work by way of means—the means of the Word of God.

The Work of the Holy Spirit in the Application of Christ's Death and Redemption
Head II is concerned with the exposition of the redemption accomplished by Christ on behalf of the elect. Again, the necessity of faith is confirmed (arts. 5–6), the basis of which is, once again, the grace of God "given [to believers] in Christ from everlasting, and not to any merit of their own" (art. 7).

Article 8 of head II is central in the transition from the purchase of redemption to the application of it: "The quickening and saving efficacy of the most precious death" of Christ extends to the elect who—and who alone—are given faith in due time. This faith is a gift of God. But more particularly, it is a gift of the Holy Spirit, "together with all the other saving gifts of the Holy Spirit" that Christ purchased by His death. By this very gift, God will also preserve His elect in the faith by the Spirit and sanctify them by the same Spirit until He will "at last bring them free from every spot and blemish to the enjoyment of glory in His own presence forever." Thus, the doctrines of final perseverance and sanctification are already implied in the nature of true faith as an irrevocable gift of the Holy Spirit, in "the incorruptibleness of the seed of God" (CD V, rej. 8).

The Work of the Holy Spirit in Regeneration
Heads III/IV treat the twin doctrines of the fall and corruption of man and of the restoration of the image of God in man. Obviously, it was the conviction of the framers of the Canons that one cannot fruitfully discuss the nature of grace and saving faith without first having a clear picture of the nature of man as fallen. It begins by describing the original state of man as in the image of God. Man was a spiritual being, "adorned with a true and saving knowledge of his Creator and of spiritual things" (art. 1). He was created holy, indeed he was endowed with all the gifts of the Holy Spirit from the beginning. When he fell into sin, "he forfeited these excellent gifts" and became utterly depraved in heart and will. This corruption was consequently passed along to posterity by birth, and not simply by imitation (art. 2), the result being, "Therefore all men are conceived in sin, and by nature children of wrath, incapable of saving good, prone to evil, dead in sin, and in bondage thereto" (art. 3).

It is noteworthy that the Reformed have no intention of denying the existence of a remnant of the image of God in man. On the contrary, "man by the fall did not cease to be a creature endowed with understanding and will, nor did sin which pervaded the whole race of mankind deprive him of the human nature" (art. 16). "There remain…in man since the fall, the glimmerings of natural light, whereby he retains some knowledge of God, of natural things, and of the differences between good and evil, and discovers some regard for virtue, good order in society, and for maintaining an orderly external deportment" (art. 4). But the elements of the *imago Dei* which remain in man as sinner are not of such power that they can offset his depravity.

Simply put, the Remonstrants put too much stock in the ability of fallen, sinful man. Therefore, the Reformed reject the idea "that the corrupt and natural man can so well use the common grace (by which they understand the light of nature), or the gifts still left him after the fall, that he can gradually gain by their good use a greater, namely the evangelical or saving grace and salvation itself" (rej. 5). Rather, they confess, "without the regenerating grace of the Holy Spirit, [all men] are neither able nor willing to return to God, to reform the depravity of their nature, or to dispose themselves to reformation" (art. 3).

In other words, the framers of the Canons understood the work necessary in order for man to believe as specific to the Holy Spirit. What the Arminians suggested, that the Spirit simply "gently advise" man to choose the good, would not do. What man needs in order to believe is nothing short of regeneration—"the regenerating grace of the Holy Spirit." Regeneration is the work of the Holy Spirit recreating and restoring the image of God in the elect. It is analogous to the monergistic work of the Spirit in the first creation, "a new creation: a resurrection from the dead, a making alive, which God works in us without our aid" (art. 12).

For this work of regeneration, the Spirit does not take into account anything in man. Since man has no ability in spiritual things since the fall of mankind—no free will with respect to salvation—this work of the Spirit, "is not to be ascribed to the proper exercise of free will, whereby one distinguishes himself above others" (art. 10). Nor is this work of regeneration the result of "prevenient grace" whereby God graciously puts sinful man in a position once again to exercise free will and to believe. This notion, that all men, as sinners, are by God "equally furnished with grace sufficient for faith and conversions" is nothing but "the proud heresy of Pelagius." Rather, this work "must be wholly ascribed to God" (art. 10)—that is, to God the Holy Spirit.

However, while the Holy Spirit uses no imagined ability in man, He does use means to bring about this radical change of the rebirth. The Spirit does not work the miracle of regeneration apart from the Word of God, "the gospel, which the most wise God has ordained to be the seed of regeneration and food of the soul" (art. 17). "What therefore neither the light of nature, nor the law could do, that God performs by the operation of the Holy Spirit through the Word" (art. 6).

Of course, the Arminians also believed in the preaching of the gospel. But they imagined a very different situation in which the gospel, the message that Christ has died for all men, is externally preached to all men, who are then all enabled in principle by prevenient, assisting, or advising grace to respond in faith, leaving it up to the individual sinner which way to decide. The theologians of Dort explain that gospel preaching in fact creates an entirely different situation:

> When God accomplishes His good pleasure in the elect or works in them true conversion, He not only causes the gospel to be externally preached to them and powerfully illuminates their mind by His Holy Spirit, that they may rightly understand and discern the things of the Spirit of God; but by the efficacy of the same regenerating Spirit, pervades the inmost recesses of the man; He opens the closed, and softens the hardened heart, and circumcises that which was uncircumcised, infuses new qualities into the will, which though heretofore dead, He quickens; from being evil, disobedient, and refractory, He renders it good, obedient, and pliable; actuates and strengthens it, that like a good tree, it may bring forth the fruits of good actions. (art. 11)

Articles 11 and 12 are at the heart of the doctrine of the work of the Holy Spirit in the Canons and among the most beautiful confessional statements of regeneration. Article 12 continues:

> And this is the regeneration so highly celebrated in Scripture and denominated a new creation: a resurrection from the dead, a making alive, which God works in us without our aid. But this is in no wise effected merely by the external preaching of the gospel, by moral suasion, or such a mode of operation, that after God has performed His part, it still remains in the power of man to be regenerated or not, to be converted or to continue unconverted; but it is evidently a supernatural work, most powerful, and at the same time most delightful, astonishing, mysterious, and ineffable; not inferior in efficacy to creation or the resurrection from the dead, as the Scripture inspired by the author of this work declares; so that all in whose heart God works in this marvelous manner are certainly, infallibly, and effectually regenerated, and do actually believe. Whereupon the will thus renewed is not only actuated and influenced by God, but in consequence of this influence, becomes itself active. Wherefore also, man is himself rightly said to believe and repent, by virtue of that grace received.

By the last statement, the Reformed sought to forestall the argument of the Remonstrants that this doctrine of regeneration would turn man into something other than a responsible being. The Reformed doctrine of regeneration does not teach that God "drags people kicking and screaming into the kingdom," but rather that it restores them to the divine image bearers they once were. Having their will renewed, they become "active"—active in believing.

While the scheme of the Arminians might seem to be intellectually more satisfying and more rational, that is not the ultimate criterion, of course. Against all rationalizing and Socinian tendencies, the Reformed explain, "The manner of this operation cannot be fully comprehended by believers in this life. Notwithstanding which, they rest satisfied with knowing and experiencing that by this grace of God they are enabled to believe with the heart, and love their Savior" (art. 13).

This leads us to a last consideration under this heading. The Remonstrants minimize the extent to which the depravity of man has progressed. This leaves him able, in principle, under the influence and "gentle advising" of the prevenient grace of the Spirit to respond in faith. "It still remains in the power of man to be regenerated or not, to be converted or to continue unconverted" (art. 12). Minimizing depravity leads them to minimize the necessity of regeneration. Regeneration is, for them, already a response of the believer, not a necessary prerequisite. The flip side of this is that the Remonstrant doctrine maximizes the ability of man to resist this process of regeneration by the Spirit. Indeed, they teach, "as respects the mode of the operation of this grace it is not irresistible" (Five Articles, art. 4). The two convictions are logically interrelated. If what man needs in order to believe is simply some measure of prevenient grace, which by definition is not saving, not effectual, not regenerating, then it follows that that particular "grace" can also be resisted.

And here lies the crux of the matter. If the operation of the Holy Spirit in regeneration can effectively be resisted, then man is ultimately more powerful than God. This is clearly what the Reformed believed. Pareus clarifies in his letter to the Synod what the Reformed really mean by their insistence that the work of regeneration ultimately cannot be resisted. He explains that for the orthodox, there is a threefold grace in regeneration: calling grace (*gratia vocans*), or external calling (*vocationis externae*); operating grace (*gratia operans*), or internal calling (*motionis internae*); and thirdly cooperating grace (*gratia cooperans*), or the grace of internal motion (*motionis quoque internae*).[2] Clearly,

---

2. Donald Sinnema, Christian Moser, and Herman Selderhuis, eds., *Acta et Documenta Synodi Nationalis Dordrechtanae (1618–1619)* (Göttingen: Vandenhoeck & Ruprecht, 2015), 1:227.

the Reformed believe that the grace of external calling can and indeed must be resisted by the unbeliever. However, the grace of internal calling is the power of God the Spirit that cannot be resisted. Indeed, this powerful grace overcomes our resistance.

The Remonstrants claim that "God in the regeneration of man does not use such powers of His omnipotence as potently and infallibly bend man's will to faith and conversion." Man may "resist God and the Holy Spirit when God intends man's regeneration and wills to regenerate him" (rej. 8). To this the Canons respond in rejection 8 by saying: "This is nothing less than the denial of all the efficiency of God's grace in our conversion, and the subjecting of the working of the Almighty God to the will of man." In effect, it is either a denial of the sinful nature of man or a denial of the divinity of the Holy Spirit. In the worst case, it is a denial of both.

The Work of the Holy Spirit in Sanctification and Perseverance
Finally, there is an indissoluble link between the true Reformed doctrine of regeneration on the one hand and of the doctrines of sanctification and final perseverance on the other. How we are brought to believe is how we are kept in the faith. If the grace of the Holy Spirit can be resisted at the outset of faith, it can also be rejected in the future. If man is the ultimate criterion in a situation of "prevenient grace" to believe or not to believe, so he is the ultimate criterion in perseverance in the faith.

Head V starts out with a dilemma—the dilemma of the Christian life. In regeneration, God by His Spirit "softens the hardened heart, and circumcises that which was uncircumcised, infuses new qualities into the will, which though heretofore dead, He quickens; from being evil, disobedient, and refractory, He renders it good, obedient, and pliable; actuates and strengthens it, that like a good tree, it may bring forth the fruits of good actions" (art. 11). Nevertheless, believers are not immediately or totally delivered "from the body of sin and from the infirmities of the flesh, so long as they continue in this world" (art. 1). This is the reality of indwelling sin (art. 3).

This situation has often produced doubt in the believer. *Will I persevere? Or will I possibly fall away from grace and lose my faith and salvation?* While the Remonstrants were of the opinion that the Reformed view of regeneration can only produce Christians who are nonchalant about their sin, the Reformed saw it differently. There is no room for self-certainty, or worse, for pride in the Christian life. Simply put, Christians could not and would not "persevere in a state of grace if left to their own strength" (art. 3).

The basic Remonstrant error of downplaying the work of the Holy Spirit as some kind of "assisting grace" enabling man to believe on his own rears its head once again with respect to the question of the perseverance of the believer. In the letter already quoted, Pareus states that by speaking of grace ("assisting grace"), the Remonstrants really deny true grace altogether.[3]

The Five Articles close with a somewhat humble statement:

> Whether [believers] are capable, through negligence, of forsaking again the first beginning of their life in Christ, of again returning to this present evil world, of turning away from the holy doctrine which was delivered them, of losing a good conscience, of becoming devoid of grace, that must be more particularly determined out of the Holy Scripture, before we ourselves can teach it with the full persuasion of our mind. (art. 5)

However, earlier in the article, the Remonstrants have already shown their hand about what they believe concerning final perseverance. In trying to safeguard free agency, they confess that "the assisting grace of the Holy Ghost…keeps them from falling," but only if "they are ready for the conflict, and desire his help, and are not inactive," making perseverance a matter of uncertainty. The Reformed reject this conditional perseverance, "that God does indeed provide the believer with sufficient powers to persevere and is ever ready to preserve these in him, if he will do his duty." They reply by saying, "This idea contains an outspoken Pelagianism, and while it would make men free, it makes them robbers of God's honor" (rej. 2).

Far from believing that the Holy Spirit simply overpowers human agency, making it in effect an ontological impossibility for the believer still to sin, the Canons actually have a quite balanced view of the Spirit's involvement in perseverance: "Although the weakness of the flesh cannot prevail against the power of God, who confirms and preserves true believers in a state of grace, yet converts are not always so influenced and actuated by the Spirit of God, as not in some particular instances sinfully to deviate from the guidance of divine grace, so as to be seduced by, and comply with the lusts of the flesh" (art. 2). It is still possible for believers to sin. This possibility, however, does not go so far as to entirely remove the work of the Spirit.

An exegetical linchpin for the Remonstrants was their insistence that Christians can in fact commit the sin against the Holy Spirit, causing them to entirely fall away from the faith (CD V, rej. 4). This, the Reformed Orthodox

---

3. "Praetextu gratiae, gratia negatur" (*Acta*, 1:217).

reject on the basis of a different and more catholic exegetical tradition, claiming that we can indeed grieve the Holy Spirit as Christians but not commit the sin against the Holy Spirit, which only the reprobate are capable of (art. 5). The problem of indwelling sin remains: "But God, who is rich in mercy, according to His unchangeable purpose of election, *does not wholly withdraw the Holy Spirit from His own people*, even in their melancholy falls; nor suffers them to proceed so far as to lose the grace of adoption, and forfeit the state of justification, or to commit the sin unto death; nor does He permit them to be totally deserted, and to plunge themselves into everlasting destruction" (art. 6, emphasis added). For believers who have backslidden, God "by the Holy Spirit again inspires them with the comfortable assurance of persevering" (art. 11).

Regeneration is that "supernatural work, most powerful," "not inferior in efficacy to creation or the resurrection from the dead," "so that all in whose heart God works in this marvelous manner are certainly, infallibly, and effectually regenerated, and do actually believe" (art. 12). But if that is the case, then it follows that "the sealing of the Holy Spirit [cannot] be frustrated or obliterated" (art. 8). It is a case of Arminian equivocation to confess the grace of the Spirit in the life of believers if that very grace is both dependent on man's future faithfulness and can be entirely lost.

Conclusion

We have seen that the Remonstrant view of salvation, though often utilizing the same vocabulary and theological categories as the Reformed, ends up being a very different system at nearly every point. This is especially true with respect to the Arminian use of "the grace of the Holy Ghost."

Ultimately, their concept of the *person* of the Holy Spirit in the economic Trinity is a different one. It makes the Spirit less than divine, less than all powerful. The same is true for their concept of the *work* of the Holy Spirit.

For the Reformed, rejecting the pernicious doctrine of the final resistibility of the work of the Holy Spirit in regeneration was ultimately a matter of doing honor to the glory of the Holy Spirit. It is no accident that the Canons close as they do with a doxology: "Now, to this one God, Father, Son, and Holy Spirit, be honor and glory forever. Amen" (CD V, 15).

CHAPTER 8

The Preservation and Perseverance of the Saints[1]

Daniel R. Hyde

The Canons of Dort "prepared the way for a dry scholasticism which runs into subtle abstractions, and resolves the living soul of divinity into a skeleton of formulas and distinctions."[2] This is how the well-known nineteenth-century Reformed historian Philip Schaff (1819–1893) described the Canons. The caricature continues. Popular anti-Calvinist George Bryson states it in his own way: "By reducing perseverance to an inevitability (as does the 5th point) all of these words of encouragement and warning are in a very real sense wasted. But in Scripture, perseverance in holiness to the end is seen as the challenge and goal of the Christian life. It should not be taken for granted."[3] Unfortunately, the caricature of "scholasticism" and "inevitability" continues in *us* because of how we talk about this doctrine in cold, sterile ways and even in how we live our lives, presuming on the preserving work of God's grace.

Of all the points of Dort's doctrine, the fifth point on preservation[4] and perseverance[5] is furthest from Schaff's caricature. Here we find the theologians, pastors, and elders assembled at Dort evidencing their ability to apply biblical doctrine to the experience of God's people. They lived this doctrine themselves, and they ministered it to those under their care. This is our life, too. As Schaff's contemporary, the Utrecht theologian Jan Jacob van Ooster-zee (1817–1892) said that this doctrine was "defended at the Synod of Dort

---

1. For a fuller exposition of the fifth point of doctrine of the Canons of Dort, see my *Grace Worth Fighting For: Recapturing the Vision of God's Grace in the Canons of Dort* (Moscow, Idaho: The Davenant Institute, 2019).

2. *The Creeds of Christendom*, ed. Philip Schaff, rev. David S. Schaff (1931; repr., Grand Rapids: Baker, 1993), 1:515.

3. George Bryson, *The Five Points of Calvinism: Weighed and Found Wanting* (Costa Mesa, Calif.: The Word for Today, 1996), 115.

4. *Conservat* (arts. 3, 7, 14); *conservantis* (art. 4); *custodia* (arts. 8–9).

5. *Perseverantia* (arts. 9, 15); *perseverantiae* (arts. 11–13).

with such warmth."[6] In the pages that follow I intend to demonstrate how Dort expressed this doctrine in a warm way.

The Context of Perseverance and Preservation

The fifth point of doctrine opens with two articles of common (catholic) Christian conviction that form the context in which preservation and perseverance are discussed: we *are* freed from our slavery to sin but *not* from our struggle with sin.

Our Freedom from Sin

Article 1 links back to the previous points of doctrine when it says, "Whom God calls [head III/IV], according to His purpose [head I], to the communion with His Son, our Lord Jesus Christ [head II], and regenerates by the Holy Spirit" (head III/IV). There's a close and strong connection grammatically between those of "whom" (*quos*) all this is true and the next statement: "He delivers *also* ("them indeed"; *eos quidem*) from the dominion and slavery of sin in this life." This past-tense, completed aspect of our freedom from sin is exemplified in Romans 6 where "our old man is crucified[7] with [Jesus]" with the immediate purpose "that the body of sin might be destroyed" (v. 6). "Destroyed"[8] is a violent verb that speaks of destruction and even annihilation.[9] It's the same word Paul uses when he says the enmity between Jew and Gentile was "abolished" (Eph. 2:15). The ultimate end is "that henceforth we should not serve sin" (Rom. 6:6). We were "servants of sin" (Rom. 6:17, 20) but are now "servants of righteousness" (Rom. 6:18) and "servants to God" (Rom. 6:22). Practically speaking, this means that you and I must "reckon... [ourselves] to be dead indeed unto sin" (Rom. 6:11). ·

Our Struggle with Sin

"Holiness" Christian traditions, though, stop with the above.[10] I cannot tell you how many emails I get each week with the latest fads to teach God's

---

6. J. J. van Oosterzee, *Christian Dogmatics: A Text Book for Academical Instruction and Private Study*, trans. John Watson and Maurice J. Evans (1870; repr., London: Hodder and Stoughton, 1891), 664.

7. Paul uses the aorist passive indicative συνεσταυρώθη.

8. Paul uses the aorist passive subjunctive καταργηθῇ.

9. καταργέω in *A Greek-English Lexicon of the New Testament and Other Early Christian Literature*, trans. William F. Arndt and F. Wilbur Gingrich (Chicago: University of Chicago Press, 1979), 417. See the comments of Thomas R. Schreiner, *Romans*, Baker Exegetical Commentary on the New Testament (Grand Rapids: Baker, 1998), 316.

10. For example, see https://www.umcmission.org/Find-Resources/John-Wesley -Sermons/Sermon-40-Christian-Perfection.

people that they can cease from consciously sinning in this life, that they can progress from a carnal Christian life to a Spirit-filled life, and that they can reach the proverbial top of the mountain in sanctification. This kind of thinking results from reading Romans 6 in isolation, but Paul also wrote Romans 7 and Philippians 3, which teach us another common truth: we still struggle with sin.[11] Article 1 concludes its statement of the biblical truth of our deliverance from sin this way: "though not altogether from the body of sin and from the infirmities of the flesh, so long as they continue in this world." Sin's dominion has been abolished; it's no longer my master. Yet sin's corruption still affects me. Thus article 2 goes on to say, "Hence spring daily sins of infirmity, and hence spots adhere to the best works of the saints." Christians are still sinful and still think, say, and do sinful things. In the words of John, "If we say that we have no sin, we deceive ourselves, and the truth is not in us" (1 John 1:8). Of course, the good news is that "if we"—as Christians—"confess our sins, [God] is faithful and just to forgive us our sins, and to cleanse us from all unrighteousness" (1 John 1:9). Because of our constant struggle with the vestiges of our sinful nature inherited from Adam, in this life we never perform a perfectly good work that is untainted by sin. Praise God that He accepts our works done in reliance on the Holy Spirit in Christ! Since we have this ongoing struggle, article 2 goes on to say that it "furnish[es] them with constant matter" to do four things.

First, "humiliation before God": "Not as though I had already attained [the glory of the resurrection], either were already perfect" (Phil. 3:12).

Second, "flying for refuge to Christ crucified": "But what things were gain to me," in my former life according to the law and the flesh, "those I counted loss for Christ. Yea doubtless, and I count all things" in this life "but loss for the excellency of the knowledge of Christ Jesus my Lord: for whom I have suffered the loss of all things, and do count them but dung, that I may win Christ, and be found in him, not having mine own righteousness, which is of the law" (Phil. 3:7–9).

Third, "mortifying the flesh more and more by the spirit of prayer, and by holy exercises of piety": I must forget "those things which are behind" (Phil. 3:13). How? "For if ye live after the flesh [my sin nature that had dominion in my former phase of life], ye shall die: but if ye through the Spirit do mortify

---

11. One pastoral question I've faced over the years is, Why does God allow sin to still dwell in His children in this life? One of the best answers I've read comes from Thomas Boston, "Why the Lord Suffereth Sin to Remain in the Regenerate," in *The Whole Works of the Late Reverend Thomas Boston of Ettrick: Sermons and Discourses on Several Important Subjects in Divinity*, ed. Samuel M'Millan (Aberdeen: George and Robert King, 1849), 6:110–24.

the deeds of the body, ye shall live" (Rom. 8:13). In the memorable words of John Owen, "Be killing sin or it will be killing you."[12] Thomas Manton said it like this: "If you enter not into a war with sin, you enter into a war with God."[13] By "the deeds of the body" Paul is not saying anything about our bodies being bad while our souls are good. He's speaking in a rhetorical way of the part for the whole. It's not just our bodies but also everything that leads up to our bodies sinning. Jesus teaches that our eyes, words, and deeds manifest the heart (Matt. 5:28; 12:34; 15:18–20); thus we need to mortify them. This is not merely changing what we look at, how we speak, and what we do. It includes these outward changes only because of an inner change. Manton said, "We must so oppose sin, that in some sort we may kill it or extinguish it, *not only scratch the face of it, but seek to root it out*; at least that must be our aim."[14] Mortification is holy war that begins deep in the heart and begins to manifest itself in looks, words, and acts. In ancient siege warfare, armies would not only use archers against their enemies on the wall or even catapults against the wall; they would use tunneling experts to dig under walls to bring them down.[15] Then they would fight hand to hand. In the same way we need to fight the sin in our hearts in order to collapse the sins of the body. We don't do this by the force of our wills or the strength of our resolve. We mortify "through the Spirit." This means that we do so in total reliance upon and only through the means that He has appointed. The Holy Spirit is the one who sanctifies us freely and merely of His grace. But the means by which He does this work are carried out by you and me.[16] The Canons tell us we mortify "by the spirit of prayer, and by holy exercises of piety." When we are feeling helpless, we need to use His means of the Word read privately and publicly, we need to hear the Word preached publicly, we need to partake of the sacraments publicly in the

---

12. "Of the Mortification of Sin in Believers," in *The Works of John Owen*, ed. William H. Goold (1850–1853; repr., Edinburgh: Banner of Truth, 1993), 6:9.

13. Thomas Manton, "Sermons Upon the Eighth Chapters to the Romans," in *The Works of Thomas Manton* (repr., Birmingham, Ala.: Solid Ground Christian Books, 2008), 12:72.

14. Manton, "Sermons Upon the Eighth Chapter to the Romans," in *Works*, 12:55.

15. For a description of "undermining," see Leif Inge Ree Petersen, *Siege Warfare and Military Organization in the Successor States (400–800 AD): Byzantium, the West and Islam* (Leiden: Brill, 2013), 286–88.

16. Manton said, "For to dream of a mortification which shall be wrought in us without our consent or endeavours, as well as whilst we are sleeping, as whilst we are waking, is to delude ourselves with a vain fancy." Manton, "Sermons Upon the Eighth Chapter to the Romans," in *Works*, 12:73. The active nature of sanctification and holiness was expressed by Hendriksen, who said, "The recipients of these favors [mentioned in vv. 1–11] must go into action." William Hendriksen, *Romans*, New Testament Commentary (Grand Rapids: Baker, 1989), 254.

midst of the congregation, we need to pray privately and on the Lord's Day in public worship and at prayer meetings, we need to join our prayers with fasting, we need to meditate on the glories of Christ, we need to engage in self-examining, and we need godly conversation and accountability.

Fourth, "pressing forward to the goal of perfection, till being at length delivered from this body of death, they are brought to reign with the Lamb of God in heaven." We are to "press toward the mark for the prize of the high calling of God in Christ Jesus," which is perfection (Phil. 3:14).

Perseverance and Preservation Defined

If article 2 were the last word, it would undoubtedly be true "by reason of these remains of indwelling sin, and the temptations of sin and of the world [that] those who are converted could not persevere in a state of grace if left to their own strength" (art. 3). Many of our evangelical brothers and sisters misunderstand this as a denial of preservation/perseverance.[17] We see something else, though, in Scripture, which article 3 states: "But God is faithful, who having conferred grace, mercifully confirms and powerfully preserves them therein, even to the end." Our heavenly Father will guard His entire church, whether dead or living, in heaven or on earth, from creation to consummation, in His almighty and ever-present power.[18] G. C. Berkouwer described this as "the eschatological perspective of this doctrine."[19]

---

17. For example, see the Assemblies of God's two statements: (1) "Assurance of Salvation" (Adopted by the General Presbytery in Session August 5 & 7, 2017). As found at https://ag.org /Beliefs/Topics-Index/Assurance-Of-Salvation (accessed August 2, 2018); (2) "An Assemblies of God Response to Reformed Theology" (Adopted by the General Presbytery in Session August 1 & 3, 2015). As found at https://ag.org/Beliefs/Topics-Index/Reformed-Theology -Response-of-the-AG-Position-Paper (accessed August 2, 2018).

18. In the words of David Pareus (1548–1622), "Perseverance is nothing else, but faith it selfe persevering to the end." "Epitome of Arminianisme: or, The Examination of the Five Articles of the Remonstrants, in the Netherlands," in *The Summe of Christian Religion, Delivered by Zacharius Ursinus*, trans. A. R. (London: Printed by James Young, 1645), 838. See *Synopsis Purioris Theologiae/Synopsis of a Purer Theology: Volume 2*, ed. Henk van den Belt, trans. Riemer A. Faber (Leiden: Brill, 2016), 263, which defines perseverance as "the continuous safe-keeping of faith, hope, and love, the deeds of which ought to last throughout one's entire life." To the question of whether saving faith includes perseverance, the Reformed orthodox answered yes because, "if not, faith would not be saving faith or justifying faith, for no-one except 'he who believes' (Mark 16:16) and no-one except 'he who endures to the end will be saved' (Matt. 24:13)." *Synopsis Purioris Theologiae*, 2:263.

19. G. C. Berkouwer, *Faith and Perseverance*, trans. Robert D. Knudsen, Studies in Dogmatics (1958; repr., Grand Rapids: Eerdmans, 1973), 11.

Initially, the 1610 document known as the Remonstrance that set in motion the series of events leading to the Synod considered final perseverance an issue that was unclear in Scripture.[20] What they were clear on was

> that those who are incorporated into Jesus Christ and thereby become partakers of His life-giving Spirit have abundant strength to strive against Satan, sin, the world, and their own flesh and to obtain the victory; it being well understood (that this is) through the assistance of the grace of the Holy Spirit, and that Jesus Christ assists them through His Spirit in all temptations, extends the hand, and—if only they are prepared for warfare and desire His help and are not negligent—keeps them standing, so that by no cunning or power of Satan can they be led astray or plucked out of Christ's hands, according to the word of Christ, John 10, "No one shall pluck them out of my hands."

The Reformed agreed on many things in this fifth point. By the time of the Synod, though, the Remonstrants were of the opinion that "true believers are able to fall through their own fault into shameful and atrocious deeds, to persevere and to die in them; and therefore finally to fall and to perish."[21] The issue, though, of such "if" language was viewing faith's interaction with grace as a hypothetical condition of final perseverance. "If" the believer is prepared for spiritual warfare, "if" the believer desires God's help, "if" the believer isn't negligent, *then* and only then will he persevere.[22] In the words of Pareus, "their assertion is not categoricall, but conditionall, that Christ, by his Spirit, is present with them, that hee stretcheth out his hand to them, and confirmes them that are inserted into him by true faith, if...."[23] What Pareus meant by "categoricall" was how Paul speaks in Romans 8: "if so be that the Spirit of God dwell in you.... If Christ be in you.... If the Spirit of him that raised up Jesus

---

20. On the debate with the Remonstrants at Dort, see Berkouwer, *Faith and Perseverance*, 39–45.

21. "Appendix H: The Opinions of the Remonstrants," in *Crisis in the Reformed Churches: Essays in Commemoration of the Great Synod of Dort, 1618–1619*, ed. Peter Y. De Jong (Grand Rapids: Reformed Fellowship, 1968), 228. See also *The Arminian Confession of 1621*, Princeton Theological Monograph Series 51, trans. and ed. Mark A. Ellis (Eugene, Ore: Pickwick Publications, 2005), 112–13.

22. See the first rejection of errors at the end of these positive articles where the Remonstrants said perseverance is not a consequence of eternal election or the historical work of Christ, but a condition of final salvation: "that the perseverance of the true believers is not a fruit of election or a gift of God gained by the death of Christ, but a condition of the new covenant, which (as they declare) man before his decisive election and justification must fulfill through his free will."

23. Pareus, "Epitome of Arminianisme," 839.

from the dead dwell in you" (vv. 9–11). These are not conditions in the hypo-thetical sense, but convey a true state of affairs. Colin Kruse comments that the possession of the Holy Spirit "is the *sine qua non* of Christian existence."[24] Thomas Schreiner comments that Paul's purpose was not to cast into doubt the believers' status but to assure: "εἴπερ (if) does not signify that some in the Roman community may be without the Spirit" and "εἰ (if) in the flow of the argument is another fulfilled condition" meaning "since."[25] Berkouwer ironi-cally said of the Remonstrant position, "If we grasp the real meaning of this objection…we have understood in principle the whole controversy."[26] Article 3 affirms that in our own strength perseverance is at best a tenable proposition, but with God our preservation is assured. This is illustrated in 1 Peter 1.

Peter speaks of *the certainty of the salvation* of God when saying our "inheri-tance" is being "reserved" by the power of God (1 Peter 1:4–5). Peter uses the verb "reserved"[27] in the perfect passive tense. The perfect tense is used less frequently than the other tenses in the New Testament; when it is, there's a reason.[28] Peter is signifying that our inheritance was accomplished in the past, and the results of that past action continue into the present.[29] The New Testament authors use the same verb to speak of something that is "kept" *until* a definite time in the future (John 2:10; 12:7; 2 Peter 2:4, 9; 3:7; Jude 6). The certainty of the saints' salvation is also confirmed by the adjectives Peter uses to describe it: "incorruptible," meaning it is imperishable and immortal; "undefiled," meaning it is pure; and "fadeth not away" or "unfading," mean-ing it does not diminish over time.

The salvation is certain along with those who participate in it—*the saved* "who are kept by the power of God" (1 Peter 1:5).[30] Peter uses a present parti-cipial verb "kept," but it's in the passive voice, meaning, God is the one active in guarding, while believers are the recipients of this action. Think of a jar of peanut butter. The peanut butter is in the jar. The lid is opened and closed by your action. The peanut butter is passive. Why is there a lid? To preserve the peanut butter inside from the air outside that causes it to go bad. This verb

---

24. Colin G. Kruse, *Paul's Letter to the Romans*, (Grand Rapids: Eerdmans, 2012), 332.

25. Schreiner, *Romans*, 413–14. See the further discussion in Kruse, *Paul's Letter to the Romans*, 333; and Schreiner, *Romans*, 395, 409–10.

26. Berkouwer, *Faith and Perseverance*, 40.

27. τετηρημένην.

28. "When it is used, there is usually a deliberate choice on the part of the writer." Daniel B. Wallace, *Greek Grammar Beyond the Basics: An Exegetical Syntax of the New Testament* (Grand Rapids: Zondervan, 1996), 573.

29. On the perfect tense, see Wallace, *Greek Grammar Beyond the Basics*, 573–82.

30. φρουρουμένους.

"kept" is both powerful and personal: it's used for a guard inside a city's walls whose job is not to let people out (2 Cor. 11:32) and for the law that kept us like captives (Gal. 3:23). The law kept us in its custody and condemned us. In the context of 1 Peter 1, though, for those who have been born again, God is now powerfully guarding us under His custody. We're under new ownership. We're no longer condemned. When the last day comes, our rightful owner Jesus will take full possession of us. Of course all illustrations break down. While God is preserving us, we're not passive like peanut butter. God is actively working out His preserving work by activating us to persevere. God's power is guarding us "through faith unto salvation ready to be revealed in the last time" (1 Peter 1:5).

All this is true because of *the certainty of the Savior*. He is *faithful* to who He is and what He has promised. He "is faithful who having conferred grace, [He] mercifully confirms and powerfully preserves them therein, even to the end" (1 Cor. 1:8–9; Phil. 1:6; 2 Thess. 3:3; 1 Peter 1:5; 5:10; Jude 24). Where did Peter get his teaching that the Savior is certain to save His people? The gospel of John records Jesus rebuking the Pharisees as false shepherds while proclaiming Himself to be the "good shepherd" (John 10:11). Jesus goes on to give three reasons that He is the certain shepherd who preserves His sheep.

First, *Jesus is the door of the sheep* (John 10:7–10): "[Amen, amen], I say unto you, I am the door of the sheep" (v. 7). He compares Himself to the false shepherd Pharisees: "All that ever came before me are thieves and robbers: but the sheep did not hear them" (v. 8). Then He explains the importance of being the door: "by me if any man enter, he shall be saved, and shall go in and out, and find pasture. The thief cometh not, but for to steal, and to kill, and to destroy: I am come that they might have life…more abundantly" (vv. 9–10).

Second, *Jesus is the shepherd of the sheep* (John 10:11–18): "I am the good shepherd" and, as such, Jesus "giveth his life for the sheep" (v. 11). In contrast, again, to the false shepherd who flees the sheep when the wolf comes near because he does not care about them (vv. 12–13), Jesus says, "I am the good shepherd" (v. 14). As this kind of shepherd, "[I] know my sheep, and am known of mine" (v. 14). Can Jesus disown what is His? Can we run away so that He who knows us so well cannot find us? Look at how powerful this image is in verse 15: "as the Father knoweth me, even so know I the Father." How does Jesus know us and we know Him? It is in the same way that the Father knows the Son and the Son knows the Father. Can the Father disown His Son? Can the Son not love the Father? You see why it's ridiculous to say a true believer can lose salvation.

Third, *Jesus is the Son of God* (John 10:28–30): "I give unto them eternal life; and they shall never perish, neither shall any man pluck them out of my hand" (v. 28). This verse in itself should eliminate all objections. "I," the eternal, almighty Son of God through whom the universe came to be "give unto them eternal life"; therefore, "they shall never perish." Literally Jesus says, "They will not perish forever."[31] This is the strongest way of saying something in Greek. Jesus uses an aorist subjunctive with an emphatic negative. How long is "never"? Forever, and ever, and ever! Because this is such an absolute statement, Jesus says "neither shall any man pluck them out of *my* hand." Not Satan. Not the false shepherds. Not even yourself. He expresses it even more strongly in verse 29: "My Father, which gave them me, is greater than all; and no man is able to pluck them out of my Father's hand." The Father gave the sheep to the Son and Jesus gives the sheep eternal life. We cannot be snatched from Jesus's or the Father's hand. No one has the right, might, ability, or authority to take us! Then in verse 30 He tells us why this is true: "I and my Father are one." This is your powerful Savior! This is a gospel that powerfully saves. What a reason to praise Him when feeling low! What a reason to tell a lost sinner there's hope in Jesus's name.

Perseverance and the Problem of Sin

In light of this, the popular slogan, "once saved, always saved" may come to mind. But is that the proper reaction to God's preserving power? Do we believe that those God in His love chose in eternity will spend an eternity loving Him? Yes, we affirm this. Yet how is this slogan so often used? It's used to say that a person who *claims* to be a Christian can live like an unbeliever his or her whole life and still be saved. Instead, articles 4–8 delve into the "existential tension"[32] between preservation/perseverance and the continuing problem of indwelling sin. Berkouwer described perseverance as "a continuity amidst all the transitoriness of our lives, as we proceed by devious paths through numberless circumstances and dangers toward the consummation, toward the day of Jesus Christ."[33]

Can I Fall into Serious Sin?

While those effectually called and regenerated cannot completely fall *from* grace—"although the weakness of the flesh cannot prevail against the power

---

31. οὐ μὴ ἀπόλωνται εἰς τὸν αἰῶνα.
32. Berkouwer, *Faith and Perseverance*, 12.
33. Berkouwer, *Faith and Perseverance*, 10.

of God"—they can fall *into* heinous sins—"yet converts are not always so influenced and actuated by the Spirit of God, as not in some particular instances sinfully to deviate from the guidance of divine grace, so as to be seduced by, and comply with the lusts of the flesh" (art. 4). We see this in the *example of the saints*: "this the lamentable fall of David, Peter, and other saints described in Holy Scripture demonstrates." David fell into adultery with Bathsheba leading him to cover it up with complicit murder by having Uriah placed at the front of the battle line (2 Samuel 11). Samson fell by selling the secret of his strength to Delilah for momentary pleasure; he underestimated her power and overestimated his (Judges 16). Peter fell after being called, trained by, and accompanying the Lord in His ministry; then he denied Jesus (Matt. 26:36–44). Peter overestimated himself, placing himself outside the very place our Lord was interrogated (Matt. 26:69–74). He shouldn't have been anywhere near that place! The same sin nature that ran through Peter's veins runs through ours. With Peter, we can be prideful: "Though all men shall be offended because of thee, yet I will never be offended…. Though I should die with thee, yet will I not deny thee" (Matt. 26:33, 35). Like Peter, while "the spirit indeed is willing…the flesh is weak" (Matt. 26:41). Our hearts are full of flammable material labeled with a big bright sign with uppercase letters: EXPLOSIVE. All it takes is the smallest spark for sin to burst out. Our sins, then, are like a cold winter that causes once fruitful trees to go dormant, suffocating our spiritual vitality.[34]

God allows this by His *righteous permission*: when believers neglect to be watchful and prayerful, "they are not only liable to be drawn into great and heinous sins by Satan, the world and the flesh, but sometimes by the righteous permission of God actually fall into these evils." If God were not in control of all aspects of our lives, there would be no hope of change. Jesus says, "You will all fall away because of Me this night" (see Matt. 26:31; cf. Zech. 13:7). When Satan demanded to have Peter that he might sift him like wheat (Luke 22:31–32), Jesus did not turn him down or say that Satan had no business asking such a thing. Our Lord was in complete control by giving Satan permission to "sift" Peter. Why? So that Peter's faith would be refined and purified and thereby enabled to strengthen his brothers in their faith after his repentance (v. 32). The Lord can allow us to fall into sin on our own accord. Knowing this and that He wants to strengthen our faith through

---

34. Herman Witsius, *The Economy of the Covenants Between God and Man: Comprehending a Complete Body of Divinity*, trans. Wíllliam Crookshank (London: R. Baynes, 1822; repr., Grand Rapids: Reformation Heritage Books, 2008), 2:57.

the experience so we'll be more assured afterward, we "must…be constant in watching and prayer" (art. 4) as Jesus said (Matt. 26:41). Watch for yourself (1 Thess. 5:6; 1 Peter 5:8) and your brothers and sisters (Gal. 6:1). Are you aware of your weaknesses? Are you concerned when a brother or sister is not in worship week in and week out? Pray (Eph. 6:18; 1 Thess. 5:6, 17). Perseverance exists in the existential tension of the Christian life. It does not exist "in a static, lifeless relationship" between God and us "but in the mobile, living relationship of the entire human life to the Father."[35]

Why Do I Feel So Far from God?

Article 5 picks up on the consequences of not watching and praying and therefore falling into "great and heinous sins." The overall result is what our forefathers called "spiritual desertion."[36] Psalm 6 expresses it in an agonizing question: "How long?" (v. 3). Psalm 32 expresses it as past pain: "When I kept silence, my bones waxed old through my roaring all the day long" (v. 3). Psalm 38 expresses it as deep pain: "For thine arrows stick fast in me, and thy hand presseth me sore" (v. 2). This affected David with feelings of distance: "My lovers and my friends stand aloof from my sore; and my kinsmen stand afar off…. Forsake me not, O LORD: O my God, be not far from me" (38:11, 21). The effects of this feeling of desertion are manifold.

By such sins we "very highly offend God." Our society talks so much about being offended, but do you realize that your sins offend God Himself? "Against thee, thee only, have I sinned, and done this evil in thy sight" (Ps. 51:4). Get over yourself and think of Him!

By such sins we "incur a deadly guilt." It's not only that you know you have sinned against God, but that you know *He* knows you've sinned! This leads us to feel mortified and petrified: "But I, as a deaf man, heard not; and I was as a dumb [mute] man that openeth not his mouth" (Ps. 38:13).

By such sins we "grieve the Holy Spirit." The Spirit who lives within us and is the down payment of our living with the triune God in eternity is grieved by our sins (Isa. 63:10; Eph. 4:30).

By such sins we "interrupt the exercise of faith." People who are paralyzed from the waist down still have life, although they cannot exercise their legs. In the same way, we still have spiritual life within us, but there are times

---

35. Berkouwer, *Faith and Perseverance*, 29.
36. Gisbertus Voetius and Johannes Hoornbeeck, *Spiritual Desertion*, trans. John Vriend and Harry Boonstra, ed. M. Eugene Oosterhaven, Classics of Reformed Spirituality (Grand Rapids: Baker Academic, 2003).

we can be spiritually paralyzed like Peter, who outside Jesus's trial was paralyzed in fear and denial when asked if he was a Christian (Matt. 26:69–75).

Through such sins believers "very grievously wound their consciences." The prophet Nathan told David, "You are the man," and then David's conscience was wounded. The apostle John assures us that "if our heart condemn us, God is greater than our heart, and knoweth all things" (1 John 3:20). Contained in this promise is the reality that our hearts *do* condemn us for our sins.

By such sins we "sometimes lose the sense of God's favor for a time." This is the worst of all experiences! "But thou, O LORD, how long?" (Ps. 6:3). "Forsake me not, O LORD" (Ps. 38:21). "Cast me not away from thy presence; and take not thy Holy Spirit from me. Restore unto me the joy of thy salvation" (Ps. 51:11–12).

Can God Renew My Backsliding?

These major effects of major sins can be reversed: "until on their returning into the right way of serious repentance, the light of God's fatherly countenance again shines upon them." It is vital to grasp that renewal is not grounded in repentance, but in the grace of God Himself. In these times our faith is like a smoldering piece of charcoal that is buried under the ashes. In these times our faith is like the sun when it is concealed by dark storm clouds; our faith runs to the corner of our hearts and is ashamed to come out.

God can renew my backsliding because I have *a renewing God*: "But God, who is rich in mercy...."[37] Nine times in Psalm 30 David invokes the name of the Lord (vv. 1–4, 7–8, 10, 12)—the name He revealed to Moses at the burning bush: "I AM WHO I AM" (Ex. 3:14 NKJV). It expresses His faithfulness to His covenant. Listen to how Matthew Henry (1662–1714) expressed the ability of God to renew us:

> If *weeping endureth for a night,* and it be a wearisome night, yet as sure as the light of the morning returns after the darkness of the night, so sure will joy and comfort return in a short time, in due time, to the people of God; for the covenant of grace is as firm as the covenant of the day.[38]

Our renewing God is faithful to His promises: "according to His unchangeable purpose of election, [He] does not wholly withdraw the Holy

---

37. See rejection 3, which states that in the richness of God's mercy He does not allow true believers to lose His Spirit, forfeit their adoption or justification, or sin against the Holy Spirit so that they are lost forever.

38. Matthew Henry, *Commentary on the Whole Bible* (1991; repr., Peabody, Mass.: Hendrickson Publishers, 1997), 782.

Spirit from His own people, even in their melancholy falls." Even when I fall into sin like David, I can pray, not hypothetically but repentantly in confidence: "Take not they Holy Spirit from me" (Ps. 51:11). God is faithful to His promises, not allowing me "to proceed so far as to lose the grace of adoption." He's brought me into His family, changing my status from orphan to son; He will not reverse this work. God is faithful to His promises, not allowing me "to proceed so far as to lose...the state of justification." I once was in a state of misery, but that was changed into a state of justification. We're not merely innocent and reverted back to Adam's garden status; we're not merely freed from guilt and punishment; no, we're positively righteous in our status and standing before almighty God. He's declared us righteous in His Son and we do not lose this! God is faithful to His promises, not allowing me "to proceed so far as to...commit the sin unto death; nor does He permit [me] to be totally deserted, and to plunge [myself] into everlasting destruction."

A Renewed People
God, "by His Word and Spirit, certainly and effectually renews them to repentance, to a sincere and godly sorrow for their sins" (art. 7).[39] There are several characteristics of a renewed people according to article 7.

First, a renewed people *seek remission*: "that they may seek and obtain remission in the blood of the Mediator." David says in Psalm 30: "O LORD my God, I cried to you for help, and you have healed me" (v. 2 ESV); "To you, O LORD, I cry, and to the Lord I plead for mercy" (v. 8 ESV); "Hear, O LORD, and be merciful to me! O LORD, be my helper!" (v. 10 ESV).

Second, a renewed people *experience God's favor*: "that they...may again experience the favor of a reconciled God." Listen to the amazing words of Psalm 30: "For his anger is but for a moment, and his favor is for a lifetime. Weeping may tarry for the night, but joy comes in the morning" (v. 5 ESV).

Third, a renewed people *adore God's mercies*: "that they...through faith adore His mercies." "I will extol you, O LORD" (Ps. 30:1 ESV); "Sing praises to the LORD, O you his saints, and give thanks to his holy name" (v. 4 ESV);

---

39. Augustine said of the elect who have fallen: "The faith of these...either actually does not fail at all, or, if there are any whose faith fails, it is restored before their life is ended, and the iniquity which had intervened is done away, and perseverance even to the end is allotted to them." Augustine, *On Rebuke and Grace*, in *A Select Library of the Nicene and Post-Nicene Fathers of the Christian Church*, ser. 1, vol. 5, *Saint Augustine: Anti-Pelatian Writings* (New York: The Christian Literature Company, 1887), 478. "For these in their love for God continue even to the end; and they who for a season wander from the way return, that they may continue unto the end what they had begun to be in good." Augustine, *On Rebuke and Grace*, 480–81.

"You have turned for me my mourning into dancing; you have loosed my sackcloth and clothed me with gladness, that my glory may sing your praise and not be silent. O LORD my God, I will give thanks to you forever!" (vv. 11–12 ESV).

Fourth, a renewed people *work out their salvation*: "that they…henceforward more diligently work out their own salvation with fear and trembling" (see Phil. 2:12). That is what David did as he "cried to" the Lord "for help, and" the Lord "healed" him; therefore he praised the Lord (Ps. 30:2 ESV). And he asks in verse 9 (ESV), "What profit is there in my death, if I go down to the pit? Will the dust praise you? Will it tell of your faithfulness? "No, but I will," is what he is saying! You can fall into sin; you cannot fall out of grace. God is a renewing God; God promises to make you a renewed people.

Preserved by a Triune God

When we think of ourselves, we can be brought to despair, but when we think of God, we can be brought to hope. We've seen the ups and downs, the joys and pains of the Christian life in the past several articles. Article 8 gives a summary:

> Thus, it is not in consequence of their own merits or strength, but of God's free mercy, that they do not totally fall from faith and grace, nor continue and perish finally in their backslidings; which, with respect to themselves, is not only possible, but would undoubtedly happen; but with respect to God, it is utterly impossible.

It then goes on to speak of the practicality of the doctrine of the Trinity for the Christian life of perseverance.[40] The doctrine of the Trinity is the guarantee of your preservation. How so? It is not in prying into the mysteries of how three can be one, but for our weakness God has revealed Himself in Scripture by teaching us that each person of the Trinity has a distinct role in our salvation. Let's pause and reflect upon the work of each person of the triune God and how that work strengthens our faith in knowing we are preserved children of God.

The work of the Father preserves: "With respect to God, it is utterly impossible, since His counsel cannot be changed nor His promise fail, neither can the call according to His purpose be revoked." God's "counsel" concerning you "cannot be changed." When the prophet Isaiah contrasted the Lord with

---

40. On this, see Ryan M. McGraw, *Knowing the Trinity: Practical Thoughts for Daily Life* (Lancaster, Pa.: Alliance of Confessing Evangelicals, 2017).

the idols of the nations, he said, "Declaring the end from the beginning, and from ancient times the things that are not yet done, saying, My counsel shall stand, and I will do all my pleasure" (Isa. 46:10). "But," one may say, "that talks about His counsel for everything in general; there's nothing there *for me*." The prophet continues further on: "For the mountains shall depart, and the hills be removed; but my kindness shall not depart from thee, neither shall the covenant of my peace be removed, saith the LORD that hath mercy on thee" (Isa. 54:10). Don't tell me that doesn't comfort or enliven you! Don't tell me Calvinism is boring, that we are the so-called frozen chosen, or that the doctrine of election is all head and no heart! God's "promise" concerning you "[cannot] fail." If the Father chose us and His choice is immutable, then His promise to us is an extension of that immutable love. What promise? "And this is the promise that he hath promised us, even eternal life" (1 John 2:25). Whose promise? Unlike our promises as fathers or the promises our fathers made to us, *the* Father's promises are never forgotten, never pushed aside because He's too busy, never said in haste, but are always realized! Further, His "calling" of you "according to His purpose [cannot] be revoked."

The work of the Son preserves: "With respect to God, it is utterly impossible, since…the merit, intercession and preservation of Christ [cannot] be rendered ineffectual." Paul praises Jesus, saying, "In whom we have redemption through his blood, the forgiveness of sins, according to the riches of his grace" (Eph. 1:7). The death of Christ on the cross, by which His blood was shed for the remission of our innumerable sins, was the final, culminating act of His active and passive obedience on our behalf (Rom. 5:18–19). How can we say that the Son of God—who came from heaven to earth, with those the Father in His counsel chose in His mind and on His heart, lived in their place all His thirty-three years, and died on the cross for their particular sins—can have that work wiped out by us? *He* merited eternal life for you—not *you* for yourself! After He did so, He went to heaven and now "maketh intercession for us" (Rom. 8:34; see also Heb. 7:25) as our "advocate" whenever we sin (1 John 2:1). Right now He is holding you in His hand, and Satan himself cannot snatch you from it (John 10:28). Satan may test you as with Job, Satan may sift as with Peter, and Satan may buffet as with Paul, but he may not snatch!

The work of the Spirit preserves: "With respect to God, it is utterly impossible, since…the sealing of the Holy Spirit [cannot] be frustrated or obliterated." He is the seal (Eph. 1:13). This means His grace in your life is authentic and guaranteed. It also means we are rendered inviolable. As Paul goes on to say of the Holy Spirit, it is "by whom you were sealed for the day of redemption" (Eph. 4:30 ESV). In addition, the Spirit is the earnest payment (Eph. 1:14).

Paul puts these two images of seal and earnest payment about us together in 2 Corinthians 1:22 (ESV), where he says that God "has also put his seal on us and given us his Spirit in our hearts as a guarantee."

Perseverance and Assurance

As the above shows, articles 4–8 of the Canons of Dort's fifth point of doctrine do not present preservation and perseverance in a cold way. We see this again in articles 9–13, where we transition from the attacks on our faith to the assurance of our faith as we strive to persevere.

Its Possibility

"Of this *preservation* of the elect to salvation and of their *perseverance* in the faith," article 9 confesses, "true believers" not only "may" but "do obtain assurance." Note well that it is actual, "true believers" who can have this assurance. The church is the continuation of the ancient covenant people and is a mixed assembly with believers and unbelievers: "Not all Israel"—meaning ethnic Israel—"are of Israel"—meaning true Israelites (Rom. 9:6).

"True believers" can have a "certain persuasion that they ever will continue true and living members of the church; and that they experience forgiveness of sins, and will at last inherit eternal life." We say with Paul, "There is therefore now no condemnation to them which are in Christ Jesus," and "I am persuaded, that" nothing "shall be able to separate us from the love of God, which is in Christ Jesus our Lord" (Rom. 8:1, 38–39). Faith contains the element of trust, but believers don't always exercise faith so that they're fully assured. Faith is rooted in the objectivity of Christ, although subjectively I may or may not feel that at any given time.[41]

"But," one may argue, "Paul was an apostle." Yes, he was. Indeed, you are assured by the same faith in the same Savior as Paul was. This is why article 9 speaks with the biblical phrase of assurance as being "according to the measure of their faith" (cf. Rom. 12:3). Some believers are spiritual babies in Christ, while others are mature adults in Christ (Heb. 5:13–14). Both have faith that contains the element of trust, but an immature, childish believer doesn't always exercise faith as a mature believer does.[42] Assurance is a possibility for all of us, although it may not be a possession yet.

---

41. Louis Berkhof, *The Assurance of Faith: The Firm Foundation of Christian Hope* (1939; repr., Birmingham, Ala.: Solid Ground Christian Books, 2004), 24.

42. Berkhof, *The Assurance of Faith*, 24.

Its Production

Where do we find this assurance? It's "not produced by any peculiar revelation contrary to, or independent [Latin, *extra*; outside] of the Word of God," as the Roman Catholic Council of Trent decreed in 1546.[43] Yet note that as Paul began, "There is therefore now no condemnation to them which are in Christ Jesus," he went on to say,

> What shall we then say to these things? If God be for us, who can be against us? He that spared not his own Son, but delivered him up for us all, how shall he not with him also freely give us all things?... Who is he that condemneth? It is Christ...who also maketh intercession for us. Who shall separate us from the love of Christ?... Nay, in all these things we are more than conquerors through him that loved us.... Nor height, nor depth, nor any other creature, shall be able to separate us from the love of God, which is in Christ Jesus our Lord. (Rom. 8:31–32, 34–35, 37, 39)

Instead of the source of assurance being revelation, article 10 points out three legitimate sources, which we recognize aren't magical remedies to take only once; they are a matter of cultivation.

First and foremost is *God's promises*: "but springs from faith in God's promises"—such as Romans 8—"which He has most abundantly revealed in His Word for our comfort."

Second, the *witness of the Spirit*: "from the testimony of the Holy Spirit witnessing with our spirit that we are children and heirs of God" (see Rom. 8:16). Romans 8:16–17 says the Holy Spirit witnesses *to* our spirit through the promises of the Word and *with* our spirit as we believe those promises and see the fruit in our lives.[44] We also recognize that this "testimony although it be not always alike powerful in believers, yet notwithstanding it manifests itself many times in their greatest humiliation and distress 'that we are children of God.'"[45]

---

43. "If any one saith, that he will for certain, of an absolute and infallible certainty, have that great gift of perseverance unto the end—unless he have learned this by special revelation: let him be anathema." Session 6, Canon 16, in *The Canons and Decrees of the Sacred and Oecumenical Council of Trent*, trans. J. Waterworth (London: C. Dolman, 1848), 46. See the rejection of error 5 in the Canons where we reject the Remonstrant teaching "that without a special revelation we can have no certainty of future perseverance in this life."

44. See also Rom. 8:9, 14–17; Gal. 4:6–7; 1 John 2:20, 27; 3:1–2, 24. The *Dutch Annotations* on Romans 8:16–17 spoke of the twofold witness of the Spirit *to* our spirits and *with* our spirits, as we see the work of His grace in our lives. *The Dutch Annotations upon the Whole Bible*, trans. Theodore Haak (London, 1657).

45. *Dutch Annotations* on Romans 8:16–17.

Third, the *good works* we do: "lastly, from a serious and holy desire to preserve a good conscience and to perform good works." As 1 John 3 says, "Hereby perceive we the love of God, because he laid down his life for us: and we ought to lay down our lives for the brethren…. And hereby we know that we are of the truth, and shall assure our hearts before him" (vv. 16, 19).[46]

Its Struggle

Does assurance mean no more spiritual doubts? Absolutely not. "Believers in this life have to struggle with various carnal doubts and that under grievous temptations they are not always sensible of this full assurance of faith and certainty of persevering" (art. 11). Just because we're forgiven doesn't mean that our faith never doubts or that we're not tempted to fall. Sin's guilt has been nullified in our lives, but we must still fight against the pollution of sin that leads to "various carnal doubts," and when it undergoes "grievous temptation," we're "not always sensible of this full assurance of faith and certainty of persevering." We see the work of temptation in 1 Corinthians 10. Everything that happened to our forefathers happened as "our examples" (v. 6) and "for our admonition" (v. 11). When Paul says, "There hath no temptation taken you but such as is common to man" (v. 13), he's speaking of their being tempted to idolatry (v. 7), to sexual immorality (v. 8), to testing Christ (v. 9), and to grumbling (v. 10). What hope is there, then, for sinners like us? Article 11 goes on to apply Paul's words from 2 Corinthians 1 to the struggles of 1 Corinthians 10:

> But God, who is the Father of all consolation, does not suffer them to be tempted above that they are able, but will with the temptation also make a way to escape that they may be able to bear it (1 Cor. 10:13), and by the Holy Spirit again inspires them with the comfortable assurance of persevering.

Its Motivation

If our God and Father of all consolation doesn't allow us to be tempted more than we can handle, provides us with the way of escaping it, and renews us by the Holy Spirit, why should we even try in the Christian life? Do we just "let go and let God"? On the contrary, "this certainty of perseverance…is so far from exciting in believers a spirit of pride or of rendering them carnally secure" (art. 12).[47] Certainty motivates us not to carelessness in godliness but

---

46. See also 1 John 3:16–19, 24; 2:3, 5; 3:10; 4:7.

47. See rejection of error 6 where we reject the Remonstrant teaching "that the doctrine of the certainty of perseverance and of salvation from its own character and nature is a cause

carefulness to godliness; not self-gratification but glorification of God; not laziness but love. We have to be aware of the "spirit of pride" within us that would turn our liberty in our Savior into a license for our sins, the grace of God for self-gratification (Gal. 5:13; 1 Peter 2:16). Have you ever said to yourself, "I can indulge in the flesh because God will forgive me?" Not only do we have to set an example to those who reject this doctrine but we have to be aware that we by nature will use the certainty of perseverance as a reason for sinning. In contrast to our natural inclination to turn certainty into an excuse for sin, article 12 proclaims in no uncertain terms that certainty is

> the real source of humility, filial reverence, true piety, patience in every tribulation, fervent prayers, constancy in suffering, and in confessing the truth, and of solid rejoicing in God; so that the consideration of this benefit should serve as an incentive [Latin, *stimulus*] to the serious and constant practice of gratitude and good works, as appears from the testimonies of Scripture and the examples of the saints.

Herman Witsius (1636–1708) would say a generation later, "Nothing is more powerful for inflaming our hearts with love to God, than to know, sense, and taste of the divine love shed abroad in them."[48] This is why when we throw our assertions back and forth with Arminian friends and they are left unconvinced, a godly life motivated by the power of God's grace will be a more powerful testimony. It is God who excites us; it's not our own doing. The God who excites us—who stimulates us to action—causes us to be excited with all our being, body and soul, mind and emotions. We see the working of the indwelling Holy Spirit in us, exciting us to live righteously. As Witsius said, "All our religion is nothing but gratitude."[49]

Article 13 goes on to say, "Neither does renewed confidence of persevering produce licentiousness or a disregard to piety in those who are recovering from backsliding." We cannot be careless because the power of God's grace is at work within us. We're new creations in Christ (2 Cor. 5:17). Instead, assurance

> renders them much more careful and solicitous to continue in the ways of the Lord, which He hath ordained, that they who walk therein may maintain an assurance of persevering, lest by abusing His fatherly kindness, God should turn away His gracious countenance from them (to

---

of indolence and is injurious to godliness, good morals, prayers and other holy exercises, but that on the contrary it is praiseworthy to doubt."

48. Witsius, *The Economy of the Covenants*, 2:78.
49. Witsius, *The Economy of the Covenants*, 2:80.

behold which is to the godly dearer than life, the withdrawing whereof is more bitter than death), and they in consequence thereof should fall into more grievous torments of conscience.

We're going to be tempted to sin, but we have the assurance of the Lord's care for us even in those temptations. We're going to struggle with motivation, but we have the Lord's promise that He's at work within us to will and to do His good pleasure. We're going to fall into sin, but we have the assurance not only that we won't fall out of grace but that our faithful God will restore and renew us again. Grace should not lead to carelessness but to carefulness.

The Means of Perseverance and Preservation

God's preserving work that leads to our perseverance is no mere academic matter of the mind. It's a daily reality. It's a tangible reality as well according to article 14, which describes God's institution and our use of means. As we saw in 1 Peter 1, God preserves our souls by His infinite and supernatural power by means of our faith.[50] Knowing the many weaknesses we've seen above, God gives tangible aids for this faith to embrace along the path of life.

He Uses Means

In the beginning God created all that exists by means of His Word (Genesis 1). His use of means was not for His sake, but for ours. Subsequently, God used the things He made to accomplish His purpose in the lives of His children. He used rain to flood the earth in judgment. He used a rainbow to signify His grace. He used a lamb and its blood to signify His mercy. John 6 tells us that Jesus used bread to feed people. Then Peter confessed that Jesus's words are the bread of our souls: "Lord, to whom shall we go? thou hast the words of eternal life" (John 6:68). Those words were the means *through* which God gave us new life: "as it hath pleased God, by the preaching of the gospel, to begin this work of grace in us" (art. 14). He still works this way in us: "so He preserves, continues, and perfects it [His work] by the hearing and reading of His Word." Twelve hundred years before Dort, Augustine's "doctrines of grace" led certain monks in southern Gaul to say that rebuke and exhortation to persevere were unnecessary.[51] Augustine reminded them that "the teachers of the churches, the apostles, were in the habit of...prescribing what things should be done, as rebuking if they were not done, and praying that they might

---

50. Witsius, *The Economy of the Covenants*, 2:76.
51. Augustine, *On Rebuke and Grace*, 473.

be done."[52] Like a sick man needs medicine so too out of love pastors must apply the rebukes of the Word and pray for the person in sin "that he may be healed...*by means of* rebuke."[53]

He Uses the Means of the Gospel
In particular, it is "by the preaching of the gospel" that the Lord has "beg[u]n this work of grace in us," meaning our being born again. By the power of the Holy Spirit God has given us new spiritual life (John 3:5–6, 8); that life came through means of the preaching of the gospel (James 1:18; 1 Peter 1:23). The translation of the Canons of Dort we're using goes on to say: "so He preserves, continues, and perfects it by the hearing and reading of His Word, by meditation thereon, and by the exhortations, threatenings, and promises thereof, as well as by the use of the sacraments." Notice the words: *Word* and *thereon*, meaning, on the *Word*. The 2011 translation of the Christian Reformed Church gives a closer reading of the latter half of the Latin text: "so God preserves, continues, and completes this work [of grace] by the hearing and reading of the gospel, by meditation on it, by its exhortations, threats, and promises, and also by the use of the sacraments."[54] This whole—hearing, reading, meditation, exhortations, threats, and promises—are linked back to the same means God used to regenerate us: by the proclamation of the *gospel*. These are linked with the clause *ita per eiusdem* (by means of the same), meaning the same gospel. *By the proclamation of the gospel* God has begun a work of grace in us *so by means of the same* gospel He continues His work of grace in us to the end.[55]

While it sounds normal to us that the gospel begins, preserves, continues, and perfects God's work of grace in us and even that we are to hear, read, meditate on, and embrace the promises of the gospel, to those of us out of

---

52. Augustine, *On Rebuke and Grace*, 473. See also p. 482. In this connection, read Canons of Dort III/IV, 17.

53. Augustine, *On Rebuke and Grace*, 489.

54. From the 2011 translation of the Christian Reformed Church. As cited at https://www.crcna.org/welcome/beliefs/confessions/canons-dort (accessed October 4, 2018). See also Wilhelmus à Brakel, *The Christian's Reasonable Service*, trans. Bartel Elshout, ed. Joel R. Beeke (Grand Rapids: Reformation Heritage Books, 1999), 4:276–77.

55. See the discussion in Mark Jones, *Antinomianism: Reformed Theology's Unwelcome Guest?* (Phillipsburg, N.J.: P&R, 2013), 47–49. For fuller treatments of law-gospel issues, see "The Puritans on Law and Gospel," in Joel R. Beeke and Mark Jones, *A Puritan Theology: Doctrine for Life* (Grand Rapids: Reformation Heritage Books, 2012), 321–33; "The Threats of the Gospel: John Owen on What the Law/Gospel Distinction is Not," in Ryan M. McGraw, *John Owen: Trajectories in Reformed Orthodox Theology* (Cham, Switzerland: Palgrave Macmillan, 2017), 71–109.

tune with seventeenth-century forms of speech, it sounds odd that the gospel is described here as having *exhortations* and *threatenings*. Thus many translations like the one we're using have tried to smooth this over by substituting "Word" in the place of "gospel." Yet this was standard fare in seventeenth-century Reformed orthodoxy. For example, immediately after the Synod, the theological faculty of the University of Leiden held public disputations from 1620–1624 on the topics of theology. The theological faculty consisted of Johannes Polyander, Antonius Walaeus, Antonius Thysius, and Andreas Rivetus—all of whom were delegates to the Synod. In Disputation 22, "On the Gospel," presided over by Polyander, we read a pristine presentation of the gospel. The word "gospel" generally means the promise of Christ, but particularly refers to the manifestation of Christ in the flesh (Mark 1) and the proclamation of reconciliation with God on the basis of the death of Christ.[56] In fact, so zealous was the faculty to guard the proper use of the gospel, this disputation said, "The destruction of unbelievers, however, is not a goal of the Gospel; that is an unconnected outcome from elsewhere, from their sins."[57] Even "the evil consequences that come about by the guilt of depraved people from the preaching of the Gospel should not be numbered among its effects."[58] At the same time, the proper use of "gospel" was affirmed and guarded: the *Synopsis* recognized that "the Gospel sometimes receives the distinguishing title of Law, because it also contains its own commands, promises, and warnings."[59] The *promises* of the gospel are obvious: justification and eternal life, citing Romans 1:17 and 1 John 2:25.[60] What about its commands and warnings? Its *commands* are repentance and faith. As Jesus said in Mark 1:15: "Repent ye and believe the gospel." Repentance can either be legal or evangelical, while faith is evangelical.[61] Finally, the gospel's *warnings* are the condemnation of unbelievers who do not obey Christ and the punishment of eternal death, citing John 3:18 and 36 as well as Hebrews 2:2–3.[62] With this, we can go on to see how article 14 mentions three ways the gospel is used to preserve, continue, and complete this work of God's grace.

First, *the gospel in public*: by the hearing and reading of the gospel. This public hearing and reading continued in the apostolic church as believers

---

56. *Synopsis Purioris Theologiae*, 1:559.
57. *Synopsis Purioris Theologiae*, 1:565.
58. *Synopsis Purioris Theologiae*, 1:567.
59. *Synopsis Purioris Theologiae*, 1:567.
60. *Synopsis Purioris Theologiae*, 1:573.
61. *Synopsis Purioris Theologiae*, 1:567.
62. *Synopsis Purioris Theologiae*, 1:573.

gathered to hear "the apostles' doctrine" (Acts 2:42) proclaimed. As Paul would later tell Timothy: "Until I come, devote yourself to the public reading of Scripture, to exhortation, to teaching" (1 Tim. 4:13 ESV).

Second, *the gospel in private*: by meditation on it. The Lord commanded Joshua to meditate on the book of the law day and night (Josh. 1:8). The psalmist extols the man who meditates on the law day and night, which causes him to be like a tree planted by the waters (Ps. 1:2). In the great psalm on the word of God, we read: "How can a young man keep his way pure? By guarding it according to your word" (Ps. 119:9 ESV). "I have stored up your word in my heart, that I might not sin against you" (Ps. 119:11 ESV). "Your word is a lamp to my feet and a light to my path" (Ps. 119:105 ESV).

Third, *the gospel in all its aspects*: by its exhortations, threats, and promises. As Paul said, "All Scripture"—not just the law, but the gospel; not just the gospel, but the law—"is breathed out by God and [therefore it is] profitable for teaching, for reproof, for correction, and for training in righteousness, that the man of God may be complete, equipped for every good work" (2 Tim. 3:16–17 ESV). We know the promise of the gospel in John 3:16, but as our forefathers said above, how about the exhortations and threats that accompany the gospel message? Paul and Barnabus *exhorted* the congregations in Lystra, Iconium, and Antioch "to continue in the faith, and saying that through many tribulations we must enter the kingdom of God" (Acts 14:22 ESV). You are called by God to "work out your own salvation with fear and trembling" (Phil. 2:12 ESV), and this exhortation is the means by which this is caused. Jesus's proclamation that "God so loved the world…that whoever believes in him should not perish but have eternal life" (John 3:16 ESV) also included these *threats*: "Whoever does not believe is condemned already" (John 3:18b ESV), and "Whoever does not obey the Son shall not see life, but the wrath of God remains on him" (John 3:36b ESV). The apostolic writer also said, "Therefore we must pay much closer attention to what we have heard, lest we drift away from it. For since the message declared by angels proved to be reliable, and every transgression or disobedience received a just retribution, how shall we escape if we neglect such a great salvation?" (Heb. 2:1–3 ESV). How is it helpful to exhort and even threaten or warn Christians? A generation later Witsius said, "These admonitions, promises, threatenings, and the like actions of God towards the elect, are so far from giving the least ground to conclude anything against their perseverance, that, on the contrary, they are powerful means for their conservation [preservation]."[63] All these aspects of

---

63. Witsius, *The Economy of the Covenants*, 2:77.

the gospel are "powerful means for [your preservation]." Paul told Titus that it was by means of sharp rebuke "that they may be sound in the faith" (Titus 1:13 ESV). The writer to the Hebrews said this was "for our good, that we may share his holiness" because it "yields the peaceful fruit of righteousness" (Heb. 12:10–11 ESV). When a believer is on a dangerous ledge, the warnings of Scripture call him or her back.[64]

He Uses the Means of the Sacraments
We celebrate our God's power through means. Not only does He preserve us by means of hearing the gospel but also by the use of the sacraments, which Thomas Watson (1620–1686) described like this: "In the Word we hear God's voice, in the sacrament we have his kiss."[65] In *baptism* we feel the Lord's grace of washing away all our sins. Every time you witness a baptism, remember your baptism, God's promise of grace to you, and your commitment to Him by faith alone! In the *Lord's Supper*, or Lord's Table or Communion, we feast with our hands, eyes, noses, and mouths upon Jesus Christ our gracious Savior.

Conclusion
What a God of grace we have! He *planned* grace for me and you, Christ *purchased* us for it, the Holy Spirit *poured* it into our hearts, and this gracious triune God *preserves* through the means of word and sacrament.

There are various attitudes toward this doctrine, but article 15 especially emphasizes the attitude of those who are comforted by it: "the spouse of Christ hath always most tenderly loved and constantly defended it as an inestimable treasure." Love and defense of this treasure are to be our outlook on this doctrine. The regenerated and converted believer has had a work of grace performed upon him by God. This causes a recognition that the perseverance of the saints is biblical, brings glory to our great God, and consoles the pious in their spiritual struggles. Our attitude is one of grateful humility for such a great benefit. Appropriately, article 15 closes with worship: "Now, to this one God, Father, Son, and Holy Spirit, be honor and glory forever. Amen."

---

64. Oosterzee, *Christian Dogmatics*, 665.
65. Thomas Watson, *A Body of Divinity* (1692; repr., Edinburgh: The Banner of Truth Trust, 2000), 21.

CHAPTER 9

Comfort and Assurance:
The Pastoral Implications of Dort

Joel R. Beeke and Ray B. Lanning

The Canons of Dort teem with practical and personal benefits that flow to us from believing great gospel truths. This is no surprise since most of the delegates to the Synod of Dort were preachers and pastors in local churches. Daily they were confronted with the needs of the members of their congregations, the questions that troubled them, and the burdens they had to bear in life.

What the Canons prove beyond all doubt is that these "doctrines of grace" afford the greatest measure of comfort and help to believers because they provide the greatest measure of certainty as to where the Christian stands with God, and why. By showing that salvation is God's work in us through Christ, by His Word and Holy Spirit, the Canons lead us to high and solid ground on which to "stand, and rejoice in hope of the glory of God" (Rom. 5:2).[1]

By contrast, the positions taken by the Arminians on the doctrines in dispute offer only generalities, possibilities, limitations, and conditions, affording only the desperate hope that by the force of will power, devotion, and a daily battle to keep from falling, at least for today one has the right to call himself a Christian. It is scant consolation to be told that we have what it takes to make the grade with God if only we try hard enough and go long enough!

In this treatment, we will show that this elusive hope must give way to something far more solid as we study the doctrines affirmed in the Canons. With emphasis on the fifth head of doctrine, we will highlight the comfort and assurance that accrue to those who embrace these scripturally grounded truths.[2]

---

1. For a good, basic introduction, see Herman J. Selderhuis, "Introduction to the Synod of Dort (1618–1619)," in Donald Sinnema et al., *Acta et Documenta Synodi Nationalis Dordrechtanae, 1618–1619* (Göttingen: Vandenhoeck & Ruprecht, 2015), 1:xv–xxxii.

2. For additional sources on the pastoral accent of the Canons of Dort, see Edwin H. Palmer, "The Significance of the Canons for Pastoral Work," in *Crisis in the Reformed Churches:*

Comfort from the Doctrine of Unconditional Election (Head I)

The Arminians' hopes vanish as soon as we turn to article 1 of the first head of doctrine, "Of Divine Predestination."[3] A blunt account is given of contemporary man's real spiritual condition and problem: "All men have sinned in Adam, lie under the curse, and are deserving of eternal death." Sin is not just one unfortunate aspect of human experience. Rather, sin is an all-encompassing, all-pervading, all-destroying power in our world, providing the spiritual and moral context in which all human beings are born, must live, and finally die.[4]

The Love of God for Sinners

We must accept this account of our natural state in order to appreciate the immense goodness of the "good news" introduced in article 2: "But in this the love of God was manifested, that He sent His only begotten Son into the world, that whosoever believeth on Him should not perish, but have everlasting life."

It may surprise the reader who has heard of the "cold, harsh Calvinism" of the Canons of Dort to discover that the Dort fathers openly declare the love of God for sinners. We have all sinned, but our sin has not quenched or diminished the love of God.

The Canons of Dort present what may be the fullest confessional account ever given of the love of God in Christ. Biblical ideas of divine justice, wrath, and condemnation are introduced only to highlight the wonder of this everlasting love.

Article 3 continues: "That men may be brought to believe, God mercifully sends the messengers of these most joyful tidings to whom He will and at what time He pleaseth." No wonder that the greatest part of Christ's earthly ministry was devoted to calling and equipping the apostles as the first

---

Essays in the Commemoration of the Synod of Dort (1618–19), ed. Peter Y. De Jong (Grand Rapids: Reformed Fellowship, 1968), 137–49; W. Robert Godfrey, "Popular and Catholic: The *Modus Docendi* of the Canons of Dordt," in *Revisiting the Synod of Dordt, 1618–1619*, ed. Aza Goudriaan and Fred van Lieburg, Brill's Series in Church History 49 (Leiden: Brill, 2011), 243–60; and Arnold Huijgen, "The Theology of the Canons of Dort: A Reassessment after Four Hundred Years," *Unio Cum Christo* 4, no. 2 (Oct. 2018): 113–15.

3. For the text used for the Canons of Dort, see *The Psalter* (Grand Rapids: Eerdmans, 2011), 96–117; in this article only the head and article are referenced.

4. Fred H. Klooster, "The Doctrinal Deliverances of Dort," in *Crisis in the Reformed Churches: Essays in the Commemoration of the Synod of Dort (1618–19)*, ed. Peter Y. De Jong (Grand Rapids: Reformed Fellowship, 1968), 52–94; and Homer C. Hoeksema, *The Voice of Our Fathers* (Jenison, Mich.: Reformed Free Publishing, 1980).

preachers of His gospel. We are reminded that the comforting and assuring gospel is preached under the direction of God in His government and providence over all things.

Some Believe, Others Do Not

Articles 4 and 5 stand together as two parts of one statement. The gospel is preached; some hearers believe it, and others do not. Those who do not believe go away unchanged, abiding under "the wrath of God." Those who embrace Jesus the Savior "are by Him delivered." They "have the gift of eternal life conferred upon them." There is no element of uncertainty, no conditions attached, no note of tentativeness. Believers possess and enjoy these precious gifts of God now and forever. The promise of the gospel is fulfilled in them and is the foundational ground of their comfort and assurance.

God's Eternal Decree: Election and Reprobation

The Canons go on to note that the doctrine of predestination (like any other truth of God's Word) can be misunderstood, misapplied, and misrepresented by "men of perverse, impure and unstable minds." Should preachers therefore set this doctrine aside and give it no place in their sermons? That would be a great loss to God's people: "To holy and pious souls [this decree] affords unspeakable consolation" (art. 6). That is, we receive great consolation from knowing that our salvation is entirely God's work in us and God's gift to us. As our salvation is sovereignly wrought in us, we say, "This is the LORD's doing; it is marvellous in our eyes" (Ps. 118:23). Sovereignly given to us, we know it cannot deceive or mislead us. It cannot be revoked by God or forfeited by us through weakness or infirmity.[5]

The Full Scope of Our Election in Christ

Article 7 presents a catalog of the contents of God's decree. God's electing love and wisdom go far beyond the mere election of some and rejection of others. In ordaining some to eternal life through Jesus Christ, God also undertakes to do all that is necessary to accomplish their redemption. He gives the elect to Christ "to be saved by Him" and "to call and draw them to His communion by His Word and Spirit."

---

5. See Peter White, *Predestination, Policy and Polemic* (Cambridge: Cambridge University Press, 1991); J. V. Fesko, *Diversity within the Reformed Tradition: Supra- and Infralapsarianism in Calvin, Dort, and Westminster* (Greenville, S.C.: Reformed Academic, 2001); and Anthony Milton, *The British Delegation and the Synod of Dort* (Woodbridge, U.K.: Boydell, 2005).

God decrees to bestow upon these elect persons "true faith, justification, and sanctification." He determines to keep or preserve them by His almighty power and "finally, to glorify them for the demonstration of His mercy and for the praise of His glorious grace." Redemption is divine in conception, divine in execution, divine in consummation, and divine in its great ends.

Uses of This Doctrine

Articles 12–17, in classic Puritan style, set forth the ways in which predestination is to be "used," or applied, by those who proclaim it and those to whom it is proclaimed. The doctrine of "unconditional election" is shown to be of great help to the Christian in various ways.

First Use: Assurance of Election

Article 12 asserts that "the elect in due time…attain the assurance of this their eternal and unchangeable election." The degree or measure of assurance may not be the same in every case, but it is right for Christians to seek it. A warning is given to those who seek some special revelation apart from what we have in Scripture. That would be "prying into the secret and deep things of God." Rather, Christians should proceed to observe in themselves "with a spiritual joy and holy pleasure, the infallible fruits of election pointed out in the Word of God—such as faith in Christ, filial fear, sorrowing for sin, hungering and thirsting after righteousness, etc." (art. 12). These qualities or attitudes of the heart are alien to fallen man and contrary to the inclinations of his nature. They are evidence of God at work in us.

Second Use: Election as a Motive for Godliness

Article 13 points out that "the sense and certainty of this election" has a paradoxical effect on a true child of God. Far from "encouraging remissness in the observance of divine commands or from sinking men in carnal security," being assured of our election in Christ only makes us more humble and undeserving in our own eyes! All the more, we adore "the depth of God's mercies," seek cleansing from sin, render thanks to God, and give Him the "ardent love" of our hearts. By contrast, "those who refuse to walk in the ways of the elect" are guilty of "rash presumption" when they boast of being God's elect.[6]

---

6. See Donald Sinnema, "The Issue of Reprobation at the Synod of Dort in Light of the History of This Doctrine" (PhD diss., University of Saint Michael's College, Toronto, 1985).

Third Use: Those Who Lack Assurance

Article 16 addresses those who are weak in faith, lack assurance and peace, and cannot see in themselves the other graces that are fruits of election. They are enjoined not to despair, much less "rank themselves among the reprobate." They must consider that "they seriously desire to be turned to God, to please Him only, and to be delivered from this body of death." These are not the attitudes and aims of reprobates! Rather, these weak and doubting Christians should persevere "in the use of the means God hath appointed for working these graces in us" and "humbly to wait for a season of richer grace." They should take comfort in the promise of God "that He will not quench the smoking flax nor break the bruised reed."

Conclusion: Let God Be God!

Article 18 concludes the presentation of the doctrine of election with a rebuke "to those who murmur at the free grace of election and the just severity of reprobation." First the authors cite the words of Paul: "Nay but, O man, who art thou that repliest against God?" (Rom. 9:20). Then they cite the words of Christ: "Is it not lawful for me to do what I will with mine own?" (Matt. 20:15). It is not for man to sit in judgment on his Maker. Let God be God!

Comfort from the Doctrine of Limited Atonement (Head II)

"As many as truly believe...are delivered and saved from sin and destruction through the death of Christ." These words sum up the teaching of the Canons of Dort, Head II, "Of the Death of Christ and the Redemption of Men Thereby."[7] Once again, Dort sounds notes of certainty and clarity regarding the salvation of all who believe in Christ. We are clearly told what

---

7. For further study of head II, see W. Robert Godfrey, "Tensions within International Calvinism: The Debate on the Atonement at the Synod of Dort" (PhD diss., Stanford University, 1974); Stephen Strehle, "The Extent of the Atonement and the Synod of Dort," *Westminster Theological Journal* 51, no. 1 (1989): 1–23; Michael Thomas, *The Extent of the Atonement: A Dilemma for Reformed Theology* (Carlisle: Paternoster, 1997); Raymond A. Blacketer, "Definite Atonement in Historical Perspective," in *The Glory of the Atonement: Biblical, Historical, and Practical Perspectives,* ed. Charles E. Hill and Frank A. James (Downers Grove, Ill.: InterVarsity Press, 2004), 304–23; Jonathan D. Moore, "The Extent of the Atonement," in *Drawn into Controversie: Reformed Theological Diversity and Debates within Seventeenth-Century British Puritanism,* ed. Michael A. G. Haykin and Mark Jones (Göttingen: Vandenhoeck & Ruprecht, 2011), 124–61; and Lee Gattiss, "The Synod of Dort and Definite Atonement," in *From Heaven He Came and Sought Her: Definite Atonement in Historical, Biblical, Theological, and Pastoral Perspective,* ed. David Gibson and Jonathan Gibson (Wheaton, Ill.: Crossway, 2015), 143–64.

we are saved from ("sin and destruction") and what has delivered and saved us ("the death of Christ").

In the years prior to Dort, two aspects of the doctrine of atonement stood at the heart of the controversy with the Arminians. First, the *extent* of Christ's atonement was disputed. Did He lay down His life only for the elect, or did He die for all mankind? Second, controversy raged around the *efficacy* of Christ's atonement—that is, the effect or result of His death. Did He "fully satisfy" for all the sins of the elect with His precious blood? Or did He only make it possible for us to be reconciled to God, if only we trust in Christ? Did Christ die for anyone in particular? Was anyone actually saved by His death?

The Dort fathers believed that Christ intentionally laid down His life for His sheep (John 10:14–15); they are thereby "delivered and saved from sin and destruction." The Arminians insisted on a "universal" or "general atonement," Christ dying for all, but not in fact securing the salvation of any. In order to be saved sinners must do their part, adding faith and repentance to the work of Christ.

More than Words

Many know this Reformed tenet as the doctrine of limited atonement. That is, it is limited in extent or scope to those for whom Christ died, but not limited in efficacy! One Reformed scholar who specialized on the doctrine of atonement, Roger Nicole, proposed a helpful alternative: definite atonement. Christ died for a *definite group* of people known to Him by name and secured a *definite result* by His death—that is, their deliverance and salvation. As Nicole points out, this usage compels Arminians to call their view more accurately indefinite atonement.[8]

More than a matter of words, it is vital to the Christian's "only comfort in life and death" to know that Christ "with His precious blood, hath fully satisfied for all my sins, and delivered me from all the power of the devil" (Heidelberg Catechism 1). But if Christ did not intend to die for me, if His death did not actually save and deliver me, that comfort quickly fades. I am thrown back on my own resources if I am to benefit from the death of Christ.

God's Infinite Mercy (arts. 1–4)

Despite our sin and hell-worthiness, there is comforting and good news that flows from Christ's definite atonement. This same God "hath been pleased

---

8. Roger Nicole, "The Case for Definite Atonement," *Bulletin of the Evangelical Theological Society* 10, no. 4 (Fall 1967): 199–207.

in His infinite mercy to give His only begotten Son, for our surety, who was made sin, and became a curse for us and in our stead, that He might make satisfaction to divine justice on our behalf." The idea of Christ's suretyship needs to be recovered for today's Christians. Think of a loan: you contracted a debt you cannot repay, but someone has cosigned the note. Christ is your Surety; He repaid your debt in full. The riches of the "eternal and infinite" Son of God have been charged to your account, dear believer!

A Promise Made to All (arts. 5–8)
Christ has commanded His servants to "declare" and "publish" this good news "to all persons promiscuously and without distinction." With the promise, they must also declare the command to repent and believe it. Those who do not believe and repent perish in their sin and unbelief. Those who believe it confess they are saved only "through the death of Christ." They know they "are indebted for this benefit solely to the grace of God, given them in Christ from everlasting."

Conclusion: The History of Redemption (art. 9)
So far the Canons have discussed this doctrine in terms of the Christian's personal experience of salvation. Now that experience is placed into a greater context, the sweep of redemptive history "from the beginning of the world to this day" and "henceforward" to the end of time. Each Christian and all Christians together as the church of Christ stand on a sure foundation: "This purpose [of God] proceeding from everlasting love towards the elect." This foundation "is laid in the blood of Christ...their Savior, who... laid down His life for them upon the cross." Our part as believers is only to "celebrate His praises here and through all eternity."

Comfort from the Doctrines of Total Depravity and Irresistible Grace (Heads III–IV)

Two great doctrines are treated together in combined Heads III and IV, "Of the Corruption of Man, His Conversion to God, and the Manner Thereof." These doctrines are known as total depravity and irresistible grace. The effects of Adam's transgression extend to all mankind, to every aspect of the human constitution. God's grace is sovereignly or irresistibly applied to all His elect; He calls them by His Word and renews them by His Spirit unto salvation in Christ.

Why take these two doctrines together? Because the first accounts for the second. If man's ruin in sin is complete, then God's remedy in Christ must be perfect. Total depravity cries out for full salvation. We cannot save ourselves. We shall perish unless God intervenes and does His work in us. Since we can do nothing, He must do all.[9]

God's Perfect Remedy in Christ (arts. 6–8)

After underscoring our complete ruin in sin in articles 1–5, the Canons go on to affirm "the glad tidings concerning the Messiah, by means of which it hath pleased God to save such as believe" (art. 6). In the worldwide preaching of the gospel, God "seriously promises eternal life and rest to as many as shall come to Him and believe on Him" (art. 8). As the word of God, the gospel promise implies a warrant to believe: God will surely do as He has promised. By grace, we sinners may take Him at His word!

Those Who Are Converted (arts. 9–10)

Despite those who reject the gospel and "refuse to be converted" (cf. art. 9), no faithful ministry of the Word goes unrewarded, as article 10 stresses: "Some who are called by the gospel obey the call and are converted"—but not because of anything they are in themselves. They are no wiser than others nor better: "It must be wholly ascribed to God, who as He has chosen His own in eternity in Christ, so He confers upon them faith and repentance, rescues them from the power of darkness, and translates them into the kingdom of His own Son." What can be more comforting than this truth when it concerns our own salvation?

Regeneration and Conversion (arts. 11–12)

Articles 11 and 12 describe the work God does in His elect by His Word and Spirit in two ways. In terms of the believer and the direction of his life, it is called "true conversion" (art. 11), from the Latin word *conversio,* meaning a "turning around" or "thorough change." In terms of what God does to produce this change, it is called "the regeneration so highly celebrated in Scripture" (art. 12). These two stand together as cause and effect. Regenerated hearers are converted by the preaching of the Word.

Articles 11–12 teach us that the Holy Spirit is at work at every point, upholding the preacher, empowering the Word, regenerating the hearer, and enabling him to believe what he hears and be converted. In all this, the Spirit applies to the elect that which they have in Christ. Detailed descriptions are

---

9. See W. Robert Godfrey, "The Corruption of Humans, and the Conversion of God with Its Way of Happening," *Saving the Reformation: The Pastoral Theology of the Canons of Dort* (Sanford, Fla.: Reformation Trust, 2019), 127–52.

given of regeneration as "a supernatural work, most powerful…most delightful, astonishing, mysterious, and ineffable," as well as of true conversion and all the Spirit must do in us to effect it (art. 11)—a work that He continues every day of our lives as Christians.

Are You Born Again? (art. 13)

The Canons offer help to anyone who asks, "How can I know I am regenerate?" The Dort fathers begin by reminding us that we cannot expect to "fully comprehend" this work of the Spirit—at least not in this life. The work is never fully done, and often we don't see what the Spirit is doing, but believers can "rest satisfied with knowing and experiencing that by this grace of God they are enabled to believe with the heart, and love their Savior." Faith in Christ and love for Christ are pearls of great price.

The Primacy of Faith (art. 14)

Here and everywhere, Dort's emphasis is on God's gift of faith. We lack many other gifts and graces and long for more evidence of conversion and regeneration. One thing is needful: faith in God, faith in His Word, and faith in Jesus Christ. True faith in Christ is the best of God's graces and gifts to us and of God's work in us: "He…produces both the will to believe, and the act of believing also." Faith is the foretoken of all other graces and the wellspring of all good works.

Grace Makes Us Gracious (art. 15)

Article 15 teaches us that we must exercise the judgment of charity toward other Christians: "Those who make an external profession of faith and live regular lives, we are bound, after the example of the apostle, to judge and speak of them in the most favorable manner." This requirement keeps Reformed churches from the error of "churches of the regenerate" in which leaders decide who is born again and who is not. "The secret recesses of the heart are unknown to us." We should pray for those "who have not yet been called…but we are in no wise to conduct ourselves toward them with haughtiness, as if we had made ourselves to differ."

Grace and Human Freedom (art. 16)

Does the irresistible "grace of regeneration…treat men as senseless stocks and blocks"? No! As the searcher of hearts, the Holy Spirit does no violence to the human will, "but spiritually quickens, heals, corrects, and at the same time sweetly and powerfully bends it." As a result, "a ready and sincere spiritual obedience begins to reign, in which the true and spiritual restoration and freedom of our will consist." If this work were not wrought in us by "the admirable Author of every good work," our situation would be hopeless. Left to himself, fallen man wills only to go on in sin.

Grace and the Means of Grace (arts. 16–17)

After stressing that God's saving work does no violence to the human will (art. 16), the Canons nevertheless conclude that God's grace is irresistible but not automatic. Article 17 highlights the way God sustains the life of body and soul. In both God "requires the use of means." We must sow and reap, mill and bake, serve and eat our daily bread. To quicken and nourish the soul, God has decreed that His Word be delivered to His people: its teachings must be proclaimed and expounded, its promises signed and sealed in the sacraments, its obligations be enforced by church discipline.

We must be kept "in the exercise of the Word," hearing it with understanding and faith, keeping and pondering it in our hearts, bringing forth the fruit of it in our lives. Both the grace of regeneration and the means by which we are regenerated are ordained in God's decree. We cannot obtain the grace if we despise or neglect the means. Once more the Canons show that our salvation is wholly of God, including the way by which He works it in us. Once more doctrine ends in comforting praise and God-centered assurance: To God alone "all the glory both of means, and of their saving fruit and efficacy is forever due. Amen."

Comfort from the Doctrine of the Perseverance of the Saints and Assurance of Salvation (Head V)

Head V of the Canons on the perseverance of the saints in grace and holiness and on the assurance of their salvation provides the apex of comfort; in fact, in all of Reformed confessional literature, we know of no section that is so packed full of comfort as this is.

Perseverance of the Saints in Grace (arts. 1–8)[10]

The Canons have already addressed perseverance in heads I (especially art. 7) and II (especially art. 8), but here in head V it is treated more broadly, profoundly, and pastorally. What a difference there is between the comfortless Arminian doctrine of conditional perseverance that ultimately leans on

---

10. Cf. Martyn McGeown, *Grace and Assurance: The Message of the Canons of Dordt* (Jenison, Mich.: Reformed Free Publishing, 2018), 271–303.

the flimsy reed of human effort and head V's robust, Reformed treatment of the saints' assured perseverance that flows out of God's almighty power in preserving His elect all the way to the end of their earthly pilgrimage and into life everlasting.

Article 1's description of the saints' experiential condition in this world stands between antinomianism, which denies the need for sanctification, and perfectionism, which denies the indwelling corruption that remains within believers. The believer is the subject of the triune grace of God that cannot fail. The saint is called according to the Father's purpose, is in communion with God's Son, and is regenerated by the Holy Spirit; nevertheless, he is not yet perfect. He is still in the process of being sanctified. Though he is delivered "from the dominion and slavery of sin in this life," he is still engaged in holy warfare against sin. "The infirmities of the flesh" still press in upon him and will do so lifelong. Though he will win the war in the end by God's grace, he will lose some skirmishes with sin along the way.

Article 2 describes these "daily sins of infirmity" as "spots [that] adhere to the best works of the saints." Unlike the unbeliever, who brushes aside his sins with self-justifying ease, even joking about them, the believer is burdened and grieved by indwelling corruptions that clings even to his "best works."[11] These daily sins humble the saint, move him to fly to Christ for refuge rather than to despair, provoke him to mortify the flesh and to be exercised in piety, and compel him to press on "to the goal of perfection." The comfort here is that this struggle against sin—a reliable mark of grace in all believers, will continue until "being at length delivered from this body of death, they are brought to reign with the Lamb of God in heaven."

This perseverance, however, as article 3 stresses, cannot be achieved through the believer's own strength. Rather—and this is the heart of the Canons' definition of perseverance—"God is faithful, who, having conferred grace, mercifully confirms and powerfully preserves them therein, even to the end." *God's faithfulness*—His track record of making no mistakes in your life, dear believer—is the bedrock of our perseverance, comfort, strength, and assurance. We can find no comfort in our faithfulness, as we are often unfaithful, but all comfort lies in God's faithfulness, for He is never unfaithful and always perfect. "As for God, his way is perfect" (Ps. 18:30)—here lies our comfort in the act of persevering; it is ultimately God's faithfulness being worked out in us. As believers, we ought to rejoice that our perseverance is not conditioned on our positive freewill response to God, for from our

---

11. Cf. Heidelberg Catechism 114.

side, salvation and perseverance are alike impossible, but from God's side of faithfulness to His own, for Christ's sake, salvation and perseverance cannot possibly fail. As believers clinging to God, we may comfort ourselves and each other that we are "confident of this very thing, that he which hath begun a good work in you will perform it until the day of Jesus Christ" (Phil. 1:6).

Articles 4–7 reflect experientially on the problem of remaining sin in the lives of God's people. These articles provide even deeper comfort, for they tell us as believers, based on God's Word, that even when we neglect the means of grace, or God forbid, fall lamentably into serious sins, as Peter and David did, God, "who is rich in mercy," will not "wholly withdraw the Holy Spirit" from us nor allow us to commit the unpardonable sin. Rather, He will preserve the seed of His regeneration alive within us, "and by His Word and Spirit" will work repentance in us, so that we will again "experience the favor of a reconciled God" and "henceforward more diligently work out [our] own salvation with fear and trembling."

God promises to preserve His neglectful, sinning saints. This is remarkable comfort despite remarkable sins that the Canons call "great and heinous" and "enormous"—sins that "very highly offend God, incur a deadly guilt, grieve the Holy Spirit, interrupt the exercise of faith, [and] very grievously wound [our] consciences." The sobering and wonderful comfort is that God's grace and love toward us in Christ is greater than all our sin against Him. This is the staggering good news of the gospel: though sin remains sin and though the sinfulness of sin is abominable in God's sight, in Christ His righteousness exceeds our unrighteousness. Though God chastises us, He will not abandon us, forsake us, or destroy us as we fully deserve. Though we may lose "the sense of God's favor for a time," God does not withdraw His eternal favor that He has decreed for us. His "unchangeable purpose of election" abides. His grace is never altogether withdrawn. He does not disinherit us as His children or cause us to "forfeit the state of justification." As Cornel Venema summarizes God's dealings with His children, "God preserves in them the imperishable seed by which He first gave them birth."[12]

Consequently, the saints' final perseverance is altogether certain and assured, as article 8 underscores, solely because of "God's free mercy" in Christ. That free mercy guarantees that genuine saints "do not totally fall from faith and grace, nor continue and perish finally in their backslidings." Rather, they shall persevere because of their triune God, "whose counsel

---

12. Cornelis P. Venema, "The Assurance of Salvation in *The Canons of Dort*: A Commemorative Essay (Part Two)," *Mid-America Journal of Theology* 29 (2018): 21.

cannot be changed, nor His promise fail, neither can the call according to His purpose be revoked, nor the merit, intercession, and preservation of Christ be rendered ineffectual, nor the sealing of the Holy Spirit be frustrated or obliterated." All glory be to the Father's preserving counsel, the Son's preserving intercession, and the Spirit's preserving seal!

Assurance of Salvation (arts. 9–15)

Articles 9–13 of the Canons deal comfortingly with a burning pastoral issue in the sixteenth and seventeenth centuries: How can believers be assured of their salvation?

Article 9 defines assurance of salvation and stresses that it ought to be normative in the lives of believers: "True believers for themselves may and do obtain assurance according to the measure of their faith, whereby they arrive at the certain persuasion that they ever will continue true and living members of the church and that they experience forgiveness of sins, and will at last inherit eternal life." As Sinclair Ferguson writes,

> Assurance is the conscious confidence that we are in a right relationship with God through Christ. It is the confidence that we have been justified and accepted by God in Christ, regenerated by his Spirit, and adopted into his family, and that through faith in him we will be kept for the day when our justification and adoption are consummated in the regeneration of all things.[13]

What a comfort such assurance is! The Dort fathers hasten to add in article 9 that believers possess it only "according to the measure of their faith." Strong faith commonly promotes full measures of assurance, whereas weak faith leaves scant measures of assurance, or in some cases no sensible assurance at all.[14]

Article 10 refutes the Roman Catholic idea that assurance is very rarely granted to a believer, and when granted it is usually in the form of a very personal special revelation "contrary to, or independent from the Word of God." Rather, similar to what the Westminster divines would write thirty years later (see Westminster Confession of Faith 18), the threefold ground of assurance of salvation consists of (1) the exercise of "faith in the promises of God, which God has revealed most abundantly in His Word for our comfort"; (2) "the testimony of the Holy Spirit testifying with our spirit that we are the children and heirs of God" (Rom. 8:16); and (3) "a serious and holy

---

13. Sinclair B. Ferguson, "The Reformation and Assurance," *Banner of Truth,* no. 643 (April 2017): 20.

14. Cf. McGeown, *Grace and Assurance,* 305–6.

desire for a good conscience and good works."[15] Again, stressing the norma-
tivity of assurance for believers, article 10 tells us that "if the elect of God
were deprived of this solid comfort that they shall finally obtain the victory
and of this infallible pledge or earnest of eternal glory, they would be of all
men the most miserable."

Like the Westminster Confession, the Canons of Dort present us with
a complex ground of assurance, which includes a primary, objective ground
(the promises of God) and two secondary, subjective grounds (the Spirit's testimony and the evidences of grace, summarized as "a godly desire for a good
conscience [inward evidences] and good works [outward evidences]").[16] For
all three kinds of assurance—the promises of God, the Spirit's testimony, and
the inward and outward evidences of grace—the believer is dependent on the
enlightening and applying ministry of the Holy Spirit, using the Word. The
more we can embrace, by the Spirit's grace, of each of these kinds of assurance the more full and robust our assurance will be. Robust, full assurance of
salvation for a true Christian is one of the greatest comforts, joys, and blessings of the Christian life. James W. Alexander said assurance "carries with
it the idea of fullness, such as of a tree laden with fruit, or of a vessel's sails
when stretched by a favouring gale."[17]

This does not mean, however, that assurance of salvation does not vary in
degree and is not at times assailed by doubt. Article 11 teaches us that "Scripture testifies that believers in this life have to struggle with various carnal
doubts and that under grievous temptations they are not always sensible of
this full assurance of faith and certainly of persevering." Happily, however,
God in His faithfulness limits the power of temptation, provides a way of
escape from it (1 Cor. 10:13), and by the Holy Spirit "again inspires them with
the comfortable assurance of persevering."

Article 12 addresses the impact and fruits that assurance produces in the
life of a Christian—particularly on his practical godliness. The Arminians
insisted that the Reformed doctrine of assurance "is a cause of indolence
and is injurious to godliness, good morals, prayers and other holy exercises."
Many Roman Catholic theologians thought it better for Christians to live

---

15. Venema, "The Assurance of Salvation in *The Canons of Dort*," 21–23.

16. For an exposition of these grounds of assurance, see Joel R. Beeke, *Knowing and
Growing in Assurance of Faith* (Fearn, Ross-shire, Scotland: Christina Focus, 2017), 75–
120; and Joel R. Beeke, *The Quest for Full Assurance: The Legacy of Calvin and His Successors*
(Edinburgh: Banner of Truth, 1999), 123–46.

17. J. W. Alexander, *Consolation in Discourses on Select Topics, Addressed to the Suffering People
of God* (repr., Ligonier, Pa.: Soli Deo Gloria, 1992), 138.

without assurance, as though it were "praiseworthy to doubt." The Reformers argued that the opposite is true. Full assurance of salvation resulting from God's grace does not make a man indifferent and proud, they said, but humble and zealous. Genuine assurance is always known by its fruits: "filial reverence, true piety, patience in every tribulation, fervent prayers, constancy in suffering, and in confessing the truth, and of solid rejoicing in God." Thus, assurance of salvation "should serve as an incentive to the serious and constant practice of gratitude and good works, as appears from the testimonies of Scripture and the examples of the saints."

As Godfrey notes, "This point is underscored in the history of Reformed people at the time of the Synod of Dort and afterward. In the Netherlands, the most committed Calvinists were called 'precisionists.' In England, they were called Puritans. Such people were clearly not secure in their sins or indifferent to holiness."[18]

Article 13 applies the truth of article 12 to those who "are recovering from backsliding." The renewal of their "confidence of persevering," the Canons say, does not promote licentiousness, but "renders them much more careful and solicitous to continue in the ways of the Lord, which He hath ordained, that they who walk therein may maintain an assurance of persevering, lest by abusing His fatherly kindness, God should turn away His gracious countenance from them, to behold which is to the godly dearer than life, the withdrawing whereof is more bitter than death."

The Conclusion of Head V

Having dealt with the comforting doctrines of the perseverance in grace and assurance of salvation, head V of the Canons concludes by briefly addressing the relationship of perseverance to the means of grace (art. 14) and the "inestimable treasure" that the doctrine of perseverance is for the church of Christ and her members. In article 14, the Canons stress for a final time how important it is to use the means of grace ordained by God for persevering in the Christian life and for pursuing comprehensive holiness and practicing true piety.[19] The Word preached and heard, the Word read and meditated on, and the Word signed and sealed in the sacraments are vital disciplines for persevering in grace.

---

18. Godfrey, *Saving the Reformation,* 163.

19. See Matthew Barrett, "Piety in the Canons of Dort," *Puritan Reformed Journal* 3, no. 1 (Jan. 2011): 223–52; Matthew Barrett, *The Grace of Godliness: An Introduction to Doctrine and Piety in the Canons of Dort* (Kitchener, Ont.: Joshua Press, 2013); and Joel R. Beeke, "The Piety of Dort," *TableTalk* 43, no. 1 (Jan. 2019): 26–29.

Nor must we neglect or forget the sacraments' role in our assurance, as article 14 says. Kevin DeYoung notes: "We often forget about baptism and the Lord's Supper as means of grace. But they are essential in the cause of gospel confidence. They remind our eyes, our hands, our noses, and our mouths of the good news we hear with our ears."[20] In the sacrament of the Lord's Supper, Christ appeals to all five of our senses in the bread and the wine and says, "Whereas you should otherwise have suffered eternal death, I have given My body to the death of the cross and shed My blood for you; and as certainly feed and nourish your hungry and thirsty souls with My crucified body and shed blood to everlasting life, as this bread is broken before your eyes and this cup is given you, and you eat and drink the same with your mouth in remembrance of Me."[21] Our Reformed and Puritan forefathers regarded the sacraments as such important means of grace to promote assurance that they often spoke of "sacramental assurance." By that terminology, they did not intend a new or another kind of assurance than that which we receive through the gospel promises being preached. Rather, they believed that we get the same Christ in the sacraments as we receive under the Word, but sometimes we get Christ better in the sacraments, since God condescends so low to assure us of His love. Thus, as the Word signed and sealed, or made visible, the sacraments serve to reinforce the assurance of grace and salvation provided by the promises of God announced in His Word.

God uses His own appointed means in gathering, saving, preserving, and assuring His elect. "As it hath pleased God, by the preaching of the gospel, to being this work of grace in us, so He preserves, continues, and perfects it by the hearing and reading of His Word" (art. 14). So it is no great mystery that those who despise or neglect these means profit little by them, if at all. They grow neither in grace nor in knowledge and therefore bear little fruit, have scant comfort, and only fleeting assurance. If you would have abundant comfort and full assurance, you should make diligent use of the means God has appointed, in the confidence that He will bless and use them in your life.

Article 15 stresses that the doctrines of perseverance and assurance, far from being peripheral to the Christian life, are repeatedly stressed in the Bible and are vital for our daily comfort and for the well-being of saving faith. The Canons stress that though Satan, the world, the ignorant, the hypocrite, and the heretic all despise these doctrines as expounded in Scripture, the body of

---

20. Kevin DeYoung, *Grace Defined and Defended: What a 400-Year-Old Confession Teaches Us about Sin, Salvation, and the Sovereignty of God* (Wheaton, Ill.: Crossway, 2019), 91.
21. Form for the Administration of the Lord's Supper, *The Psalter*, 138.

true believers—here called "the spouse of Christ"—has "always most tenderly loved and constantly defended [them] as an inestimable treasure"—that is, a treasure beyond value, a treasure that comforts us as nothing in this world can, a treasure that unlike anything else moves believers to worship their faithful, triune God and give Him all the glory for their salvation.

And so the Canons conclude on "a high note of doxology"[22] and comfort, ending in the triune God Himself: "Now, to this one God, Father, Son, and Holy Spirit be honor and glory forever. Amen."

Conclusion of the Whole

The conclusion appended to the Canons is also comforting and assuring. After explaining the historical context in which they were written, in the midst of a theological battle between the Reformed and the Arminians ("Remonstrants"), the authors declare confidently that they have drawn the material for the Canons directly from the Scriptures: "This doctrine the synod judges to be drawn from the Word of God and to be agreeable to the confessions of the Reformed churches"—that is, the Belgic Confession of Faith and the Heidelberg Catechism.[23]

The conclusion then goes on to point out how unjust their Arminian accusers have been, after which it reassuringly states that all the approved delegates at the Synod of Dort have signed this document, without exception. Finally, the Synod exhorts all ministers to handle and conduct themselves with regard to the doctrines expounded in the Canons "piously and religiously… to the glory of the divine Name, to holiness of life, and to the consolation of afflicted souls…and the edification of those who hear them. Amen." How fitting that even in the closing sentences of a rather polemical conclusion, the Canons return one more time to the theme of comfort and edification.

In conclusion, though not structured along the theme of comfort as explicitly as the Heidelberg Catechism, the Canons of Dort present comfort to believers in every head of doctrine, culminating particularly in its views of perseverance and assurance in the final head. Far from being cold, harsh, or dry, the Canons are packed with language, doctrine, and pastoral counsels that are warm, compassionate, encouraging, assuring, and, above all, full of biblical and practical comfort for afflicted consciences and established saints.

---

22. McGeown, *Grace and Assurance,* 319.

23. In general, Scripture proofs appear in the Canons only when what they affirm adds to the statement of a doctrine found in the Belgic Confession or Heidelberg Catechism. See the "Index of Cross References to the Three Forms of Unity" found in *The Psalter,* pp. 118–21.

CHAPTER 10

Preaching the Doctrines of Dort

Cornelis P. Venema

Not long before writing this essay on preaching the doctrines of Dort, I was asked to prepare two sermons on the first main point of doctrine as part of a sermon series in my home church. During a meeting of the church's pastors, it was suggested that I preach on the Canons' teaching about not only God's sovereign and merciful decision to save His people in Christ (election) but also God's sovereign and just decision to leave others in their sins (reprobation). My response to this suggestion was to offer a different approach. On the one hand, I declined to take up the challenge to address directly the topic of reprobation in either of my sermons. And on the other hand, I decided to focus attention upon three articles that emphasized the assurance believers ought to cultivate regarding their election and salvation. In the course of my reflection upon how I would preach on the theme of God's sovereign and merciful election, I was reminded concretely of the importance of the question. This question takes two distinct forms.

The first and most obvious form of the question is whether or not the scriptural teachings of unconditional election, definite atonement or particular redemption, radical depravity, effectual calling, and the perseverance of the saints ought to be openly taught in the preaching of the gospel.[1] Should those

---

1. Today, these points are often summarized in English-speaking circles by the acronym TULIP (Total depravity, Unconditional election, Limited atonement, Irresistible grace, and the Perseverance of the saints). Unfortunately, this acronym is of recent vintage, changes the order of the five points, and also employs terminology (especially in the case of "total depravity," "irresistible grace," and "limited atonement") that does not adequately express the Reformed view. For critical assessments of the value of this acronym, see Richard Muller, *Calvin and the Reformed Tradition: On the Work of Christ and the Order of Salvation* (Grand Rapids: Baker Academic, 2012), 58–62; and Kenneth J. Stewart, *Ten Myths about Calvinism: Recovering the Breadth of the Reformed Tradition* (Wheaton, Ill.: IVP Academic, 2011), 75–96. I will have occasion in what follows to explain why the terminology of "limited atonement" and

who preach include these doctrinal themes as explicit features of the content of their gospel proclamation? If these themes are essential to the biblical gospel of God's gracious work in the salvation of His people, it seems clear that they ought to be openly set forth in the preaching of the Word of God. If they belong to the "whole counsel of God" (Acts 20:27 NKJV), then they surely must be addressed. Since the confessions of the church, including the Canons of Dort, summarize the teaching of Scripture, the preaching of the gospel should be regulated by them. The only issue is how these doctrines should be presented.

The second form of the question is whether or not the doctrines of grace also have implications for the *manner* in which the gospel of Jesus Christ is proclaimed. In this form of the question, the focus is not as much upon how the teaching of election informs *the content* of gospel preaching, but how this teaching shapes *the way* the gospel is ministered. If the Canons of Dort rightly express what the Scriptures teach about God's purpose of election, it is important to recognize that this has profound implications not only for *what* is preached but also for *how* the gospel is communicated. Though this may seem like a fairly abstract way of defining the question, we will find that the Canons address both of these forms of the question in their five main points of doctrine. In some instances, the Canons address how the doctrines of grace should be presented in the preaching of the gospel. In other instances, the Canons address how the doctrines of grace stand behind, undergird, and lend urgency as well as power to the preaching of the gospel.

Before the adoption of the Canons of Dort in the early seventeenth century, the sixteenth-century Reformers had already grappled with the question as to how the doctrine of election ought to be treated in the teaching of the church.[2] Since the theme of election often raises a number of difficult theological questions, some argued (e.g., Philip Melanchthon) that it would be better to avoid the topic altogether or perhaps restrict the discussion of it to the narrow precincts of the Christian academy. Interestingly, John Calvin, whose name is frequently linked in popular imagination with the topic of predestination, directly addresses this question in his *Institutes*. Calvin observes

---

"irresistible grace" are especially misleading designations of two of the main points adopted by the Synod of Dort.

2. For an extensive treatment of the way Calvin and later Reformed theologians addressed the subject of the preaching of predestination and election, see Pieter L. Rouwendal, *Predestination and Preaching in Genevan Theology from Calvin to Pictet,* vol. 1: Studies in the History of Church and Theology, ed. Andreas J. Beck (Kampen, The Netherlands: Summum Academic Publications, 2017).

that there are two kinds of persons who fail to do justice to this theme. On the one hand, there are those whose unbridled curiosity lands them in a labyrinth of their own making from which there is no escape. Rather than remain within the boundaries of what Scripture teaches us, they "unrestrainedly… search out things that the Lord has willed to be hid in himself."[3] Against this temptation, Calvin wisely counsels us to seek to know only what God in His wisdom has decided to reveal for our benefit. On the other hand, there are those who, fearful of rash presumption in the handling of the doctrine of election, avoid the subject altogether. Such persons think it best to avoid this topic the way sailors carefully avoid a reef at sea. In Calvin's estimation, this timidity in handling the doctrine of election amounts to a kind of "anxious silence" that questions the wisdom of the Holy Spirit's teaching in the school of the Scriptures.[4] Since the Holy Spirit teaches us about God's gracious election, we would be remiss not to consider the usefulness of this teaching.

Though it is often overlooked, the controversy regarding the doctrine of election in the Reformed churches in the Netherlands began in response to Arminius's preaching through the book of Romans. During the course of his preaching, Arminius took exception to the prevalent Reformed view of election. In Arminius's estimation, the traditional formulation of the doctrine created serious pastoral problems, especially in regard to the assurance believers may have of their election and salvation.[5] On the one hand, the teaching of unconditional election encouraged what Arminius described as a "careless certainty" regarding God's gracious purpose of election. Since the prevalent Reformed view emphasized the unconditionality of election, Arminius believed it invited believers to be assured of their salvation in a presumptuous fashion. Since God's gracious election does not depend upon the sinner's choice to persevere in the way of faith, it tempts preachers to diminish the seriousness of the gospel call to conversion. Moreover, when this teaching is joined to an Augustinian reading of Romans 7:14–25, believers are encouraged to rest their confidence in God's gracious purpose of election, even

---

3. *Institutes of the Christian Religion,* ed. John T. McNeill, trans. Ford Lewis Battles (Philadelphia: Westminster Press, 1960), 3.21.2.

4. Calvin, *Institutes,* 3.21.4.

5. James Arminius, *Declaration of Sentiments,* in *The Works of James Arminius,* trans. James Nichols and William Nichols (Grand Rapids: Baker, 1986), 1:637–38. Keith D. Stanglin and Thomas H. McCall, *Jacob Arminius: Theologian of Grace* (Oxford: Oxford University Press, 2012), 182, describes the topic of assurance as a "point of departure" for Arminius's formulation of an alternative doctrine of election to the prevalent Reformed view.

though their lives exhibit little fruit in the way of good works.[6] The preaching of unconditional election, therefore, permits believers to be assured of their election and salvation even when their lives belie their profession. On the other hand, the Reformed view of God's absolute, eternal, and immutable will to elect some persons to salvation and at the same time to reprobate others inevitably occasions doubt on the part of some believers regarding their election. According to Arminius, the preaching of the Reformed doctrine of election creates two insoluble pastoral problems: either an idle presumption regarding salvation or an anxious uncertainty regarding God's gracious favor.

One of the characteristic traits of the Canons is their sensitivity to the implications of the doctrines of grace for the preaching of the gospel. In each of the five main points of doctrine, there are articles that address the question of how these doctrines should be set forth in preaching. At the same time, each main point considers the significance of what is affirmed for the way the gospel should be preached. Accordingly, my approach to the topic of preaching the doctrines of Dort will be to follow the sequence of the five main points, noting how their respective articles answer both forms of the question before us.[7]

Unconditional Election: Preaching the Joyful Message of the Gospel with Confidence

If there were any doubt about the importance of the doctrine of election for preaching, it is dispelled in the opening articles of the first main point of doctrine. These articles do not immediately take up the topic of unconditional election, but begin with a clear statement of the gospel that is to be joyfully announced to all people. Even though all people have sinned in Adam and lie under the judgment of God, the gospel announces God's unmerited love in sending His Son into the world to save those who deserve condemnation and death. The aim of gospel preaching is to bring fallen sinners to faith in Jesus Christ. For this purpose, "God mercifully sends proclaimers of this very joyful message to the people He wishes and at the time He wishes" (art. 3). Since

---

6. *The Seventh Chapter of St. Paul's Epistle to the Romans,* in *The Works of James Arminius,* 2:659.

7. For an earlier essay on the Canons' teaching regarding the preaching of election, see Peter Y. De Jong, "Preaching and the Synod of Dort," in *Crisis in the Reformed Churches: Essays in Commemoration of the Great Synod of Dort, 1618–1619,* ed. Peter Y. De Jong (Middleville, Mich.: Reformed Fellowship, 1968, 2008), 143–67. De Jong's essay focuses upon how the doctrines of grace should form an important part of the content of what is preached, giving less attention to the implications of these doctrines for the manner in which the gospel is to be preached.

no one can believe in Christ without hearing the good message of the gospel, God appoints preachers to be His ambassadors, graciously summoning those who hear the gospel to believe in Christ for salvation.

The theme of unconditional election arises in the first main point of doctrine as an answer to this question: How is it that some respond in faith to the gospel's invitation to believe in Christ, whereas others remain willfully unbelieving in the face of the overtures of the gospel? How do we account for this twofold response to the preaching of the gospel, that some believe and are saved while others disbelieve and remain under condemnation and death? The Canons answer this question in two ways. On the one hand, they emphasize that the "cause or blame" for unbelief lies wholly with those who willfully reject the promise of salvation through Christ. On the other hand, the Canons insist that those who believe unto salvation do so by virtue of God's gracious and eternal decision to grant them the gift of faith. According to the Canons, "the fact that some receive from God the gift of faith within time, and that others do not, stems from His eternal decision.... In accordance with this decision He graciously softens the hearts, however hard, of His chosen ones and inclines them to believe, but by His just judgment He leaves in their wickedness and hardness of heart those who have not been chosen" (art. 6).

The importance of this affirmation for the preaching of the gospel can scarcely be exaggerated. When God's ambassadors call fallen sinners to faith in Jesus Christ, they do so in the confidence that God will unfailingly draw His chosen people to Himself. What undergirds the gospel call to faith in Christ is the conviction that God will graciously grant the response that this call demands. Since God's gracious election of His people in Christ takes place not on the basis of foreseen faith but "for the purpose of faith, of the obedience of faith, of holiness, and so on," the preaching of the gospel does not depend for its fruitfulness upon anything fallen sinners are required to do in their own strength. Rather, God graciously communicates all the benefits of salvation to His own as the "fruits and effects" of election.[8]

In addition to the confidence that election grants to preachers in their proclamation of the gospel, the first main point of the Canons explicitly addresses the way the theme of election should be handled in preaching. In article 14,

---

8. It must be observed that such "fruits" are not the principal ground of the believer's assurance. Though such fruits "confirm" the genuineness of faith, the principal grounds for full assurance are the promises of the gospel, together with the testimony of the Holy Spirit. This is evident in the fifth main point of doctrine, article 10, which identifies "the promises of God which he has very plentifully revealed in His Word for our comfort" as the first and foremost basis for assurance.

which bears the title, "Teaching Election Properly," preachers are encouraged to treat the doctrine of election "with a spirit of discretion," and to do so in a way that simultaneously magnifies God's glory and comforts believers:

> Just as, by God's wise plan, this teaching concerning divine election has been proclaimed through the prophets, Christ Himself, and the apostles, in Old and New Testament times, and has subsequently been committed to writing in the Holy Scriptures, so also today in God's church, for which it was specifically intended, this teaching must be set forth—with a spirit of discretion, in a godly and holy manner, at the appropriate time and place, without inquisitive searching into the ways of the Most High. This must be done for the glory of God's most holy name, and for the lively comfort of His people.

Since the teaching of divine election is proclaimed throughout the Scriptures, it should likewise be set forth by those who preach and teach the gospel in the church today. However, the doctrine of election should be presented wisely and discretely, at the proper time and place, and without any inappropriate searching out of the ways of God. The preaching of election must not mute the joyful message that all preachers are called to announce—namely, that God has sent His Son into the world to make atonement for the sins of His people and that all who believe in Him shall not perish but have eternal life.

Though article 14 provides a general exhortation to handle the doctrine of election with discretion, it does not illustrate directly how such discretion will manifest itself in preaching. However, it is significant that this article is located within a series of articles that provide several concrete illustrations of what such discretion entails.

In the two articles that precede article 14, for example, the Canons address the way believers may cultivate the assurance of their election and salvation. Recognizing that some believers may struggle to obtain full assurance, the Canons encourage believers to be assured of their election, "not by inquisitive searching into the hidden and deep things of God, but by noticing within themselves, with spiritual joy and holy delight, the unmistakable fruits of election pointed out in God's Word such as a true faith in Christ, a childlike fear of God, a godly sorrow for their sins, a hunger and thirst for righteousness, and so on" (art. 12). Rather than encouraging believers to an inappropriate searching out of the ways of God, preachers ought to call believers to "make their calling and election sure" (cf. 2 Peter 1:10–11) by observing the fruits of God's grace at work in them. Because those whom God elects are also those whom He brings to faith and repentance, such faith and repentance are like fruits that spring from a good tree. Such fruits of the work of God's grace in believers are telltale marks of their calling and election. These articles (14–15) clearly aim to answer the Arminian accusation that the doctrine of election makes believers careless. Rather than encouraging carelessness, the doctrine of election encourages believers "to humble themselves before God, to adore the fathomless depth of His mercies…and to give fervent love in return to Him who first loved them" (art. 15). Through the preaching of the gospel, including the teaching about election, believers are urged to grow in their assurance as they "walk in the ways of the chosen."

In the articles following article 14 of the first main point, similar illustrations are provided of a nonspeculative, pastorally comforting, and God-glorifying approach to the preaching of election. When believers struggle with doubts and temptations, even the temptation to "count themselves among the reprobate," they should be urged to continue to use the means of grace and to wait upon God's mercy (art. 16).[9] When they do not find themselves making much progress in holiness, they must be reminded of God's gracious promise that "He will not snuff out a smoldering wick and that He will not break a bruised reed." At the same time, the biblical teaching of reprobation engenders a spirit of soberness, even fear, on the part of those who "do not seriously turn to God" or respond as they ought to the gracious overtures of the gospel.

The Canons' pastoral emphasis upon preaching the comfort of the gospel comes to particularly powerful expression in article 17. This article was added to the first main point of doctrine in order to respond to a common accusation that the Arminians brought against the Reformed view. According to the Arminians, the Reformed teaching offered no comfort to godly parents

---

9. The Canons' treatment of how the topic of reprobation is to be handled in the preaching of the gospel is reminiscent of the sentiment expressed earlier in the Second Helvetic Confession, chapter 10:

> And although God knows who are His, and here and there mention is made of the small number of elect, yet we must hope well of all, and not rashly judge any man to be a reprobate. For Paul says to the Philippians, "I thank my God for you all" (now he speaks of the whole Church in Philippi), "because of your fellowship in the Gospel, being persuaded that he who began a good work in you will bring it to completion at the day of Jesus Christ. It is also right that I have this opinion of you all" (Phil. 1:3 ff.)….
>
> And when the Lord was asked whether there were few that should be saved, he does not answer and tell them that few or many should be saved or damned, but rather he exhorts every man to "strive to enter by the narrow door" (Luke 13:24): as if he should say, "It is not for you curiously to inquire about these matters, but rather to endeavor that you may enter into heaven by the straight way."

whose infant children were called out of this life in their infancy. In their estimation, this doctrine implied that "many infant children of believers are snatched in their innocence from their mother's breasts and cruelly cast into hell so that neither the blood of Christ nor their baptism or the prayers of the church at their baptism can be of any use to them."[10] The answer to this accusation in article 17 provides an especially important illustration of the way the doctrine of election should be handled in the church's preaching. Rather than treating election in an improperly inquisitive manner, the authors of the Canons offer a robust statement of the undoubted assurance such parents may have regarding the election and salvation of their children:

> Since we must make judgements about God's will from His Word, which testifies that the children of believers are holy, not by nature but by virtue of the gracious covenant in which they together with their parents are included, godly parents ought not to doubt the election and salvation of their children whom God calls out of this life in infancy (art. 17).

Rather than speculatively inquiring into the secret will of God regarding such children, their parents should be encouraged through the church's preaching of the rich and sure promises that God has made respecting their children. Whatever judgment is made about such children, it must be a judgment made upon the basis of God's revelation or Word. No room may be left to speculate about God's gracious will concerning them.[11]

Particular Redemption or Definite Atonement: Preaching Christ's Work of Atonement and Its Sure Promise

The second main point of doctrine offers some especially important comments on the way election impacts the preaching of the gospel. It addresses the way Christ's work of atonement was designed by God to effectually redeem

---

10. Conclusion: *Rejection of False Accusations.*

11. The most frequently quoted Scripture texts in support of this affirmation at the Synod were Gen. 17:7; Acts 2:39; and 1 Cor. 7:14. These texts are cited in the Dutch edition of the *Acta* of the Synod. For more extensive treatments of the background and significance of article 1/17, see W. Robert Godfrey, "A Promise for Parents: Dordt's Perspective on Covenant and Election," in *Church and School in Early Modern Protestantism: Studies in Honor of Richard A. Muller on the Maturation of a Theological Tradition,* ed. Jordan J. Ballor, David S. Sytsma, and Jason Zuidema (Leiden/Boston: Brill, 2013), 373–86; Erik A. De Boer, "'O, ye Women, Think of Thy Innocent Children, When They Die Young!' The Canons of Dordt (I, 17) between Polemic and Pastoral Theology," in *Revisiting the Synod of Dordt,* ed. A. Goudrian and F. van Lieburg, (Leiden: Brill, 2011), 261–90; and Cornelis P. Venema, *Christ and Covenant Theology: Essays on Election, Republication, and the Covenants* (Phillipsburg, N.J.: P&R, 2016), 214–55.

all those whom He has chosen to save. Of the five points, undoubtedly this point is the most controversial among those affirmed in the Canons. For this reason, those who agree with the other four points but demur from this one are often called "four-point Calvinists."[12] Perhaps the most significant reason some demur from the teaching of particular redemption is the fear that this teaching "limits" the scope of Christ's atoning sacrifice and thereby imperils the church's ability to herald to all sinners the joyful message of the gospel. If Christ's atoning death was designed only to procure the salvation of the elect, the universal and gracious invitation of the gospel is undermined. Indeed, some allege that the teaching of particular redemption must inevitably discourage preachers from issuing the gospel invitation to all with the promise that whoever comes to Christ in faith will assuredly be saved.

In remarkable contrast to these concerns, the second main point begins in a way that mimics the opening articles of the first point. After noting that God's justice requires that satisfaction be made for the sins we have committed "against His infinite majesty," the Canons declare that God in His boundless mercy has provided the necessary satisfaction through the death of His Son upon the cross (arts. 1–2). In the following articles, the Canons emphasize the infinite value and worth of Christ's atoning sacrifice. Utilizing traditional language, the Canons affirm that Christ's atoning death was "more than *sufficient* to atone for the sins of the whole world" (emphasis mine, art. 3).[13] Even though Christ's work of atonement is *efficient* unto the salvation

---

12. See, e.g., Millard Erickson, *Christian Theology* (Grand Rapids: Baker, 1983), 825–41, esp. 834–35. Erickson doesn't describe himself as a "four-point Calvinist," but that is essentially his position.

13. The Canons' use of the language "sufficient for all" reflects a common expression, which is found already in Peter Lombard's *Sentences*: pro omnibus…sufficientiam; sed pro electis…. ad efficaciam (sufficient for all, but efficient for the elect). Since this language was liable to various interpretations, its presence in the Canons illustrates the authors' desire to leave room for some diversity of opinion among those who affirm particular redemption. Remarkably, Calvin himself, in his comments on 1 John 2:2 (*Calvin's Commentaries* [1844–1856; repr., Grand Rapids: Baker, 1981], 22:173) rejected this language as liable to misunderstanding. For treatments of the extent or design of the atonement in Calvin and later Calvinism, including the Amyraldian view of hypothetical universalism, see W. Robert Godfrey, "Reformed Thought on the Extent of the Atonement to 1618," *Westminster Theological Journal* 37/2 (1975): 133–71; Peter L. Rouwendal, "Calvin's Forgotten Classical Position on the Extent of the Atonement: About Efficiency, Sufficiency, and Anachronism," *Westminster Theological Journal* 70/2 (2008): 317–35; G. Michael Thomas, *The Extent of the Atonement: A Dilemma for Reformed Theology from Calvin to the Consensus (1536–1675)*, Paternoster Biblical and Theological Monographs (Carlisle: Paternoster, 1997); Brian G. Armstrong, *Calvinism and the Amyraut Heresy: Protestant Scholasticism and Humanism in Seventeenth-Century France* (Madison: University of Wisconsin Press, 1969); Richard Muller, *Christ and the Decree: Christology and Predestination in Reformed*

of the elect alone, this does not imply that His sacrifice was insufficient to the need of all lost sinners. Accordingly, in the preaching of the gospel by Christ's ambassadors, the promise of salvation through faith in Christ must be presented to all:

> Moreover, it is the promise of the gospel that whoever believes in Christ crucified shall not perish but have eternal life. This promise, together with the command to repent and believe, ought to be announced and declared without differentiation or discrimination to all nations and people, to whom God in His good pleasure sends the gospel. (art. 5)

In this striking declaration, the Canons affirm the propriety of preaching the gospel universally and indiscriminately to all sinners. Through the preaching of the gospel, the promise of salvation in Christ is presented to sinners, who are urged to respond in faith. Since Christ's work of atonement is sufficient for the salvation of all, the gospel invitation may extend the promise of salvation to all, summoning them to respond properly in faith and repentance.[14] That some refuse to do so is not owing to any deficiency in the sacrifice of

---

Theology from Calvin to Perkins (Grand Rapids: Baker Publishing, 2008), 33–35; and Roger Nicole, "Moyse Amyraut (1596–1664) and the Controversy on Universal Grace: First Phase (1634–1637)" (PhD diss., Harvard University, 1966).

14. The Canons' affirmation of the universal sufficiency of Christ's atonement expresses a general consensus among Reformed theologians from Calvin and his contemporaries until the time of the Synod of Dort. Though the Canons' teaching on definite atonement seems incompatible with the Amyraldian understanding of "hypothetical universalism," it does not exclude other forms of hypothetical universalism that were represented among the delegations to the Synod of Dort, including that of John Davenant, a member of the English delegation. According to the Amyraldian view, the atoning work of Christ was provided by God for the salvation of *all* lost sinners on condition of faith (hence, "hypothetical"). However, since God has determined to grant the condition of faith to the elect alone, the death of Christ is only effectual to their salvation. In the Amyraldian view, there is a disjunction between God's will to provide a universal, indefinite atonement for all sinners, and His will to grant the requisite faith to the elect alone. While the Canons seem clearly at odds with Amyraldian hypothetical universalism (though without expressly condemning it), they do not rule out the position espoused by John Davenant. According to Davenant, the universal sufficiency of Christ's atonement provides a warrant for an indiscriminate preaching of the gospel to all lost sinners, calling them to embrace the gospel promise in Christ by faith in order to be saved. However, the will of God expressed in the gospel call to all lost sinners must be distinguished from God's intentional and effectual will to save the elect by granting them the requisite faith whereby they come to benefit from Christ's work on their behalf. For an extensive treatment of the Canons' teaching in relation to various forms of hypothetical universalism, including Davenant's, see Muller, *Calvin and the Reformed Tradition,* 126–60; and Richard Muller, *Dictionary of Latin and Greek Theological Terms: Drawn Principally from Protestant Scholastic Theology,* 2nd ed. (Grand Rapids: Baker Academic, 2017), q.v. "universalismus hypotheticus," 381–83.

Christ. Rather, those who remain unbelieving have only themselves to blame for their willful refusal to embrace the gospel's promise (art. 6). But those who genuinely believe in Christ unto salvation receive this favor from God's grace alone "given them in Christ from eternity" (art. 7).

The most important article in the second main point of doctrine is article 8, which declares that "it was the entirely free plan and very gracious will and intention of God the Father that the enlivening and saving effectiveness of His Son's costly death should work itself out in all His chosen ones, in order that He might grant justifying faith to them only and thereby lead them without fail to salvation." This article not only underscores the particularity of Christ's work of atonement, but it also explicitly notes the implications of this truth for the preaching of the gospel. Because Christ's atonement was, according to God's design and intention, given to effect the salvation of the elect, the preaching of the gospel will prove unfailingly fruitful as God's appointed means to grant faith and salvation to His chosen from "every people, tribe, nation, and language." Christ's atoning death for His people will not be frustrated, but will "effectively redeem" those whom God graciously chooses to save. By His work of atonement, Christ has ensured that those for whom He offered Himself a sacrifice for sin will be cleansed by His blood and preserved to the end.

Thus, rather than limiting Christ's work of atonement, the Canons emphasize both the *unlimited sufficiency* of Christ's satisfaction to the salvation of all sinners and its *unfailing efficacy* for the salvation of all God's chosen people. From the perspective of the teaching of the Canons, the Arminian view is one that is most aptly described as a doctrine of limited atonement. Though the Arminian view affirms that Christ's atonement was for all, it simultaneously teaches that it remains inefficacious to the salvation of any sinner, unless or until it becomes effectual by an independent act of the sinner's will. According to the Arminian teaching, "the necessity, usefulness, and worth of what Christ's death obtained could have stood intact and altogether perfect, complete and whole, even if the redemption that was obtained had never in actual fact been applied to any individual."[15]

Thus, the teaching of definite atonement in no way prevents preachers from declaring the gospel promise to all lost sinners. But it does more than this. It fortifies Christ's ambassadors to preach out of the conviction that Christ will surely draw all those for whom He died through the ministry of His Spirit. Moreover, it provides a sure *warrant* for the gospel promise itself. The gospel promise amounts to more than preaching "if you believe, you will

---

15. Canons of Dort II, rej. 1.

be saved." The promise may not be reduced to the simple declaration "Christ has made it possible for you to be saved, though your actual salvation depends upon your independent determination to believe and to continue to do so." No, when believers are called to trust in Christ, they are called to believe that He has *fully satisfied for all their sins.* They do not embrace a gospel promise that is simply conditional and provisional, as though Christ were not the one whose work of atonement ensures the salvation of those who entrust themselves to Him in faith. They are called to embrace Christ, trusting that He has not only procured their right to be saved but will also ensure that every benefit belonging to salvation is imparted to them. To use the language of the author of Hebrews, believers trust the gospel promise that Christ is able to save them to the uttermost (Heb. 7:25). Christ's work promises those who believe in Him all that is necessary to enjoy full and final salvation. As John Murray so concisely and eloquently puts it,

> [Christ] could not be offered as Savior and as the one who embodies in Himself salvation full and free if He had simply made the salvation of all men possible or merely had made provision for the salvation of all. It is the very doctrine that Christ procured and secured redemption that invests the free offer of the gospel with richness and power. It is that doctrine alone that allows for a presentation of Christ that will be worthy of the glory of His accomplishment and of His person. It is because Christ procured and secured redemption that He is an all-sufficient and suitable Savior.[16]

Radical Depravity and the Effectual Call: Preaching the Gospel to All in the Power of the Spirit

Some of the most important statements regarding the doctrines of grace in relation to preaching are found in the third and fourth main points of the Canons.[17] These points, which treat the topics of the radical depravity of fallen sinners and the effectual ministry of Christ's Spirit in their conversion, are of special relevance to preaching and preachers. They remind preachers that those whom they address with the call of the gospel are spiritually dead,

---

16. John Murray, *Redemption Accomplished and Applied,* 2nd ed. (Grand Rapids: Eerdmans, 2015), 63–64.

17. The Canons combine the third and fourth main points of doctrine because the real point of divergence between the Arminian and Reformed views emerges most clearly in the fourth point. The Arminian or Remonstrant view acknowledges that fallen sinners are incapable of saving themselves apart from God's prevenient grace. However, this grace can always be resisted and is therefore ineffectual to ensure the salvation of any fallen sinner.

incapable of and unwilling to perform any saving good. The ministry of the gospel does not presume that fallen sinners are able to do anything in their own power to save themselves. They also emphasize that the gospel call must be extended to all sinners seriously, urgently, and compassionately. And, consistent with what we have already found in the earlier points of doctrine, the fourth point encourages preachers to preach with the expectation that the Holy Spirit will work in regeneration and conversion to draw lost sinners to faith in Christ. Because preaching is the means the Spirit uses as the "seed of regeneration," the ministry of the gospel is powerful to save those whom God has chosen in Christ.

Before describing the way the Spirit effectually calls those whom God has chosen in Christ, the third main point emphasizes that the gospel alone is able to grant salvation to fallen sinners. Due to the fall into sin, "all people are conceived in sin and are born children of wrath, unfit for any saving good, inclined to evil, dead in their sins, and slaves to sin" (art. 3). Neither the "light of nature" remaining in sinners after the fall nor the law of God is adequate as a means of restoring them to favor with God (arts. 4–5). Thus, the only hope of salvation for fallen sinners lies in the power of the gospel of Jesus Christ.[18] Since fallen sinners are incapable of doing any saving good upon the basis of the light of nature or the law of God, the gospel of Jesus Christ offers the exclusive remedy for them to be reconciled and restored to fellowship with God. The gospel of Jesus Christ—the announcement of His saving work of atonement and the call to faith and repentance—is the means God has appointed to grant salvation to His people.

Within the setting of this emphasis upon the saving power of the gospel, the Canons make a remarkable statement regarding the seriousness and sincerity of the call of the gospel that is extended indiscriminately to all lost sinners. They respond directly to the Remonstrant claim that the Reformed view militates against the genuineness of the gracious call of the gospel. According to the Remonstrants, if God unconditionally elects to save some lost sinners but not others, the gospel call becomes disingenuous. Neither God nor preachers who issue the call of the gospel in His name can genuinely express a desire that all would believe in Christ unto salvation. In their judgment, the doctrine of unconditional election calls into question the sincerity of the gospel call with respect to those whom God has not chosen. How

---

18. Canons of Dort, III/IV, 6: "What, therefore, neither the light of nature nor the law can do, God accomplishes by the power of the Holy Spirit, through the Word or the ministry of reconciliation. This is the gospel about the Messiah, through which it has pleased God to save believers, in the both the Old and the New Testament."

can God express a gracious disposition toward all in the call of the gospel when He does not will to save all? Contrary to the Arminian charge that the Reformed view undermines the ability of preachers to call all lost sinners to salvation through faith in Christ, the Canons insist that

> all who are called through the gospel are called seriously [*serio vocantur*]. For seriously and most genuinely [*Serio enim et verissime*] God makes known in His Word what is pleasing to Him [*quid sibi gratum sit*]: that those who are called should come to Him. Seriously He also promises rest for their souls and eternal life to all who come to Him and believe. (art. 8)

By using language almost identical to that of the Remonstrants in their description of the gospel call, the Canons expressly aim to rebut the claim that the Reformed view of unconditional election is incompatible with a compassionate presentation of the gospel to all.[19]

There are several observations that may be made regarding the Canons' affirmation of the sincerity of the gospel offer. First, though the authors of the Canons were convinced that the sincerity of the gospel offer does not contradict the scriptural teaching of unconditional election, they do not attempt to provide a theological explanation as to how this is so. They simply affirm what the Scriptures teach about the graciousness of the gospel call without granting the Arminian charge that this is inconsistent with the Reformed view of election.[20] Second, it should be noted that the Arminian view does not avoid the problem that is often alleged against the Reformed view—namely, that it represents God's will as it is expressed in the call of the gospel in a way that is out of harmony with His particular purpose of election. According to

---

19. The Opinions of the Remonstrants declare that "whomever God calls to salvation, he calls seriously, that is, with a sincere and completely unhypocritical intention and will to save" (as quoted in De Jong, *Crisis in the Reformed Churches,* 265). The subtle difference in viewpoint between this opinion and the Canons lies in the phrase "intention and will." Though the Canons speak of what God declares in His Word to be pleasing to Him, they do not say that He "intends" to draw all whom He calls to Himself.

20. For an extensive treatment of the biblical basis for the free offer of the gospel, see John Murray, "The Free Offer of the Gospel," in *Collected Writings of John Murray,* (Carlisle, Pa.: Banner of Truth, 1982), 4:114–31. For an extensive treatment of the way Reformed theologians have defended the distinction between God's will that is revealed in the gracious call of the gospel and God's will of decree to save those whom He elects, see Muller, *Calvin and the Reformed Tradition,* 107–25; John Piper, "Are There Two Wills in God? Divine Election and God's Desire for All to Be Saved," in *The Grace of God, the Bondage of the Will,* ed. Thomas Schreiner and Bruce A. Ware (Grand Rapids: Baker, 1995), 1:107–32; and Robert Lewis Dabney, "God's Indiscriminate Proposals of Mercy, As Related to His Power, Wisdom, and Sincerity," in *Discussions of Robert Lewis Dabney* (Carlisle, Pa.: The Banner of Truth, 1982), 1:282–313.

the Arminian view, God wills (absolutely and antecedently) to save all fallen sinners upon the basis of Christ's work of atonement, to be sure. This allegedly undergirds the genuineness of the gospel's call to all sinners to believe in Jesus Christ and be saved. However, the Arminian view also declares that God simultaneously wills (conditionally and consequently) to save only those specific sinners who independently choose to embrace the gospel promise by faith. Remarkably, God's will as it relates to the specific persons He elects does not comport with His absolute will to save all fallen sinners.[21] And third, when the Canons affirm the sincerity of the gospel call to all lost sinners, they do so in the light of what the Scriptures teach regarding God's gracious disposition toward all lost sinners. The sincere gospel offer focuses upon *what God reveals concerning what would be genuinely pleasing to Him*, not upon *what God has particularly willed to effect* in the salvation of His chosen people.[22] According to the teaching of the Canons, we must distinguish between two aspects of the will of God. On the one hand, the gracious call of the gospel reveals that God genuinely desires that all fallen sinners should respond in faith to the gospel call and so be saved. On the other hand, God's purpose of election expresses His gracious intention to save those toward whom He chooses to be merciful.

The Canons' affirmation of the sincere gospel offer is of the greatest importance for the preaching of the gospel. When the gospel is preached and sinners are called to faith and repentance, Christ's ambassadors are not only permitted but also obliged to extend this call with heartfelt compassion. The word of the gospel is to be ministered as a joyful message to all its recipients. Even as the apostle Paul expressed his heartfelt desire that his kinsmen according to the flesh would be saved (Rom. 10:1), so the gospel preacher ought to minister the gospel with a similar desire.[23] Those who are

---

21. Cf. Richard Muller, "Grace, Election, and Contingent Choice: Arminius' Gambit and the Reformed Response," in *The Grace of God, the Bondage of the Will*, 2:274: "According to this doctrine [the Arminian], God genuinely wills that which he knows will never happen, indeed, what he wills not to bring about!"

22. In Reformed theology, the obligations of the gospel call to faith and repentance are understood to belong within the orbit of God's "preceptive" will, and not His "decretive" will. For a discussion of this distinction between God's will of precept and His will of decree, see Louis Berkhof, *Systematic Theology* (Grand Rapids: Eerdmans, 1941), 76–77. Regarding these aspects of God's will, Berkhof observes that the decretive will of God is "that will by which He purposes or decrees whatever shall come to pass, whether He wills to accomplish it effectively (causatively), or to permit it to occur through the unrestrained agency of His rational creatures." God's preceptive will "is the rule of life which God has laid down for His moral creatures, indicating the duties which he enjoins upon them" (77).

23. Cf. Calvin, *Institutes,* 3.23.1, which appeals to the opinion of Augustine that "we ought to be so minded as to wish that all men be saved."

privileged to herald the gospel should do so with a heart that is compassionate toward all. The preaching of the gospel is nothing if not an earnest and sincere entreaty to all to believe in Jesus Christ and so be saved.

After this strong affirmation of the sincerity of the gospel call, the fourth main point of the Canons describes the way in which the Holy Spirit accompanies the preaching of the gospel by effectually persuading those whom God elects to respond to the gospel in faith and repentance. Contrary to the Arminian view, which insists that God's grace is always resistible and ineffectual as long as sinners choose to reject the gospel call, the Canons maintain that God "effectively calls" the elect to Himself in time, granting them faith and repentance by the ministry of the Spirit. The work of the Spirit in conversion is powerful, inexpressible, and supernatural. When the Spirit grants new birth to spiritually dead sinners, He "penetrates into the inmost being of man, opens the closed heart, softens the hard heart, and circumcises the heart that is uncircumcised" (art. 11). For this reason, the Canons' view of the work of the Spirit in conversion is not aptly described by the usual language of "irresistible grace." Whereas this language suggests that sinners are overpowered by the gracious operations of the Holy Spirit, the Canons consistently speak of the Spirit's ministry as an "effectual" *persuasion*.[24] When the Spirit works through the call of the gospel in the case of God's chosen ones, He "infuses new qualities into the will, making the dead will alive, the evil one good, the unwilling one willing, and the stubborn one compliant; He activates and strengthens the will so that, like a good tree, it may be enable to produce the fruits of good deeds" (art. 11). Though all lost sinners are unwilling and unable to respond properly to the call of the gospel until and unless they are granted a new birth through the ministry of the Spirit, those who are graciously and effectively converted by the Spirit respond freely and actively in the way of faith and repentance.[25]

---

24. The language of "persuasion" mitigates against any view of the Spirit's ministry with the Word as a coercive one. This is a common sentiment in the Reformed confessions and is nicely set forth in the Westminster Confession of Faith, chap. 10.1:

> All those whom God hath predestinated unto life, and those only, he is pleased, in His appointed and accepted time, effectually to call, by His Word and Spirit, out of that state of sin and death, in which they are by nature, to grace and salvation, by Jesus Christ; enlightening their minds spiritually and savingly to understand the things of God, taking away their heart of stone, and giving unto them a heart of flesh; renewing their wills, and, by His almighty power, determining them to that which is good, and effectually drawing them to Jesus Christ; yet so, as *they come most freely*, being made willing by His grace. (emphasis mine)

25. Article III/IV.12 concludes with these words: "And then the will, now renewed, is not only activated and motivated by God but in being activated by God is also itself active.

Perhaps the most important statement regarding the relation between election and preaching in the fourth point is article 17. In this article, the Canons link God's purpose of election directly to His use of means in effectually calling believers through the ministry of the gospel. In the ordinary realization of His saving purpose in time, God is pleased to use the preaching of the gospel as the "seed of regeneration":

> Just as the almighty work of God by which He brings forth and sustains our natural life does not rule out but requires the use of means, by which God, according to His infinite wisdom and goodness, has wished to exercise His power, so also the aforementioned supernatural work of God by which He regenerates us in no way rules out or cancels the use of the gospel, which God in His great wisdom has appointed to be the seed of regeneration and the food of the soul. For this reason, the apostles and the teachers who followed them taught the people in a godly manner about this grace of God, to give Him the glory and to humble all pride, and yet did not neglect meanwhile to keep the people, by means of the holy admonitions of the gospel, under the administration of the Word, the sacraments, and discipline. (art. 17)

The Spirit's work in conversion is not immediate, since it is ordinarily effected through the ministry of the means of grace, principally the preaching of the gospel with its earnest call to faith and repentance.

Accordingly, even though the doctrine of election is often alleged to encourage passivity on the part of the church's ministers in carrying out the work of missions and evangelism, the Canons offer no encouragement to such passivity. Since the Spirit works through the means of gospel preaching to grant salvation to those whom God elects, the church and its ministers are obliged to proclaim the good news to all lost sinners. Failure to preach the gospel with compassion, urgency, and relentlessness exhibits a failure to recognize that such gospel preaching is the ordinary means by which God grants His grace to those whom He has chosen. When the ordinary means of grace are not ministered energetically, with the prayer that the Holy Spirit would cause these means to be effectual to the salvation of lost sinners, the church presumes "to test God by separating what He in His good pleasure has wished to be closely joined together" (art. 17).

For this reason, man himself, by that grace which he has received, is also rightly said to believe and to repent."

The Perseverance of the Saints: Preaching as a
Means of Preservation

The fifth and last point of doctrine in the Canons, which affirms God's gracious preservation of those whom He elects to save, emphasizes the role of preaching in a way that echoes the fourth point. Just as God is pleased to use the ordinary means of grace, especially preaching, to grant regeneration and conversion by the effectual work of the Holy Spirit with the Word, so He is pleased by means of preaching to enable believers to persevere to the end in faith and repentance.

In the opening articles of the fifth main point, the Canons acknowledge that believers struggle throughout their lives with "daily sins of weakness" (art. 2). In some instances, believers fall into serious sins, as is witnessed in Scripture by the grievous cases of David in the Old Testament and Peter in the New Testament. Such sins grieve the Holy Spirit and may even entail the suspense of the exercise of faith for a season (art. 5). However, God in His boundless mercy does not take His Holy Spirit from those whom He calls according to His unchangeable purpose of election. Believers may be assured that God will preserve His chosen ones in the way of faith and repentance to the end. Believers, were they left to their own resources, would undoubtedly fail to persevere to the end, but God graciously preserves them in the way of salvation. Believers may be sure that God's "plan cannot be changed, His promise cannot fail, the calling according to His purpose cannot be revoked, the merit of Christ as well as His interceding and preserving cannot be nullified, and the sealing of the Holy Spirit can neither be invalidated nor wiped out" (art. 8).

Within the setting of this robust emphasis upon the assurance believers may have of God's preserving grace, the Canons also maintain that such assurance should not be confused with a careless and lackadaisical presumption. Far from inducing believers to a careless disregard for godliness, God has appointed the use of the means of grace, especially preaching, to ensure their perseverance: "Just as it has pleased God to begin this work of grace in us by the proclamation of the gospel, so He perseveres, continues, and completes His work by the hearing and reading of the gospel, by meditation on it, by its exhortations, threats, and promises, and also by the use of the sacraments" (art. 14). The role of preaching in the perseverance of believers has implications for preachers and believers alike. For preachers, it serves to remind them of the urgency and seriousness of their calling to preach the Word in season and out of season (2 Tim. 4:2). Such preaching must comfort believers with the assurance of God's preserving grace and at the same time warn and admonish the unbelieving and disobedient to turn in repentance and faith to God. For believers, the Canons' emphasis upon the role of preaching in perseverance serves as a reminder to them to make diligent use of the means of grace. God only preserves His chosen people as they make appropriate use of the preaching of the gospel and the reception of the sacraments. Contrary to the common Arminian complaint that the Reformed view of election is an inducement to carelessness in the Christian life, the Canons accent the responsibility of believers to be disciplined throughout their lives by the ministry of the gospel.

Summary

My review of the five main points of the Canons provides ample evidence that the authors were particularly anxious to address the implications of these doctrines for the preaching of the gospel. Contrary to the way these doctrines are often handled, the authors of the Canons demonstrate throughout that they were motivated by a profound pastoral interest in the way the gospel of Jesus Christ should be joyfully and confidently proclaimed to all lost sinners. This is evident in respect to both forms of the question regarding preaching these doctrines that I identified in the introduction to this essay.

With regard to the question, Should the doctrines of grace be explicitly set forth in the church's preaching of the gospel? the Canons' answer is a resounding "Yes, indeed!" However, the Canons consistently emphasize the need to present the Scripture's teaching of election in a discreet, non-speculative manner. The preaching of the gospel of God's gracious election of His people in Christ must always direct believers to what God has revealed in His Word. Rather than tempting believers to speculate in an unbridled way about God's secret purposes, such preaching points them to the joyful gospel message of salvation through faith in Christ. Two principal themes should invariably govern any presentation of the scriptural teaching regarding God's gracious election of His people in Christ. First, preaching the doctrines of grace must aim to magnify the sheer graciousness of God's saving work in Christ. The glory of the triune God's saving purpose and work must be paramount in the ministry of the gospel. In all of the respective works of God the Father, God the Son, and God the Holy Spirit, God's initiatives and accomplishments in the salvation of His elect people ought to be preeminent. In this way, believers will be taught to humble themselves in the presence of the God of their salvation. And second, preaching the doctrines of grace will also prove to be a great comfort to believers. Rather than base their confidence of salvation in their own works, believers ground their assurance of salvation upon God's gracious work in Christ and the promises that are in Him. When the doctrines of grace are properly presented in preaching, God is praised for His undeserved mercy in Christ, and believers find their comfort in His invincible love (cf. Rom. 8:28–39).

However, what is perhaps most remarkable about the Canons' teaching is the way they underscore the implications of the doctrines of grace for the *way* the gospel should be preached. In the course of my survey of the Canons, I identified several features of such preaching.

First, when preachers announce the joyful message of the gospel that God so loved the world that He gave His Son so that whosoever believes in Him may not perish but have eternal life, they may do so with *confidence* that God will unfailingly draw His chosen people to faith in Christ according to His purpose of election.

Second, the promise of the gospel of Jesus Christ, which must be indiscriminately proclaimed to all lost sinners, does not declare merely that Christ's work of atonement makes it possible to be saved if only you would do something to make it effectual to your salvation. No, the gospel promise in Christ is that He is a perfect Savior, whose atoning sacrifice procures and secures the salvation of all those who trust in Him. Christ is a Savior who saves to the uttermost all who come to Him (Heb. 7:25), trusting that He will grant them every spiritual blessing through the ministry of His Spirit.

Third, those who preach the gospel may declare seriously and compassionately to all lost sinners what would please God—namely, that they come to Him through faith in Christ. The urgent and sincere summons of God should be extended through preaching that is born of a heartfelt desire and prayer that all lost sinners be saved (Rom. 10:1).

Fourth, gospel preachers may uncompromisingly summon lost sinners to faith and repentance out of the conviction that God is pleased by the ministry of the Spirit of Christ to grant what the gospel call requires to all whom He chooses to save. Even though lost sinners are spiritually dead, incapable of performing any saving good, the preaching of the gospel will be accompanied by a powerful working of the Spirit, who with the Word effectually regenerates and converts lost sinners.

And fifth, contrary to the Arminian accusation that the doctrine of election encourages carelessness or undermines the assurance of salvation, the preaching of the gospel in the power of the Spirit is the means God is pleased to use to preserve His people in a lively faith to the end. In short, gospel preaching, when undergirded by the doctrines of grace, should with joyful confidence call all lost sinners to embrace the sure promise of the gospel. Such preaching is energized by the conviction that God will unfailingly cause this means to accomplish His saving purposes in Christ.

CHAPTER 11

Proclaiming Joyful Tidings: Dort, Evangelism, and the Sovereignty of God

Jon D. Payne

The sun was disappearing fast behind the hazy Delhi horizon. We needed to move quickly if we were going to reach Pastor Dorsey before sundown. It was my first time to India. The sights, sounds, and smells of Hindustan overwhelmed my suburban American senses. My friend and guide, an Indian seminarian, hailed us a ride in a beat-up motorized rickshaw. Our driver weaved through Delhi traffic like a NASCAR champion, repeatedly coming within inches of sundry vehicles, pedestrians, animals, and objects in the road. We even swerved around an enormous elephant. My friend was calm. I pretended to be. He was used to the pandemonium. I most definitely was not.

When we finally arrived at our destination, it was obvious we'd entered a rough section of the city. It was a Delhi slum—tens of thousands of people living in miserable squalor. My friend told me to stay close. People stared. I followed him apprehensively through the narrow, winding path that snaked through the wretched slum. There were makeshift dwellings on both sides of us and a streamlet of sewage and human waste running under our feet. The smell was almost unbearable.

After walking for several minutes, nervously wondering how deep we would go into this dubious shantytown, we suddenly stopped. I heard singing. I leaned forward and glanced into a dwelling where I witnessed a beautiful and unforgettable scene. Pastor John Dorsey, a seventy-three-year-old Presbyterian missionary-pastor, was sitting on a small stool in a dimly lit room surrounded by about twenty small children. He was leading them in gospel songs. After the singing he read from the Scriptures. He shared with the children the timeless message of hope—the *gospel*—in their native tongue. I will never forget what I saw that evening. The late Pastor Dorsey's commitment to reaching the lost with the good news of Jesus Christ was unparalleled. He was an evangelist at heart, sharing the gospel numerous times a week. What may be surprising to some, however, were his theological convictions. Pastor Dorsey was a Calvinist—a predestinarian. Indeed, he heartily subscribed to the Canons of Dort (CD).

Some will wonder, "How can this be? Aren't divine predestination and gospel evangelism mutually exclusive?" As a new believer, I posed this very question to my Reformed friends when they introduced me to the doctrines of election and predestination. "Unconditional election can't be true," I insisted. "And if it is true," I added, "then evangelism is superfluous, since the elect are sure to be converted with *or without* our evangelistic efforts." I argued that the doctrine of predestination unavoidably fosters indifference toward missions. Furthermore, it necessarily compromises a free offer of the gospel. Like many others, I considered Calvinism to be "logically anti-missionary."[1] A popular evangelical scholar expressed my sentiments well:

> If [Calvinism] is correct, then we need not get excited about missions for several reasons. First of all, God does not love the whole world in a redemptive sense, but only the elect. Second, Christ only died for the elect, not the world. Third, no one has the faith to believe unless God gives it to him. Fourth, God has willed to give faith only to a select few, "the frozen chosen." Fifth, when God's power works on the hearts of the unbelievers He wants to save, there is absolutely nothing they can do to refuse it. God's power is irresistible…. If all these were true—thank God they are not—it would be understandably hard to muster up much enthusiasm for missions or evangelism.[2]

Ironically, the very theological categories that I thought undermined faithful evangelism are those that I now believe powerfully fuel it. Indeed, far from quenching zeal for evangelism, election and predestination are doctrines that kindle and maintain it. History is chalked full of passionately evangelistic men and women who believed the same.

John Calvin, the great Genevan Reformer (1509–1564), was a leader in the sixteenth-century missions and church-planting movement in Europe. He trained and sent hundreds of missionary-pastors to preach the gospel and establish biblical churches in France, Poland, Italy, and Hungary.[3] He even

---

1. William Estep, "Calvinizing Southern Baptists," *Texas Baptist Standard*, March 26, 1997. Quoted in Kenneth J. Stewart, "Calvinism and Missions: The Contested Relationship Revisited," *Themelios* 34.1 (April 2009).

2. Norman Geisler, *Chosen But Free: A Balanced View of Divine Election* (Minneapolis: Bethany House Publishers, 1999), 136.

3. Carter Lindberg, *The European Reformations* (Oxford: Blackwell Publishing, 1996), 281–87.

sent missionaries to Brazil, a distant land understood to be "the ends of the earth" in mid-sixteenth-century Europe.[4] Or what about the fiery itinerant evangelist John Knox (1514–1572)? The Scottish Reformer's belief in predestination did not hinder him from boldly proclaiming the unsearchable riches of Christ in the churches and heather-laden moors.[5] During the First Great Awakening, notable Calvinists George Whitefield (1714–1770) and Jonathan Edwards (1703–1758) were tireless gospel evangelists.[6] Indeed, they led thousands of people to Christ on both sides of the Atlantic. Many aren't aware that Edwards spent eight years on the colonial frontier as a missionary to the Mohawk and Mohican Indians.[7] Moreover, celebrated missionaries such as David Brainerd (1718–1747), Henry Martyn (1781–1812), Adoniram Judson (1788–1850), and John Paton (1824–1907) all embraced the doctrines of sovereign grace. In all of these examples from church history, faithful evangelism was not hindered but energized by a belief in the biblical doctrines of election and predestination. Their devotion to Christian mission stemmed from the Synod of Dort's conviction that

> election is the unchangeable purpose of God, whereby, before the foundation of the world, He hath out of mere grace, according to the sovereign good pleasure of His own will, chosen, from the whole human race...a certain number of persons to redemption in Christ. (CD I, 7)

Therefore, election and predestination are not impediments to evangelism, as some would argue. On the contrary, they make evangelism profoundly meaningful and wonderfully successful through the efficacious working of God's life-giving Spirit and Word.

To be sure, the Synod of Dort was not chiefly concerned with questions related to Christian evangelism and the missionary task. The Dutch ecclesiastical assembly was convened primarily to respond to the destructive Arminian errors of the Remonstrants.[8] Nevertheless, in the following pages the reader

---

4. See Michael Haykin and Jeffrey Robinson Sr., *To the Ends of the Earth: Calvin's Missional Vision and Legacy* (Wheaton, Ill.: Crossway, 2014).

5. Jane Dawson, *John Knox* (New Haven, Conn.: Yale University Press, 2015).

6. Joseph Tracy, *The Great Awakening: A History of the Revival of Religion in the Time of Whitefield and Edwards* (1842; repr., Edinburgh: Banner of Truth, 2019).

7. See Jon D. Payne, "Jonathan Edwards: Missionary to the Indians," in William M. Schweitzer, ed., *Jonathan Edwards for the Church: The Ministry and the Means of Grace* (Welwyn Garden City, U.K.: Evangelical Press), 115–35.

8. For further reading, see Peter Y. De Jong, ed., *Crisis in the Reformed Churches: Essays in Commemoration of the Great Synod of Dort, 1618–1619* (Middleville, Mich.: Reformed Fellowship Inc., 1968); Aza Goudriaan and Fred van Lieburg, eds., *Revisiting the Synod of Dordt (1618–1619)*

will discover that the Canons of Dort furnish important truth related to the foundation, means, and motivation of biblical missions and evangelism.

Sovereign Grace: An Indestructible Foundation for Evangelism

The doctrine of divine sovereignty, which includes unconditional election and predestination, is the glorious *and necessary* foundation of all biblical evangelism. Or is it? As already mentioned, many assert that Dort's teaching on election and predestination is a perennial foil to faithful outreach—a wet blanket upon the fires of evangelistic zeal.[9] After all, how could anyone be motivated to share the gospel if, as the Canons assert, "some receive the gift of faith from God and others do not receive it [based upon] God's eternal decree?" (CD I, 6). If God is sovereign and predestination is true, then why evangelize?

Evangelism and Total Depravity

What many who ask these questions fail to take into account, however, is the fundamental biblical doctrine of total depravity. Indeed, understanding the reality of mankind's wretched and helpless spiritual condition puts the grace of election and predestination in an entirely new light. In our natural state—that is, in Adam—we are all dead in transgressions and sins (Eph. 2:1; Col. 2:13). Our fallen sinful condition renders us incapable of seeking God or responding to His overtures of grace (Eph. 2:1–3). The apostle Paul writes in Romans 3:10–12 (NKJV):

> There is none righteous, no, not one;
> There is none who understands;
> There is none who seeks after God.
> They have all turned aside;
> They have together become unprofitable;
> There is none who does good, no, not one.

(Leiden: Brill, 2011); Homer C. Hoeksema, *The Voice of Our Fathers* (Grand Rapids: Reformed Free Publishing Association, 1980); and Daniel R. Hyde, *Grace Worth Fighting For: Recapturing the Vision of God's Grace In the Canons of Dort* (Lincoln, Neb.: The Davenant Press, 2019).

9. Presbyterian and Reformed believers are sometimes referred to as the "frozen chosen." This pejorative title is sometimes merited, even if stemming from an Arminian perspective. Indeed, the Reformed can often lack zeal in worship and evangelism as a misunderstanding and misapplication of God's sovereignty, thinking it fosters spiritual apathy and evangelistic indifference. Rightly grasped and routinely contemplated, however, God's sovereign grace is high-octane fuel for evangelism. It always has been. Belief in divine election certainly did not slow down the prophets and apostles in their evangelistic endeavors. Nor, as mentioned above, did it discourage the Magisterial Reformers. God's absolute sovereignty in salvation should not hamper our enthusiasm for evangelism either. It should drive it.

Humanity is held captive by the world, the flesh, and the devil (Eph. 2:1–3). Every part of us is corrupted by original and actual sin. Bavinck explains that sin "holds sway over the whole person, over mind and will, heart and conscience, soul and body, over all one's capacities and powers. A person's heart is evil from his or her youth and a source of all kinds of evils."[10] There is truly no health in us. Indeed, contrary to popular opinion, we are not born with an inherent inclination to love and serve God. No, quite the opposite. We are naturally hostile toward God (cf. Rom. 8:7–8). Left to ourselves, we are His rebellious and stiff-necked enemies (cf. Gen. 6:5; Rom. 5:10).

The Canons of Dort highlight the doctrine of human depravity.[11] The first head of doctrine begins with a clear and sobering paragraph on the miserable fallen state of mankind. It also affirms God's just and sovereign right to leave "the entire human race in sin and under the curse, and to condemn them on account of their sin" (art. 1). In other words, God was not required to save anyone. He owes His sinful rebel creatures nothing. It would have been "no injustice" for God to leave us all in our willful defiance. We are morally depraved insurgents in God's world. We deserve nothing less than God's righteous judgment.

Similar to the way Paul opens his epistle to the Romans, the Canons start by highlighting the righteousness of God and the universal depravity of mankind (Rom. 1:18–3:20). However, it's not until the third and fourth heads of doctrine that the Canons deal at length with humanity's sinful condition:

> Man was originally created in the image of God and was furnished in his mind with a true and salutary knowledge of his Creator and things spiritual, in his will and heart with righteousness, and in all his emotions with purity; indeed, the whole man was holy. However, rebelling against God at the devil's instigation and by his own free will, he deprived himself of these outstanding gifts. Rather, in their place he brought upon himself blindness, terrible darkness, futility, and distortion of judgment in his mind; perversity, defiance, and hardness in his heart and will; and finally, impurity in all his emotions. (CD III/IV, 1)

Humanity was created with original righteousness, but that righteousness was lost when our first parents sinned against God. We are all inheritors of Adam's original sin. We are born with wicked hearts, darkened minds, wayward

---

10. Herman Bavinck, *Reformed Dogmatics* (Grand Rapids: Baker Academic, 2006), 3:119.
11. See in this volume chapter 5 by Christopher J. Gordon.

affections, and obstinate wills. God's word is crystal clear when it states that we were "by nature children of wrath, like the rest of mankind" (Eph. 2:3 ESV).

A biblical understanding of total depravity, therefore, helps us to view predestination in a completely different light, both in terms of salvation and the proclamation of salvation through missions and evangelism. Predestination, in relation to human depravity, lays a sure foundation for the gospel of free grace. It highlights the fact that our fallen sinful condition makes us incapable of saving ourselves. Thus, God must *purpose* and *accomplish* our salvation monergistically. God must plan it. God must do it. If not, we are lost forever. Unless God purposes and effectually calls sinners unto salvation in Christ, all hope would be lost. John Murray elucidates:

> The fact that calling is an act of God, and of God alone, should impress upon us the divine monergism in the initiation of salvation in actual procession. We become partakers of redemption by an act of God that instates us in the realm of salvation, and all the corresponding changes in us and in our attitudes and reactions are the result of the saving forces at work within the realm into which, by God's sovereign and efficacious act, we have been ushered. The call, as that by which the predestinating purpose begins to take effect, is in this respect of divine monergism after the pattern of predestination itself. It is of God and of God alone.[12]

Salvation *apart from* divine predestination necessarily makes salvation a joint venture. God does His part and we do ours—a kind of salvation partnership. But that is impossible. No one seeks for God in an unregenerate state. Dead people don't seek. Like Lazarus in the tomb after four days, we are dead until raised by the life-giving word of Christ (John 11:33–34). Salvation is by grace alone, not by works. Nor does God work in our lives as a response to "foreseen faith…[the] obedience of faith, holiness, or any other good quality of disposition in man, as the pre-requisite, cause or condition on which it depended" (CD I, 9). No, we do nothing to elicit God's mercy. Our only boast is the sovereign grace of God.

> For by grace you have been saved through faith, and that not of yourselves; it is the gift of God, not of works, lest anyone should boast. For we are His workmanship, created in Christ Jesus for good works, which God prepared beforehand that we should walk in them. (Eph. 2:8–10 NKJV)

---

12. John Murray, *Collected Writings of John Murray* (Edinburgh: Banner of Truth, 1977), 2:166.

Without God's sovereign, saving decrees, the proclamation of the gospel would fall upon only deaf ears and hard hearts. No one would ever believe the gospel if not for God's sovereign choice and the Spirit's application of Christ's life-giving grace. No amount of emotional pleading or artful persuasion can lead a depraved sinner to faith in Christ. Sovereign grace is the only remedy for mankind's depraved spiritual condition. John Murray writes:

> This doctrine [of mankind's spiritual inability] does not hinder evangelism. One of the greatest hindrances to the spread of the gospel is the lack of it. It is only on the presuppositions of total depravity and complete human impotence that the full glory and power of the gospel can be declared.[13]

Only those whom God has chosen in Christ "before the foundation of the world" will respond to the gospel (Eph. 1:4; cf. Matt. 25:34). Only those who are predestined according to God's eternal purpose will receive the "riches of his grace" (Eph. 1:5, 7). Only those who are "appointed to eternal life" will believe (Acts 13:48 NKJV). And only those who were given to Christ by the Father in eternity past will come to Him in the future and live with Him forever. Jesus declares:

> I am the bread of life. He who comes to Me shall never hunger, and he who believes in Me shall never thirst. But I said to you that you have seen Me and yet do not believe. All that the Father gives Me will come to Me, and the one who comes to Me I will by no means cast out. For I have come down from heaven, not to do My own will, but the will of Him who sent Me. This is the will of the Father who sent Me, that of all He has given Me I should lose nothing, but should raise it up at the last day. And this is the will of Him who sent Me, that everyone who sees the Son and believes in Him may have everlasting life; and I will raise him up at the last day. (John 6:35–40 NKJV)

Confident Evangelism

Election and predestination establish a sure foundation for missions and evangelism. God *shall* save His people from their sins (Matt. 1:21). Therefore, believers should evangelize with confidence—not confidence in themselves or in the latest evangelistic techniques—but confidence in the sovereign purpose of God and in the execution of His purpose through the Spirit-empowered proclamation of His efficacious Word. We go forth and make

---

13. Murray, *Collected Writings*, 2:88.

disciples in confidence, knowing that Christ will "lose not one" of those whom the Father has given Him.

As a new believer steeped in Arminian perspectives, I was deeply worried about my evangelistic inadequacies. I was led to believe that every missed opportunity brought blood on my hands. I thought people were going to hell because of my failure to share the gospel with them (or at least to share it effectively). But a right view of predestination taught me differently. I learned that I could trust God with my evangelistic successes *and failures*. Whether or not a person comes to saving faith in Christ is not ultimately up to me, though I am privileged to participate in the mission. God is in control. We are totally dependent upon God in evangelism. Christ is sovereignly building His church. We go forth to make disciples of all nations, confidently and humbly clinging to the promise that "all authority in heaven and on earth has been given to [Christ]" (Matt. 28:18–20 ESV).

I've heard it said that we should believe in God's sovereignty, but evangelize as if He's not sovereign. Perhaps we will be more motivated to share the gospel if we imagine that the salvation of souls is left up to us. This is certainly not how the ascended Jesus wanted Paul to carry out his mission in Corinth when He told him, "Do not be afraid, but go on speaking and do not be silent, for I am with you, and no one will attack you to harm you, *for I have many in this city who are my people*."[14] Jesus wanted Paul to evangelize with holy confidence, knowing that there were many unregenerate elect in Corinth who needed to hear and, by God's sovereign grace, believe the gospel. The sovereignty of God in salvation cultivates both zeal and steadfastness in evangelism. Thus, believers should never pretend that God is not sovereign when they evangelize. That is like pretending that God is not God. J. I. Packer explains:

> The supposition seems to be that you cannot evangelize effectively unless you are prepared to pretend while you are doing it that the doctrine of divine sovereignty is not true…. This is nonsense…. So far from inhibiting evangelism, faith in the sovereignty of God's government and grace is the only thing that can sustain it, for it is the only thing that can give us the resilience that we need if we are to evangelize boldly and persistently, and not be daunted by temporary setbacks. So far from being weakened by this faith, therefore, evangelism will inevitably be weak and lack staying power without it.[15]

---

14. Acts 18:10, emphasis added.
15. J. I. Packer, *Evangelism and the Sovereignty of God* (Downers Grove, Ill.: InterVarsity Press, 2008), 14.

The evangelistic task without the foundation of divine predestination is like building a house upon the sand. Unless the Lord builds the house on the foundation of His eternal love in Christ, we labor in vain to reach the nations (Ps. 127:1). Apart from God's sovereign decree, even the most sophisticated attempts to reach the lost are futile. No one would ever come to Christ apart from God's electing grace and power. From start to finish, "salvation belongs to the Lord" (Jonah 2:9 ESV). "Moreover whom He predestined, these He also called; whom He called, these He also justified; and whom He justified, these He also glorified" (Rom. 8:30 NKJV).[16]

Clothed with this truth, believers spread the gospel with prayerful confidence. The salvation of souls is ultimately not up to us. Salvation is in God's hands. That is an encouragement and a comfort to the church. It cultivates confidence in evangelism. It's also a reminder that we can be messengers without being manipulators.

Therefore, a better question than If God is sovereign, why evangelize? is Why evangelize if He is not?

The Means of Evangelism

Predestination is the foundation of gospel evangelism, the divinely decreed bedrock of Christian mission. Without it the Great Commission becomes a fruitless ambition. No one can be saved apart from God's sovereign, predestinating, regenerating grace. But we are still left wondering *how* the elect are brought to saving faith in Christ. How is the finished redemptive work of Christ applied *in time* to those who were chosen by God *before time*? By what means is the church called "to make disciples of all nations"?

Some from an Arminian perspective argue that *if* predestination is true, secondary means are superfluous. "Why bother with means," they taunt, "if God is sovereign?" Others from a hyper-Calvinistic perspective have maintained that *because* predestination is true, secondary means are unnecessary. Ironically, they too ask, "Why bother, if God is sovereign?"

A story from church history that highlights the latter view is found in the life of William Carey (1761–1834), the father of modern missions. As a young pastor Carey attended a ministers' fraternal where he argued for the importance and urgency of overseas missions—to take the gospel to heathen lands. But an older minister interrupted Carey before he could finish: "Young man,

---

16. Hoeksema states, "It is all of God in Christ, therefore. Our election, our redemption, the purchase of all the blessings of salvation, the actual bestowal of those blessings, from faith through justification and sanctification and preservation to eternal glory—all is sovereignly and effectually bestowed upon us by God in Christ." *Voice of Our Fathers*, 375.

sit down! You are an enthusiast. When God pleases to convert the heathen, he'll do so without your aid or mine."[17]

The apostle Paul answers both the Arminian and hyper-Calvinistic perspectives in his epistle to the Romans. After laying a solid doctrinal foundation for the universal depravity of mankind in chapters 1–3 and the redemption that comes by grace through faith in Christ in chapters 3–8, Paul expounds upon God's "purpose of election" in chapter 9. One might read the apostle's teaching on election and conclude that missionary preachers, evangelistic believers, and the objective means of grace are unnecessary for the conversion of souls. But Paul debunks this notion in chapter 10. After making the declaration in Romans 10:13 (ESV) that "everyone who calls on the name of the Lord will be saved," the apostle writes,

> How then shall they call on Him in whom they have not believed? And how shall they believe in Him of whom they have not heard? And how shall they hear without a preacher? And how shall they preach unless they are sent? As it is written:
>
> > "How beautiful are the feet of those who preach the gospel of peace,
> >
> > Who bring glad tidings of good things!" (Rom. 10:14–15 NKJV)

It's not *apart* from preachers, but *through* them that the elect hear the gospel of Jesus Christ and believe. God could have written the gospel in the clouds for all to see. He could have rained down gospel tracts from heaven or sent personal visions to everyone. But these are neither the ways nor the means through which God has chosen to save His people. It is through the "folly" of preaching that God is pleased to save His elect (1 Cor. 1:21). It is through the preaching of the gospel and the faithful administration of the sacraments that Christian disciples are made (cf. Matt. 28:18–20). The Canons are clear about this:

> And that men may be brought to believe, God mercifully sends the messengers of these most joyful tidings to whom He will and at what time He pleases; by whose ministry men are called to repentance and faith in Christ crucified. "How then shall they call on Him in whom they have not believed? And how shall they believe in Him of whom they have not heard? And how shall they hear without a preacher? And how shall they preach except they are sent" (CD I, 3).

---

17. Stephen Neill, *A History of Christian Missions* (London: Penguin Books, 1964), 222–26.

And to whom are these "joyful tidings" meant to be proclaimed? Where is the church commanded to send missionary pastors to preach the gospel?

> The promise of the gospel is that whosoever believes in Christ crucified shall not perish, but have eternal life. This promise, together with the command to repent and believe, ought to be declared and published to all nations, and to all persons promiscuously[18] and without distinction, to whom God out of His good pleasure sends the gospel (CD II, 5).[19]

From our finite human perspective, we do not know who will believe the gospel. Thus, we freely and joyfully announce that "whoever believes in Him should not perish but have everlasting life." And we know that when someone truly believes the gospel, they were predestined to do so before the foundation of the world (cf. John 6:38–40, 44; Eph. 1:4). The "whoever believes"—the free offer of the gospel—is not compromised *in any way* by God's sovereign grace. In fact, the preacher's invitation to believe would be empty without it.

In accord with other historic Reformed creeds and confessions that emerged from the sixteenth and seventeenth centuries, the Canons of Dort underscore the centrality of the means of grace for missions and discipleship. They did not make the Roman Catholic error, which views missions as efficacious merely through the priestly administration and operation of the church (*ex opere operato*). Nor did they swing the other direction and marginalize the means of grace, regarding them as divorced from the reality of the salvation they proclaimed and signified. Rather, the framers of the Canons understood the word and sacraments to be that which the Spirit of God efficaciously employs to apply redemption to God's elect.[20]

---

18. The word "promiscuously" doesn't seem to fit here. In its primary definition, it refers to a person characterized by transient sexual behavior with many partners. In its secondary definition, however, it refers to an indiscriminate approach to something. Here, of course, it refers to gospel evangelism that is indiscriminate of age, ethnicity, class, or social status.

19. In this article we see allusions to Matt. 28:18–20; John 3:16; and Acts 2:38–39.

20. The Westminster Standards also include prayer as a means of grace. The Shorter Catechism states in question 88 that "the outward and ordinary means whereby Christ communicateth to us the benefits of redemption are, His ordinances, especially the Word, sacraments, and prayer; all which are made effectual to the elect for salvation." Prayer plays a vital role in evangelism and missions. R. B. Kuiper maintained, "To be never so diligent in bringing the evangel to the lost, and not to pray that God may bless the evangel to their hearts unto salvation, is the height of folly, for only God the Holy Spirit can effectually by the Word call sinners to repentance." R. B. Kuiper, *God-Centered Evangelism* (Edinburgh: Banner of Truth, 1966), 151.

As the almighty operation of God whereby He brings forth and supports this our natural life does not exclude but requires the use of means by which God in His infinite mercy and goodness has chosen to exert His influence, so also the aforementioned supernatural operation of God by which we are regenerated in no way excludes or subverts the use of the gospel, which the most wise God has ordained to be the seed of regeneration and food of the soul. Wherefore, as the apostles and the teachers who succeeded them piously instructed the people concerning this grace of God, to His glory and to the abasement of all pride, and in the meantime, however, neglected not to keep them, by the holy admonitions of the gospel, under the influence of the Word, the sacraments, and discipline; so even now it should be far from those who give or receive instruction in the Church to presume to tempt God by separating what He of His good pleasure has most intimately joined together. For grace is conferred by means of admonitions; and the more readily we perform our duty, the more clearly this favor of God, working in us, usually manifests itself, and the more directly His work is advanced; to whom alone all the glory, both for the means and for their saving fruit and efficacy, is forever due. Amen. (CD III/IV, 17)[21]

God uses messengers and objective means to save, gather, nourish, and protect His elect. The messengers of the good news, however, are not only lawful ministers of the gospel. All believers are commanded to be evangelistic, and a right understanding of God's sovereignty should never "lessen the urgency, and immediacy, and priority, and binding constraint, of the evangelistic imperative."[22]

The Motivation of Evangelism

R. B. Kuiper, in his classic book *God-Centered Evangelism*, writes, "In the course of its history the Christian Church has been actuated by various motives in the spread of the gospel. Many of these motives were noble, but others—it must be admitted were ignoble."[23] For instance, Kuiper mentions colonialism and the inducement for material wealth and earthly power as ungodly motivations for missions displayed throughout history. Wrong motivations also may include

---

21. Earlier in article 6 it states, "What, therefore, neither the light of nature nor the law could do, that God performs by the operation of the Holy Spirit through the word or ministry of reconciliation; which is the gospel concerning the Messiah, by means whereof it has pleased God to save such as believe, as well under the Old as under the New Testament."

22. Packer, *Evangelism and the Sovereignty of God*, 38.

23. R. B. Kuiper, *God-Centered Evangelism: A Presentation of the Scriptural Theology of Evangelism* (Edinburgh: Banner of Truth, 1978), 95.

a lust for adventure, a craving for attention, or a "display of personal piety."[24] Rightly understood, however, the sovereignty of God in salvation reorients the believer's motivations for evangelism. It liberates the believer's heart to focus on God's love and glory as principal motivations for evangelism rather than guilt, fear, or self-promoting exhibitions of piety. As Kuiper explains,

> Love for God and His Christ will induce, yes compel, God's child to devote himself wholeheartedly to the spread of the evangel because he knows that its ultimate end will be the glorification of God in Christ. Through evangelism the day will be hastened when "every tongue shall confess that Jesus Christ is Lord, to the glory of God the Father" (Phil. 2:11). That is the chiefest concern of him who loves God.[25]

The apostles were motivated by the love of God as they carried out the Great Commission. Paul wrote, "The love of Christ compels us" (2 Cor. 5:14 NKJV). It was God's ineffable love for His elect, clearly expressed in the propitiatory death of His Son, that motivated the apostles to reach the lost. They were moved by the good news expressed in the Canons of Dort that since we cannot "deliver ourselves from God's anger, God in His boundless mercy has given us as a guarantee His only begotten Son, who was made to be sin and a curse for us, in our place, on the cross, in order that He might give satisfaction for us" (CD II, 2). The apostles did not minister out of misguided motivations. It was not even primarily out of duty that they proclaimed the gospel.[26] They were motivated by love *for* God; that is, love for His glorious nature and His sublime works of creation and redemption. And they were motivated by the love *of* God—God's eternal love for His elect. With confidence in the evangelistic task, knowing that its success was grounded in the infinite love and eternal counsels of His sovereign God, Paul expressed, "I endure all things for the sake of the elect."[27]

In addition to the love of God, the glory of God is meant to be a chief motivation for evangelism. Not that the church's evangelism in any way furnishes to God a glory that He doesn't already possess. For God is "all sufficient, not standing in need of any creatures which He hath made, nor deriving any glory from them, but only manifesting His own glory in, by,

---

24. Kuiper, *God-Centered Evangelism*, 96–97.

25. Kuiper, *God-Centered Evangelism*, 105.

26. "Love for God and His Christ guarantees on the part of the believer loving, hence genuine and devoted, in distinction from external and legalistic, obedience to the divine command to evangelize the nations." Kuiper, *God-Centered Evangelism*, 103.

27. 2 Tim. 2:10 NKJV.

unto, and upon them."[28] We reflect God's resplendent glory and spread His fame when we share the gospel with our next-door neighbors and take it to the nations. Evangelism is not about us. It's about God. It's about His glory and renown, not ours. When God's grace and glory become our focus and aim, they form the wind in our evangelistic sails. An evangelistic outlook that places confidence in God's predestinating love and divinely instituted means will reject the new fads of evangelical manipulation. Instead, what will be cultivated is a humble confidence in God's sovereign purpose and ordinary means to save the elect and fill the earth "with the knowledge of the glory of the LORD, as the waters cover the sea" (Hab. 2:14). The Canons of Dort instill this confidence again and again, while standing as a sure defense of the gospel that we are called to preach and share.[29] Compelled by God's love and glory, we confidently take the gospel to the world.

Conclusion

The vision of Rev. Dorsey sharing the gospel with those dear children in Delhi, India, will be etched on my mind forever. It was a glorious scene. It was Calvinism in action. Rev. Dorsey's passion to reach the lost was contagious, and to this day it inspires me to boldly share the good news that God loves rebel sinners and sent His beloved Son to live, die, and rise for them. Heralding the magnificent news that Christ fulfilled God's law with His sinless life, satisfied God's justice with His atoning death, and burst through the gates of hell with His glorious resurrection, all to redeem undeserving sinners, is one of the great privileges of the Christian life. How, then, can we neglect so great a privilege?

Rev. Dorsey's zeal for evangelism was not squelched by his belief in the classic Reformed view of predestination, which the Canons of Dort clearly explicate. On the contrary, it was fueled by it. Armed with the ordinary means of grace and motivated by God's sovereign love and glory, the elderly missionary-pastor confidently went forth in mission. He believed that "the message of the cross is foolishness to those who are perishing, but to us who are being saved it is the power of God" (1 Cor. 1:18 NKJV). It was Dorsey's conviction, along with the Canons of Dort, that God's sovereign grace "does not exclude but requires the use of means...by which we are regenerated... which the most wise God has ordained to be the seed of regeneration and

---

28. Westminster Confession of Faith, II.2.
29. See CD I, 7; III/IV, 10.

food for the soul."[30] In other words, God ordains the means as well as the ends of salvation.

The Canons of Dort constitute a courageous and historic defense of the gospel. They also support—*and even encourage*—its proclamation through evangelism and world mission. Proclaiming the joyful tidings of Christ to the world, therefore, is not inconsistent with the theological system of the Canons. Evangelism is the logical and faithful outworking of its teaching.

> *Pity the nations, O our God,*
> *Constrain the earth to come;*
> *Send your victorious Word abroad,*
> *And bring the strangers home.*

> *We long to see your churches full,*
> *That all the chosen race*
> *May with one voice and heart and soul,*
> *Sing your redeeming grace.*[31]

---

30. CD III/IV, 17.

31. Isaac Watts "How Sweet and Awesome Is the Place," in *The Trinity Psalter Hymnal*, ed. Alan D. Strange, Derrick J. Vander Meulen (Willow Grove, Pa.: Trinity Psalter Hymnal Joint Venture, 2018), 425.

CONTRIBUTORS

Joel R. Beeke
Dr. Beeke (PhD, Westminster Seminary, Philadelphia) is president and professor of systematic theology and homiletics at Puritan Reformed Theological Seminary, a pastor of the Heritage Reformed Congregation in Grand Rapids, Michigan, coeditor of *Puritan Reformed Journal*, editor of *The Banner of Sovereign Grace Truth*, editorial director of Reformation Heritage Books, president of Inheritance Publishers, and vice president of the Dutch Reformed Translation Society. He has written and coauthored over one hundred books, edited another one hundred books, and contributed 2,500 articles to Reformed books, journals, periodicals, and encyclopedias. He is presently working on publishing a four-volume *Reformed Systematic Theology* (Crossway) with Paul Smalley. He regularly speaks at conferences around the world. He and his wife Mary have been blessed with three married children and four grandchildren.

Kevin J. Bidwell
Kevin J. Bidwell is the minister of Sheffield Presbyterian Church (EPCEW) in Sheffield, England. His PhD work is published as "The Church as the Image of the Trinity": A Critical Evaluation of Miroslav Volf's Ecclesial Model. Dr. Bidwell has edited the Westminster Standards into modern English (without revisions). It is entitled *The Westminster Standards for Today: Recovering the Church and Worship for Everyday Christian Living.* He has ministered the gospel in more than forty countries and a recent focus is the equipping of pastors in Uganda and East Africa. He is married to his wife, Maria, and they are blessed with two daughters.

Lyle D. Bierma
Dr. Bierma is the P. J. Zondervan Professor of the History of Christianity at Calvin Theological Seminary in Grand Rapids, Michigan. He joined the faculty in 1999 after nineteen years of teaching doctrine and church history at Reformed Bible College (now Kuyper College) in Grand Rapids. As a child, he spent several years in Nigeria as part of a missionary family, and more recently he has done short-term teaching stints at seminaries in Nigeria, Brazil, India, Serbia, and Indonesia. In addition to teaching, Dr. Bierma oversees the PhD program at Calvin Seminary. He is the translator or cotranslator of ten German, Dutch, and Latin books and the author of *The Covenant Theology of Caspar Olevianus, The Doctrine of the Sacraments in the Heidelberg Catechism, An Introduction to the Heidelberg Catechism,* and *The Theology*

of the Heidelberg Catechism: A Reformation Synthesis. Lyle is married with two grown children and four grandchildren.

John V. Fesko

Dr. Fesko serves as professor of systematic and historical theology at RTS Jackson. From 2009 to 2019 he was academic dean and professor of systematic theology at Westminster Seminary California. Before moving to Westminster California, Dr. Fesko was pastor of Geneva Orthodox Presbyterian Church for ten years. His academic interests include early modern Reformation and post-Reformation theology, the integration of biblical and systematic theology, as well as soteriology, especially the doctrine of justification. His most recent publications include *The Spirit of the Age, Death in Adam, Life in Christ, The Trinity and the Covenant of Redemption, The Covenant of Redemption, The Theology of the Westminster Standards, Songs of a Suffering King,* and *Beyond Calvin: Union with Christ and Justification in Early Modern Reformed Theology,* among many others. Dr. Fesko and his wife, Anneke, have three children and reside in Jackson, Mississippi.

W. Robert Godfrey

Dr. Godfrey has taught church history at Westminster Seminary California since 1981. He taught previously at Gordon-Conwell Theological Seminary, Stanford University, and Westminster Theological Seminary in Philadelphia. He was the third president of Westminster Seminary California. As of 2017 he is president emeritus and professor emeritus of church history. Rev. Godfrey is a minister in the United Reformed Churches in North America. He has spoken at many conferences including those sponsored by the Lausanne Committee for World Evangelization, the Philadelphia Conference on Reformed Theology, and Ligonier Ministries. Dr. Godfrey currently serves as chairman of the board for Ligonier Ministries. He is the author of many books, including *Learning to Love the Psalms, An Unexpected Journey, Reformation Sketches, Pleasing God in Our Worship, God's Pattern for Creation,* and *John Calvin: Pilgrim and Pastor.* Dr. Godfrey and his wife, Mary Ellen, have three grown children, including two sons who are ministers in the United Reformed Churches in North America.

Christopher J. Gordon

Rev. Gordon is pastor of Escondido United Reformed Church (URC) in Escondido, California. He pastored the Lynden United Reformed Church from 2004 to July 2012. Rev. Gordon is lecturer in practical theology at Westminster Seminary California. He is also the president and featured teacher of the radio program *Abounding Grace Radio.* He and his wife, Darcy, have four children, Kendal, Collin, Zachary, and Lucy.

Sebastian Heck

Sebastian Heck was born and raised a Roman Catholic in the Black Forest region of southern Germany. He was converted in the United States and subsequently became Reformed through a study of Scripture and reading Reformed resources. Sebastian received his theological training from a German seminary (MDiv), as well as at Westminster Theological Seminary in Philadelphia (PhD studies). Sebastian was ordained in the Presbyterian Church in America to be a church-planting pastor in Heidelberg in 2010 and was installed as the first indigenous pastor of the Free Evangelical-Reformed Churches in Germany in 2018. Rev. Heck is behind the endeavor *Reformation2Germany*, which seeks to establish a Reformed church in Germany, a theological seminary, and a publishing house. He and his wife, Isabel, have been married since 2000 and have three teenaged children: Sophia, Tabea, and David.

Michael S. Horton

Dr. Horton is the J. Gresham Machen Professor of Systematic Theology and Apologetics. He has taught apologetics and theology at Westminster Seminary California since 1998. In addition to his work at the seminary, he is the founder and host of the *White Horse Inn*, a nationally syndicated, weekly radio talk-show exploring issues of Reformation theology in American Christianity. He is also the editor-in-chief of *Modern Reformation* magazine. Dr. Horton is the author/editor of more than twenty-five books, including a series of studies in Reformed dogmatics published by Westminster John Knox. He is an ordained minister in the United Reformed Churches in North America and lives in Escondido with his wife, Lisa, and four children.

Daniel R. Hyde

Rev. Hyde is pastor of Oceanside United Reformed Church in Carlsbad /Oceanside, California. He also serves as associate fellow in theology and liturgics and as director of the Reformed & Presbyterian Studies Program at Greystone Theological Institute in Corapolis, Pennsylvania. Among his books are *Grace Worth Fighting For: Recapturing the Vision of God's Grace in the Canons of Dort*, *God in Our Midst: The Tabernacle and Our Relationship with God*, *Welcome to a Reformed Church: A Guide for Pilgrims*, and *Jesus Loves the Little Children: Why We Baptize Children*. He has also contributed chapters to *John Owen: Between Orthodoxy and Modernity*, *The Ashgate Companion to John Owen's Theology*, and *A Puritan Theology: Doctrine for Life*. Rev. Hyde is married to Karajean and they have four children: Cyprian, Caiden, Daxton, and Sadie.

Ray B. Lanning

Rev. Lanning is minister of the Word in the Reformed Presbyterian Church of North America, is retired from active service, and is living in Grand Rapids, Michigan. Rev. Lanning served congregations in North Carolina, Florida, and Michigan in several branches of the North American family of Presbyterian and Reformed churches (ARPC, PCA, CRC, RPCNA). In retirement Rev. Lanning continues to work as an editor for Reformation Heritage Books, has contributed chapters and articles to various published works, and is the author of *Glorious Remembrance: The Sacrament of the Lord's Supper as Administered in the Liturgy of the Reformed Churches* (RHB 2017).

Jon D. Payne

Dr. Payne is senior pastor of Christ Church Presbyterian (PCA) in Charleston, South Carolina. Before planting Christ Church in 2013, he was senior pastor of Grace Presbyterian Church (PCA) near Atlanta, Georgia, from 2003 to 2013. Dr. Payne also serves as executive coordinator of the Gospel Reformation Network, a board member of the Heidelberger Society, and a trustee with the Banner of Truth Trust. Dr. Payne is series coeditor of and contributor to the Lectio Continua Expository Commentary on the New Testament and author/editor of numerous books including *John Owen on the Lord's Supper, In the Splendor of Holiness: Rediscovering the Beauty of Reformed Worship for the 21st Century* (translated into Spanish, Burmese, Chinese, Portuguese, and Italian), and *A Faith Worth Teaching: The Heidelberg Catechism's Enduring Heritage*. He and his wife, Marla, have been married for twenty-one years and have two teenage children, Mary Hannah and Hans. They reside in Mt. Pleasant, South Carolina.

Cornelis P. Venema

Dr. Venema is president and professor of doctrinal studies at Mid-America Reformed Seminary, Dyer, Indiana. He also serves as an associate pastor at Redeemer United Reformed Church in Dyer and is coeditor of the *Mid-America Journal of Theology* and contributing editor of a column on doctrine for the monthly periodical *The Outlook*. Dr. Venema has written numerous books and articles including *But for the Grace of God* and *An Exposition of the Canons of Dort*. He is married to Nancy, and they have four children and thirteen grandchildren.